1

THE SECOND COMING OF "*TRUMP THE FIRST*"
DEAR LEADER OF THE BANANA REPUBLIC
OF THE DISUNITED STATES OF AMERICA
Part II Second Edition
By Axel de Landalay

In memory of a once-great country that could have lived a long time with its multiple chronic diseases, dysfunctional government, and flawed democracy but committed collective suicide when it found out that its people had split personalities that could no longer live together in the same reality.

TABLE OF CONTENTS

PART II - THE ADVENT OF "*TRUMP THE FIRST*"

Donald Trump

The GOP's anti-democratic past.........................

PART III – THE SECOND COMING OF TRUMP

ACT I - The setup - Setting up the stage......................... 94

ACT II - The Confrontation

ACT III - The climax

ACT IV - The plot is revealed

ACT V - The Resolution

PART II

THE ADVENT OF "TRUMP THE FIRST," DEAR LEADER OF THE BANANA REPUBLIC OF THE DISUNITED STATES OF AMERICA

"If we don't win on November 5, I think our country is going to cease to exist. It could be the last election we ever have. I actually mean that." Donald Trump, in case he does not win.

"We are going to win four more years. And then after that, we'll go for another four years." Donald Trump, in case he wins.

We should always heed the words of wannabe dictators because they tend to do exactly what they say.

THE SECOND COMING
OF DONALD TRUMP

For the Republicans, Donald J. Trump represents the Party's messianic hope to fulfill its long-awaited agenda to establish a fascist form of government in America. For this fulfillment to be realized, the messiah must first disappear to give the faithful time to prepare for his Second Coming, where he will re-appear in all his glory.

In his first coming, when Jesus Christ came to earth, he did not have time to fulfill all the prophesies foretold by the Jewish prophets. For the faithful, Jesus's return is therefore expected so that he can complete all the prophecies as described in Revelation. For this reason, for more than two thousand years, Christians have been preparing for Jesus's return to reign in all his glory over all the nations of the earth.

As the new Messiah, Donald Trump also did not have time to accomplish all the goals of the Republican Party and had to disappear for a while. In a sense, Donald Trump losing the 2020 presidential election was a blessing in disguise, for his temporary departure gave the faithful time to prepare for his second coming when he will be re-elected in all his glory to reign over what is left of America. How? Two reasons:

- First and foremost, Donald Trump's personality.
- Second, the radical metamorphosis of the Republican Party into a sect.

Except that, in this master plan, Republicans are forgetting one crucial element:

Donald Trump is not a Republican:
His only Party is himself.
The Republican Party is
dead, Kaput, Mort,
Muerto,

WHO IS DONALD J. TRUMP?

What's in a name?

TRUMP: from the Old French "*Trompe*" meaning *"horn"* or "*trumpet*" to become "*tromper*", in Middle French meaning "*to deceive.*" or "*Fraud,*" which gave us "*trumpery*" form the French "*tromperie*" meaning deception, worthless nonsense, rubbish, trash, fooling talk or actions, delusive , shallow, beliefs that are superficially or visually appealing but of little value.

DERIVED EXPRESSION: The verb phrase *trump up* means "*to concoct with the intent to deceive,*" to invent or make up a story.

Rarely does such a name describe a person's character and personality so aptly as Donald Trump, former President of the United States and Republican front-runner to the 2024 Presidential election.

In the meantime, adore or loath him, Donald Trump will without a doubt stand out as one of the most .... (Fill in the blanks) political figures of this century.

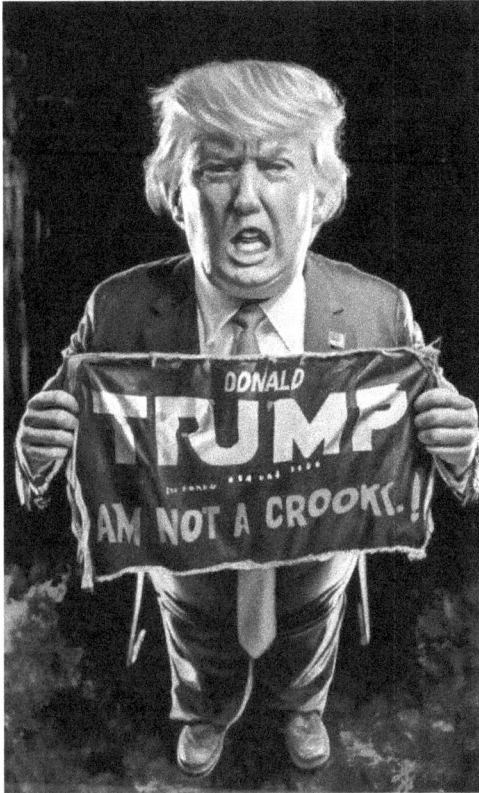

If you cannot forget Nixon's famous declaration, "*I am not a crook,*" following the Watergate scandal that ended his presidency, it is because that is how history remembers him. By the same token, when Trump says that he is *"The Most Honest Human Being God Has Ever Created,"* there is a good chance that because of his pathological lying, he will enter the history books as **the most dishonest U.S. president that God ever created**.

But if that generic description of Donald Trump resembles too much of a future Wikipedia entry, how would you describe a person as complex, or as some would say, as simple as Donald Trump?

So, here is a challenge:

How would you best describe Donald Trump to someone who has never heard of him? Of course, unless someone has been living under a rock for the past decade, such a person would be hard to find, but let's pretend anyway.

The most common approach would be to compare him to other famous people, an animal, or use a variety of character traits that would best describe the person. Finding one single entity that encompasses most of Trump's character attributes in another human being is a challenge, given his behavioral uniqueness. So, the real question to properly describe Donald Trump is **not to ask who he is but what he is.**

Therefore, by comparing Trump's behavior to any other living creature, there is only one that stands the comparison perfectly: **a virus** and, more specifically, the

THIEVE-15 virus

First comment: the comparison is not derogatory. Viruses are unique and remarkable in their own way, just like Trump.

But before you label the comparison between Donald Trump and a virus preposterous, outrageous, or surprising, consider this:

- Viruses are considered **semi-intelligent** because they can mutate, just like Trump.
- Viruses **don't have a brain**, but they are smart to react to their environment, just like Trump.
- There is **no consciousness** in viruses, just like in Trump.
- As their name suggests, viruses are viral. They can spread fast and very easily infect hosts presenting

compatibility or some weaknesses, making them more susceptible to becoming infected. Viruses are normally host specific, with a preference for those offering the best chance to survive. What differentiates the THIEVE-15 virus is that it is a **non-discriminatory equal opportunity host seeker**: Any host will do as long that it can serve its purpose of benefiting the virus itself.

Examples of how the THIEVE-15 virus has found fertile ground in infecting hosts by gender, age, and race:

- A significant number of people aged 65 or older are more exposed to being infected by the THIEVE-15 virus. As being more conservative, this host category finds echoes in Trump's reminiscing about the good old days of law and order, economic growth, and America first.

- As far as gender susceptibility to the THIEVE-15 virus is concerned, Republican women, thanks to Trump's success in overturning the Roe v. Wade Supreme Court abortion ruling, the virus has a stronghold in this particular type of host. However, since Trump has changed sides 14 times on the abortion topic, many of these affected host groups may enter into remission.

- Of all potential hosts particularly susceptible to getting infected by the THIEVE-15 virus, White Evangelical Christian was the easiest to infect and probably the type of host most resistant to any form of vaccine. Since accepting assertions without proof was already in their DNA, the THIEVE-15 virus found in this group was the perfect host to infect others with similar critical thinking deficiency.

- Race is also a big factor in the susceptibility to catching the THIEVE-15 virus. White people without college degrees are particularly receptive to catching the virus. Having no natural defense against B.S., the virus has easily infected this host group that Trump is particularly fond of: "*I love uneducated people.*" In addition, the THIEVE-15 virus has contaminated large fringed segments of white Americans who fear being replaced by immigrants of different races and ethnicities.

Other fertile infection grounds where the THIEVE-15 virus finds easy hosts are among the bitter, resentful, angry, fearful, neurotic, economically and socially left behind, and conspiracy advocates. But let us not forget a special type of host made of self-serving politicians: the former Republican Party, which now deserves special attention.

Ordinarily, viruses do not mutate to become cancerous. However, certain viruses become potent to the point of causing cancer in the host, which is exactly the case for the Trump virus once it had infected the Republican Party host.

Here is exactly how the four stages of cancer describe perfectly well the way the THIEVE-15 virus infected the Republican Party and spread metastatically to finally kill its host.

- **Stage Zero**: Precancerous change. After Trump was elected president, one can start to perceive subtle changes in the Republican Party's traditional fashion of governing. At this stage, Trump is nothing more than a lump.

- **Stage One**: The tumor is usually small and hasn't grown outside of the organ it started in. At this stage, the "*Trump* *lump"* has mainly infected the GOP and has not yet reached the electoral base of the Republican Party.

- **Stages 2 and 3**: The tumor is larger and has grown outside of the organ it started in by spreading to nearby tissue. The GOP contamination is starting to spread to the Republican base, which in turn affects the major GOP organ by making it weaker and more susceptible to stop functioning.

- **Stage four**: Metastatic spread. The cancer has spread through the lymphatic system of the Republican Party and changed its DNA.

- **Left untreated**, cancer eventually kills its host. **And that is exactly what happened to the now-defunct Republican Party.**

Questions and answers about the THIEVE-15 virus.

- **Where does the name THIEVE-15 come from?**
  The word *"Thieve"* means *"to rob"* or *"to steal,"* like when one belongs to a sect that robs you of your individuality, your way of thinking, your worldview, and your moral values. More specifically, it is an acronym for:

Virus origin:	**T** rump
Contamination risk	**H** igh
Contamination type	**I** nfectious
Spreading rate	**E** xponential
Pathogen type	**V** irus
Outbreak type	**E** pidemic (see note)
The year the virus started	2015

Note: Epidemic stage because it only affects the United States but could become a pandemic if the virus mutates and infects other countries with mini-Trumps.

- **How is the THIEVE-15 virus different from the COVID-19 virus?**

COVID-19 is a respiratory virus that can only be transmitted from person to person. In addition to being able to infect the same way, the THIEVE-15 virus has the particularity of being able to infect without physical contact because of its ability to infect the brain at a distance through social media, especially if you consume information, news, and fake news without protection like common sense, skepticism, and critical thinking.

- **How does THE THIEVE-15 virus affect the brain?**

Soon after being infected, the hosts start to experience changes in the way they think and relate to others. The hosts' behaviors are not much different from those who just joined a sect: They experience a sense of euphoria, belonging, purpose, energy, and dedication to the cause in the belief that they know something that others do not, confident in the knowing that they alone possess the truth. All those new feelings raised their dopamine level, rendering them more aggressive and hermetic to any other point of view that contradicts their beliefs. But how is this possible?

Recent research in neuroscience has put in evidence that dopamine has an unsuspected effect on the way the brain works, which led to a new theory called *"predictive coding."* At the cognitive level, the brain generates models, or beliefs, about what information it should be receiving. These beliefs get translated into predictions about what should be experienced in order to make sense. When the information received does not conform to what was predicted, the brain goes into a *"prediction error mode"* to determine the causes of the discrepancies. This *"predictive coding"* would, in part, explain how perception works and how it can alter reality. For this reason, it appears that there is no point in arguing with a person infected by the virus because no amount of evidence can tripwire the *"predictive coding"* that tells the brain that the new information received is an error.

Before long, the brain is completely hooked on the elevated dopamine level, and the host starts to show signs of a new syndrome called **SSPTS** (**S**erve, **S**pread, and **P**rotect **T**rump **S**yndrome).

A Syndrome is a group of symptoms that consistently occur together, like opinions, emotions, and behaviors. More specifically, SSPTS has the effect:

✓ To inhibit some cognitive functions, such as common sense or critical thinking.
✓ To alter the perception of reality by living in a fantasy world born out of your own wishes of what that reality should be.
✓ To completely erase any sense of self-worth and self-respect: this is why some people (Ted Cruz, Mike Pence) who have been insulted and ridiculed by Trump keep crawling back to kiss the Dear Leader's ring in a submissive display of love and devotion.
✓ The effect of SSPTS on the brain reward system is particularly evident among Republican politicians who, for political expediency and interest, have changed their stripes from being anti-THIEVE-15 to the most avid supporters of the virus.

- ✓ Another consequence of the THIEVE-15 elevating the dopamine level is that it also affects the part of the brain that regulates and alters the **brain's reward system**, which affects the way we engage in social interactions. For anybody who feels ignored, lonely, frustrated for being misunderstood, socially or economically isolated, finding others who share the same views, feelings, or desires is comforting and rewarding. After the rewarding experience, the prefrontal cortex assesses the entire event and tries to repeat it by seeking the original stimulus or action that created the feeling. This type of experience is even more evident among people addicted to social media who find in the sharing and validation of their views rewarding and addictive. It is, in fact, the same process that hooks people to drugs or any addiction, being food, sex, the exercise of power, or a sect.

- **How do I know if I am infected with THIEVE-15, and what are the symptoms?**
- ✓ Self-examination to determine if you have been infected by the virus is very difficult since the host does not feel differently and is not aware that his brain has been altered to think differently.
- ✓ However, friends and family are often the first ones to notice behavioral signs of something amiss in a person infected by the THIEVE-15 virus.
- ✓ There is, however, one way to get an idea of whether you are more susceptible to catching the THIEVE-15 virus. Take *the "How to subvert democracy self-test"* at the end of this book. If your score is between 20 and 24, you have a great chance of being already infected or at risk of catching it.

✓ **Warning**: Being intelligent or educated is not a protection against THIEVE-15 and SSPTS. In fact, the virus will make you dumber, but the good news is that you won't even be aware of it.

- **Can THIEVE-15 be transmitted from person to person?**

Person-to-person contact is not the primary source of infection by the THIEVE-15 virus. The virus is more likely spread by misinformation, conspiracy theories, and social media those algorithms act as an echo chamber for the things you want to believe to be true.

- **Is there a vaccine against THIEVE-15**

There is no known vaccine against THIEVE-15, but prevention could go a long way in catching the virus. If you have no natural immune abilities such as common sense, critical thinking, or anti-B.S. strategies, you are at high risk of catching the THIEVE-15 virus.

- **Is there a treatment for THIEVE-15**

Like for any addiction, recovering from the virus could be long, difficult, and painful, and something you cannot do alone unless something drastic happens in your life. A good place to start is by educating yourself and taking stock of who you really are, your core values, and what is important to you.

- **What can I do to protect myself against THIEVE-15?**

As we are all day long assailed by information and misinformation requiring our attention, protecting yourself against the hijacking of your values and beliefs is almost mission impossible. One place to start is to begin to cut off all stimuli and validation of your beliefs on social media. Next, diversify your sources of information and validate them with independent sources.

- **Can the THIEVE-15 mutate?**

Yes, the THIEVE-15 virus has mutated into many variants in places where mini-Trumps have found fertile terrain, such as populism.

- **Can you get infected by the THIEVE-15 twice?**

Like any virus, having been infected once does not offer any type of immunity against getting re-infected. When you stop experiencing the symptoms of the virus, you could be in remission, but you are not cured; if you don't change your environment or keep frequenting the same already infected people, chances that the virus that had laid dormant comes back stronger than ever before. This happens very frequently (William Barr, former Trump Attorney General).

- **Is there a long THIEVE-15?**

This is a good question. At its highest infection, the virus had infected tens of millions of Americans. Today, the numbers have strongly diminished, suggesting that a great number of those infected have gone into remission and are now virus-free. There is always a risk of re-contamination, but it appears that the virus has lost its potency and that the hard-core of those infected have difficulties in infecting new others.

End note

Like most viruses, the **THIEVE-15** just won't disappear on its own. Since as of to date no vaccine has been found, the only hope to see it stop spreading is to achieve herd immunity. Nobody knows for sure when the infection will reach critical mass to stop spreading, but with about one-third of Americans infected, the virus already shows signs of difficulty in finding new hosts to spread beyond its base.

However, the true test of the virus's potency for reaching epidemic status will happen on November 5th, 2024 when the U.S. presidential election will be used as a test to reveal the full extent of the contagion. At that time, two scenarios are possible:

1. As for many viruses, vaccines are usually found by inoculating potential hosts with a small dose of the pathogen to invoke an immune response to fight the virus. In this case, all the mildly infected hosts (independents) along with those who have developed an immunity to the virus will together reach a critical mass in number to reach herd immunity.

2. In the second scenario, in a Zombie apocalypse style, the number of people infected by the virus overwhelms those who had remained sane until complete extinction. Because if there is one thing viruses do well, it is to eliminate everything that is a threat to their survival.

There is no point in blaming the THIEVE-15 virus. Anything a virus does is for itself and to defend its interest. The host is only a means to achieve its goals: to survive and prosper.

In the same way, you cannot say
that you are anti-plague or anti-cholera;
being anti-Trump is meaningless: Trump just is.

COULD THE REAL DONALD J. TRUMP PLEASE STAND UP!

Aside from virus comparison, one of the best ways to judge one's character is to examine how a person sees himself. For a narcissist like Donald Trump, we already know that he sees himself as the most intelligent human being ever created by God. But perhaps the self-assessment that will enter the history books will be this one:

"I am the most honest human being, perhaps, that God ever created," D. Trump.

Yes, indeed, this quote deserves to be listed in the Guinness Book of Records, not because it is a record of some sort, but because it is the funniest joke ever uttered by a politician that will stay unchallenged for a long time, if ever. Yes, Donald Trump has a sense of humor after all, even if it is a sick one.

But who is Donald Trump? Many people and books have attempted to portray the man in its complexity and contradictions by opposing what he is and what he is not. But what will stand out is his legacy in his role of attempting to change the soul of America forever.

For this reason, the following is an attempt to bring water to the mill to all those who are considering re-electing Donald Trump as the next president to represent us and our country to the world. With that purpose in mind, one place to start is to consider how Donald Trump sees himself.

HOW DONALD TRUMP SEES HIMSELF

**Captain America superhero saving us
by making America Great Again, Again**

Some countries in the Americas and other shithole countries, to use Trump's terminology, are envying us for the luck of having the original of all the wannabe mini-Trumps of the planet. But this has nothing to do with luck. We have elected him once and are ready to re-elect him again, eyes wide open because right from the horse's mouth, he told us the many reasons why he is the best man for the job:

- *"My two greatest assets have been mental stability and being, like, really smart,"*
- *"Would qualify as not smart, but genius....and a very stable genius at that!"*
- *"I always told people, you know I'm a very smart guy. I got good marks. I was all this, I went to the best college: the Wharton School of Finance, which to me is like the greatest business school,"*
- *"I'm speaking with myself, number one, because I have a very good brain, and I've said a lot of things... I know what I'm doing, and I listen to a lot of people, I talk to a lot of people, and at the appropriate time, I'll tell you who the people are. But I speak to a lot of people. My primary consultant is myself, and I have, you know, I have a good instinct for this stuff,"*
- *"I'm not changing. I went to the best schools. I'm, like, a very smart person. I'm going to represent our country with dignity and very well. I don't want to change my personality -- it got me here,"*
- *"I'm, like, a smart person. I don't have to be told the same thing in the same words every single day,"*
- *"I try to step back and remember my first shallow reaction. The day I realized it can be smart to be shallow was, for me, a deep experience."*
- *"I could negotiate peace in the Middle East – very few other people could,"*
- *"I think I'm almost too honest to be a politician,"*

- *"I don't want to brag, but I just completed a jig-saw puzzle in just 1 week, and the box said from 1 to 4 years."*
- *"You'd be shocked if I said that in many cases, I probably identify more as a Democrat."*
- *"What do you have to lose? It's going to be tremendous. We're going to have jobs, we're going to bring back the wealth, we're going to take care of our military, we're going to take care of our vets. We're going to start winning again."*
- *"I'm intelligent. Some people would say I'm very, very, very intelligent.".*
- *"I'm like a smart person. I don't have to be told the same thing in the same words every single day for the next eight years."*
- *"I'm the most successful person ever to run for the presidency, by far. Nobody's ever been more successful than me. I'm the most successful person ever to run.*
- *"I will prevent WWIII very easily, very easily….and you can have WWIII, by the way."*

In addition, in his own words,

- *"I know more about ISIS than the generals do."*
- *"I know more about lawsuits than I do? I'm the king."*
- *"Nobody knows more about trade than me."*
- *"I understand politicians better than anybody."*
- *"Nobody knows the government system better than I do."*
- *"I'm the king of debt. I'm great with debt. Nobody knows debt better than me."*

- *"Nobody in the history of this country has ever known so much about infrastructure as Donald Trump."*
- *"I think I know about it (the economy) better than [the Federal Reserve]."*

The only thing Donald Trump admitted: *"Nobody knew health care could be so complicated."* That is probably why he did not repeal *"Obama Care"* with *"Trump Care"* as he had promised.

With all that knowledge within one person, we should be so lucky to have Donald Trump as president again. But for those who are still sitting on the fence, here comes the kicker:

"I am the most honest human being,
perhaps, that God ever created," and
"I will be the greatest jobs president that God ever created."

We should seize on our chance while it is still time because God will never create a human as perfect as Donald Trump again.

HOW DO AMERICANS SEE DONALD TRUMP

Watching the news media gives you the impression that candidate Donald Trump is at the apex of his popularity. Polls after polls tell you how Trump has left all other presidential in the dust, how each indictment has raised his profile, lined his pockets, and how he will crush Joe Biden for the 2024 presidential.

However, serious studies into the American public's perception of Donald Trump as a presidential contender show a more nuanced reality. In truth, little has changed over the years in the way the general voters have perceived Donald Trump.

Several PEW research have put the following in evidence:

"*Trump remains broadly unpopular with the public: 63% of Americans have an unfavorable opinion of the former president, while 35% view him favorably. A year ago, Trump's rating stood at 60% unfavorable.*" [1]

Although every indictment against Trump has been an opportunity to line his pockets, 65% of adults think the charges are serious, including 51% who said they are very serious and 14% who said they are somewhat serious. Only 24% said they were not serious, including 17% who said they 2were not serious at all.

---

[1] July 2023 PEW poll
[2] ABC News/Ipsos poll.

More telling is that a majority of Americans say Trump should be prosecuted on Federal Criminal Charges linked to the 2020 Election. [3]

Apart from Trump's unconditional and Forever Trumpists, for those who dislike the man with a passion, qualifiers are more colorful:

"Obtusely offensive, arrogantly insulting, compulsively dishonest, vaingloriously conceited, behaves like a petulant child, has next to no geographical or worldly knowledge, he has zero empathy, is vindictively nasty, and hateful, degrading towards women, and many minority groups, can be ignorantly racist, brutishly and selfishly greedy, acrimoniously narcissistic, but most alarmingly of all, he is seriously divisive, he is a Buffon and a dick."

The most unsettling poll findings are that most Republicans would vote for Trump even if he's convicted of a crime. This admission means that there is a real possibility that Trump could run the country from inside a jail, like a mafia boss, unless, of course, he pardons himself.

"Memo to myself: I got to get re-elected president, God damn it! It is the only way to stay out of jail." From Trump's little voice in his head.

---

[3] Quinnipiac University National Poll

HOW DO MENTAL HEALTH PROFESSIONALS SEE DONALD TRUMP.

Question: Is Donald Trump a sane person?

There are two theories to this question.

One is that Donald Trump is afflicted with several psychological disorders.

Another is that Trump is not a delusional, narcissistic, psychopath, sociopath, but that in truth, worse than that.

We already know that dozens of psychologists have diagnosed Donald Trump as a narcissistic/psychopath/sociopath with character traits that share all dictators. Even those who know him personally well, like family members, label him as

"A petty, pathetic little man — ignorant, incapable, out of his depth, and lost to his own delusional spin."[4]

Let's call a cat a cat: Donald Trump is a textbook narcissist, just like his father, Fred Trump Sr., who also was a sociopath.

So, where does Donald Trump stand?

The originality of Donald Trump is that he exhibits character traits that overlap the clinical definition of narcissism, sociopath, and psychopath. In a sense, Donald Trump is a hybrid type of animal that encompasses most of the characteristics that define either one of the following three psychological disorders.

---

[4] Quote from Mary L. Trump in her book "*Too much and never enough*".

Sociopath traits

- Lack of remorse.
- Charming
- Intelligent
- Liars
- Manipulative
- Narcissistic
- No Long Relationships
- Spontaneous
- Lack of Love
- Highly Competitive

Narcissist traits

- Superiority and entitlement
- Exaggerated need for attention and validation
- Great need for control
- Lack of responsibility
- Lack of boundaries
- Lack of empathy
- Perceiving everything as a threat
- Emotional reasoning
- Fear of rejection and ridicule
- Anxiety
- Deeply repressed shame
- Inability to be genuinely vulnerable
- Inability to communicate or work as part of a team

Psychopath traits [5]

- Cold indifference to the feelings of others.
- Pathological Lying and Manipulation.
- Lack of Morality and Rule-breaking.
- Lack of empathy and Cold-Heartedness.
- Narcissism and False Superiority Complex.
- Gaslighting and Psychological Bullying.
- Lack of Contrition and Self-Serving Victimhood.
- Irresponsibility and disregard for social norms, rules, and obligations.
- Persistent irresponsibility.
- Failure to follow social norms for law-abiding behavior may provide grounds for imprisonment.
- Fraud that manifests itself through repeated lies, use of false names, or fraud by others for the sake of gain or pleasure.
- Morbid lying/broad-mindedness.
- Very low frustration threshold and low aggression threshold, .
- Irritability and aggression manifested through repeated fights
- Pronounced tendency to blame others or to come up with explanations of the behavior that creates problems.
- Lack of realistic future planning.
- Reckless indifference to one's own or others' safety.
- Lack of remorse.
- Smoothness / superficial charm.
- Self-centered, with great thoughts about self-worth.
- Bluffing, use of manipulation.
- Lack of depth of emotion.

"Our society is moving in the direction of permitting, reinforcing, and in some cases actually valuing some of the traits listed in the Psychopathy Checklist." Robert Hare.

---

[5] Source: Hare - Psychopathy checklist

Dictators like Adolf Hitler, Mao Zedong, Josef Stalin, and Pol Pot, just to name those directly responsible for the death of millions of people, all have at least one thing in common: They were all narcissists and psychopaths.

Dictators are also fed by grand delusions regarding their self-importance. In most instances, they see themselves or are seen by their supporters as a "*Messiah*" of some sort, a savior, a protector, a liberator, whose mission is to rescue them from something. Attributions that dictators embraced eagerly since they all were also narcissists. Some, like Stalin, Mao Zedong, or Kim Jong-un of North Korea, have even reached God-like status.

Seeing themselves as "*very special*" people deserving of admiration, they have extreme difficulties empathizing with the feelings and needs of others. In short, they display all the characteristics associated with Narcissistic personality disorder.

Most dictators are also paranoid, which often translates to physically eliminating anybody who does not toe the line or is seen as a potential threat. They constantly require some proof of allegiance and loyalty. But for them, loyalty is a one-way street.

Being preoccupied with their achievements and abilities, they are extremely vindictive and more likely to try to punish those who express any negativity or criticism towards their performance.

To reach their goals, dictators make it a policy to exploit others to do their bidding or to cover up their nefarious deeds. In that way, they never take responsibility and never, never have to apologize for anything.

Finally, being the worrying, emotional, and anxious type, always on the defensive, dictators tend to complain all the time. This character trait explains why Bill Mahar has made it a habit of calling Trump "a *whining little bitch"*.

In conclusion, in the same way that you don't have to be a chicken to recognize an egg, it does not take a psychoanalyst to recognize that Donald J. Trump embodies all the personality traits associated with dictators.

WHEN CHARISMATIC MEETS DEMAGOGUE

Charismatic: a person with particular traits that attract, inspire, or fascinate others. A personal magic of leadership arousing exceptional popular loyalty or enthusiasm for a public figure (such as a political leader). Merriam-Webster.

Martin Luther King Jr., Napoleon Bonaparte, Nelson Mandela, Hitler, Winston Churchill, Mahatma Gandhi, and Fidel Castro were all charismatic leaders. However, even if they share some character traits, their legacy goes from one extreme to another. But why?

One possible answer could be that the difference between them does not lie in what they have in common, but in a character trait that is lacking. Indeed, if they all have confidence, clarity of vision, self-awareness, and communication skills, the missing ingredients that make a difference are empathy and compassion.

Donald Trump, for one, is definitely a charismatic person. Still, since his sense of empathy and compassion is virtually nil, he will never be in the same league as other great leaders or some U.S. presidents. However, that character deficiency is compensated by another formidable character trait that explains his popularity: he is a demagogue.

Demagogue: a leader who makes use of popular prejudices and false claims and promises in order to gain power. Merriam-Webster

The problem with demagogues is that once they have tasted one drop of power, they get drunk and addicted to it and will never give it up.

WHEN PATHOLOGICAL MEETS DELUSIONAL

Pathological: being such to a degree that is extreme, excessive, or markedly abnormal. Merriam-Webster.

With thousands of "*Pinocchios*" and "*Pants on Fire*" from fact-checkers who make it their business to sort out truths, half-truths, hyperboles, and blatant lies, Donald Trump would win the Hall-of-Fame as the Mother of all liars. By the end of his term, Donald Trump had accumulated 30,573 untruths (euphemism for lies), **an outstanding 21 lies per day**.

Sure, we expect lies from politicians, but the fact that it does not make a dent of a difference in their ability to get elected to represent us says more about us than them, as proven by the cases of Georges Santos, elected to Congress in the 2022 Mid-Term election.

Georges Santos lied about where he went to school, his criminal status in Brazil, his athletic accomplishments, being Jewish, the timing of his mother's death, lying to investors., where he worked, being robbed of his rent money, campaign finances, about his name, and owning several rental properties for example, did not faze any electors whatsoever. So it appears that how much of a douchbag you are does not matter as long as he belongs to your tribe, which proves again that in a democracy, the weak link is the voters.

As entertainment, there is no doubt that Pinocchio-Trump memes have made the heydays of late-night television shows, stand-up comics, and viral video producers of all stripes. But before judging, perhaps we should pause and try to discern the difference between pathological liars and compulsive liars because, although often used interchangeably, the terms "*pathological liar*" and "*compulsive liar*" differ. The difference is in the motive for lying.

If pathological liars are generally motivated by a desire to gain attention or sympathy, compulsive liars, on the other hand, have no recognizable motive for lying and will do so no matter the situation.

Some of Trump's lies are ridiculous, like when he claims to be the healthiest and fittest President in history when a picture of his bums while playing golf could be mistaken as one of those funny photos of obese people shopping at Walmart. No wonder he went ballistic when Nancy Pelosi called him "*morbidly obese*."[6] Trump is not used to being on the receiving end of name-calling. Besides that, why did he even have to write his own health report presented by his doctor, Ronny Jackson, who had to make it more credible by adding that Trump was so healthy he could live to 230 years of age? Imagine that!

This kind of lying is why trying to define what type of liar Donald Trump, in truth, is can be challenging. Because Trump's lies are never anecdotal nor benign and always seem to have the

---

[6] A medical term in which you have a body mass index (BMI) higher than 35. BMI and used to estimate body fat and determine if you are at a healthy body weight for your size.

motive of benefiting him, no matter how trivial or outlandish. In that respect, Donald Trump is both a pathological and a compulsive liar, a sort of a hybrid kind of animal or mutant with the following characteristics that we can all recognize:

- Aside from seeking sympathy, adoration, or attention, Trump does not need any particular reason to lie.
- Donald Trump is always either a hero or a victim of his story.
- Trump's lies are often outlandish or unbelievable, and when they are not, you have to wonder, what's his point for lying?
- Trump's stories may change. Often because we have videos or recordings of what he did or said that contradict his lies. In this case, Trump usually pivots to say that if we don't like this story, he has another one.
- After repeating the same lie in ad nauseam, Trump often ends up believing in his own fantasy. The scariest thing is that, at the same time, he manages to convince others.

Delusional: something that is falsely or delusively believed or propagated. Merriam-Webster.

Donald Trump suffers from a psychiatric condition called malignant narcissism, manifested by an extreme intolerance of realities that do not fit his wishful view of the world. In other words, "Donald Trump is dangerously mentally ill and temperamentally incapable of being president." The symptoms of malignant narcissism that President Trump purportedly manifests are many and include antisocial behaviors, sadism, lack of conscience, and manipulative and aggressive tendencies."[7] That is a pretty strong diagnostic for someone who

---

[7] Quoted from John Gartner, a psychotherapist at Johns Hopkins University

admitted to never having personally interviewed[8] Donald Trump. But do you have to be a chicken to recognize an egg?

However, as problematic as such a diagnosis could be for a person who once occupied the most powerful office of the free world, some psychiatric professionals dare to further diagnose Donald Trump as a person with a delusional and malignant narcissism condition with paranoid and grandiose features, a condition plagued by both Adolf Hitler and Joseph Stalin. However, even without such an extreme diagnosis, it remains a fact that over 70,000 people self-identifying as *"mental health professionals"* did sign a petition declaring that *"Trump is mentally ill and must be removed."* when he was still in office. Scary stuff when you consider that Trump is not finished yet with his bid to re-conquer power in 2024. That prospect raises a disturbing question: How could such a pathological condition square with Trump's millions of followers?

Without sounding like an explanation coming out of a treatise in psychiatry, the reason is twofold:

Following is an excerpt of an interview given to The Scientific American by Forensic psychiatrist Bandy X.. Lee explaining the outgoing president's pathological appeal.

- *"**Narcissistic** symbiosis refers to the developmental wounds that make the leader-follower relationship magnetically attractive. The leader, hungry for adulation to compensate for an inner lack of self-worth, projects grandiose omnipotence—while the followers, rendered needy by societal stress or developmental injury, yearn for a parental figure. When such wounded individuals are*

---

[8] An American Psychiatric Association's modification of a 1970s-era guideline, known as the Goldwater rule.

given positions of power, they arouse similar pathology in the population, creating a lock and key relationship."

- *"**Shared psychosis** or induced delusions occur when a highly symptomatic individual is placed in an influential position. The person's symptoms can spread through the population through emotional bonds, heightening existing pathologies and inducing delusions, paranoia, and propensity for violence, even in previously healthy individuals."*

The consequence: *"There is great injury, anger, and re-directable energy for hatred, which Trump harnessed and stoked for his manipulation and use. The emotional bonds he has created facilitate shared psychosis at a massive scale."*

The takeaway is that the relationship between Trump and his supporters is one of interdependence similar to cult members who are emotionally bonded with their leader and refuse to see any other truth as a psychological protection against pain and disappointment of the reality of their life.

SECOND THEORY

The second school of thought regarding Trump's so-called psychological and mental deficiencies is just another con, a smoke screen to a more nefarious strategy for regaining and keeping power. Forget all the medical jargon to explain Trump's mental state. He knows exactly what he is doing. The simple explanation is that Trump is not detached from reality and is quite capable of discerning right from wrong and truth from a lie. He simply does not care. All his actions are geared toward one thought: What's in it for me?

In that respect, being portrayed by his detractors as mentally unstable has served him well; he is the victim. A role that reinforces his supporters in their conviction that their hero has been cheated of his just reward as the defender of the aggrieved and the victimized.

So, continuing to portray Trump as the megalomaniac who thinks he is smarter, richer, and stronger than anyone else just fortifies his grandiose and superior persona from his admirers.

UPDATE

As we are entering 2024 and both candidates are starting in earnest a long and exhaustive presidential campaign, one thing is becoming evident:

Donald Trump is becoming more and more unhinged, delusional and wacko

His perpetual ranting, outlandish assertions, and physical behavior all point to a scary conclusion:

Donald Trump is losing it, and his mental state of paranoia and dementia poses a real threat to America, as proven by his paranoid thirst for revenge if re-elected.

"We will root out the communists, Marxists, fascists, and the radical left thugs that live like vermin within the confines of our country, that lie and steal and cheat on elections and will do anything possible — they'll do anything, whether legally or illegally, to destroy America and to destroy the American dream."

But all this is not new. Already, back in 2017, psychiatrists, psychologists, and other mental health professionals concluded in **"*The Dangerous Case of Donald Trump* that Trump's mental health posed a "*clear and present danger*" to the nation."**

To which Trump may reply:

"Many psychologists believe that I am a narcissistic psychopath who only thinks of himself. Fooled you! I am the most unselfish, caring person that God ever created." From Trump's little voice in his head.

HOW DO HISTORIANS SEE DONALD TRUMP

According to C-SPAN[9], a list of 142 historians and other experts in rating U.S. presidents used a criterion of ten leadership qualities to rate the performance of Donald Trump.

First, the good news: According to historians, Donald Trump is only rated as **the worst president for "moral authority"** and **"administrative skills."**

The worst president in all categories goes to James Buchanan, who helped precipitate the Civil War. So, Donald Trump still has a second chance to become the worst president ever if he succeeds in getting re-elected in 2024.

According to historians who have rated all 47 United States presidents so far, Donald J. Trump ranked fourth from worst, just Franklin Pierce[10].

However, we should here take a pose and make a distinction between being a bad president and a bad person because one does not imply the other. Being the most hated does not necessarily reflect a person's character, since such sentiment

---

[9] C-SPAN 2021 Historians Survey of Presidential Leadership

[10] According to C-SPAN's 2021 President Historians Survey.

could be inspired by many different reasons than his character traits.

America, for sure, had a lot of presidents with questionable ethics, some of whom did terrible things that we would rather forget. In determining which presidents were bad people, we should put in a special box those who displayed character traits that they shared with many of their compatriots of the time, such as racism, since many would argue that you could be a racist and a good person at the same time. Thomas Jefferson, James Monroe, Andrew Johnson, Millard Fillmore, Calvin Coolidge, and Woodrow Wilson, for instance, all fall within that category, with special recognition to those who caused the death of hundreds of thousands of people:

- **Andrew Jackson** waged war on the Creek and Cherokee tribes to take their land. His troops killed vast numbers of Native Americans, including women and children, and forced 46,000 Native Americans out of their homes and onto reservations.
- **James Polk,** one of the evilest American presidents, was responsible for the deaths of 25,000 Mexicans.
- **James Buchanan** for paving the way for the Civil War, which resulted in 1.5 million casualties.
- **William McKinley** was another evil American president who crushed the Philipino, seeking independence at the cost of tens of thousands of people killed in direct combat and hundreds of thousands more who died from diseases contracted in concentration camps.

Of those presidents, not particularly racists, but whose actions were a mixed bag of good and evil:

- **Franklin D. Roosevelt** is one of our most popular presidents despite doing some questionable bad things, like ordering the forced relocation of more than 100,000 Japanese-Americans to internment camps after Japan bombed Pearl Harbor. Why didn't he do the same thing for the other citizens of Axis power's descent, such as Germans and Italians?
- **Harry S. Truman** is also a popular president whose legacy will be forever tinted for choosing to drop atomic bombs on the Japanese cities of Hiroshima and Nagasaki, killing between 130,000 and 226,000 mainly civilian people in 1945 while choosing to refuse the offer from Japan to surrender with one condition, that the Japanese Emperor Hirohito not be tried as a war criminal.
- **Dwight D. Eisenhower** was another popular president for his leading role in liberating Europe. But as president, he should be held responsible for authorizing a 1953 CIA-orchestrated coup to topple the Iranian government, resulting in the coronation of the Shah, political murders, and ultimately the rise of Muslim extremism.
- **Lyndon B. Johnson** for orchestrating the false flag " *Bay of Tonkin incident*" and launching the U.S. into a full-scale involvement in the Vietnam War that cost the lives of between 1,4500,000 to 3,595,000 on both sides in the three former French colonies of Vietnam, Laos, and Cambodia.
- **Richard Nixon** for lying in pretending to be willing to end the Vietnam War but, in fact, expanding it for political purposes at the cost of the loss of an additional 22,000 American lives.

- **George W. Bush,** for his false flag excuse to invade Iraq that, did cost the lives of at least a quarter of a million people.

So, considering that Trump's saga is not yet over, where will he fit in the aforementioned list of evil-doers? It all depends on whether or not he will be true to himself in the next presidential election.

Aside from being the only president ever to be impeached twice by the House of Representatives, his attempt to overthrow the Constitution, his 13 indictments, and 91 criminal charges, Donald Trump is in a class of his own.

"No president has ever done what I've done…not even close."

An understatement. Although, that is probably not what Trump had in mind when he uttered that comment. But the fact remains that because of all his transgressions and perhaps because of them, Trump remains the darling and poster child of political victims to millions of Americans.

But one of the main reasons Trump is at the very bottom of the list is credited for his monumental failure in the way he handled the COVID-19 epidemic. The U.S. had weeks of warning about the impending health tsunami that was about to hit the country. But Trump just could not focus on what to do, preferring to blame others for his lack of action by repeating his mantra:

"I don't take responsibility at all."

Let's hope that voters will remember that statement when it comes to electing the next president of our great country.

One last thing: Another group of historians and experts consulted by Siena rated

Trump last among all presidents when it came to integrity and intelligence.

Unless you want a dumbass and a crook to represent you, you now know for whom not to vote in the next presidential election. And if you cannot bring yourself to vote for any alternative candidate, stay at home and sit on your hands, but do not complain later and play the victim when your country just got flushed down the toilet because you are complicit.

HOW DOES THE WORLD SEE DONALD TRUMP?

The answer in two pictures

As chaos and a threat to the world   **As a Bozo and a sad scary clown**

To ask if Trump Donald Trump was unpopular across the world during his tenure as the most powerful man on the planet is like asking if the Pope is catholic. Aside from countries where mini-Trumps are surfing on the populist wave, Donald Trump was broadly loathed as a dangerous buffoon that, in a tantrum, could start bombing the shit of some country. A possibility serious enough that prompted General Mark Milley, chairman of the Joint Chiefs of Staff in the Trump Administration, to call his Chinese counterparts, promising to warn them first if he were ordered to attack China. Scary stuff indeed.

Of course, our visceral reaction as Americans is to say, "*Who cares?*" even if that sentiment reflects on the global image of Americans and how people think of the U.S.. But even if we pretend not to care, it is depressing to think that others believe that the greatest country on earth has elected a moron to represent them. This is certainly not what Trump had in mind when he said, "*Make America Great Again.*"

More alarming was the fact that the greatest negative attitude towards the U.S. was among some of our closest allies in Europe and elsewhere: countries like Spain, the UK, France, and Germany, where Trump was compared with Vladimir Putin and Xi Jinping. When your closest friends start to compare your leader with the leaders of two of the most undemocratic countries in the world, we should begin to pay attention.

But that was in the past. What about the future?

According to a recent Pew research, America's image abroad rebounded with the transition from "*President Chaos*" to "*President Normal.*" But for the future, anyone who thought that the Trump presidency was disastrous, including many Americans and most allies, is foreseeing a return of Trump 2.0 as cataclysmic not only for the U.S. but for the world at large. Here are some of the policy changes Trump muses of doing."

- **Withdrawing from NATO**. Not a veiled threat, considering his disdain for any multinational agreement. That should cause lots of worries for Taiwan and South Korea.

- Pulling the rug under Ukraine's support and military assistance, presumably to please his role model and mentor Vladimir Vladimirovich Putin. Thus, his prediction "*If I'm president, I will have that war settled in one day, 24 hours*".

- **Pull out of the Paris Accord** on climate change (again), or at least scrap all the previous U.S. regulations supporting carbon reduction and expand the use and exploration of fossil energy.

- **Reinstating the policy of separating migrant families at the U.S.-Mexico border**. *"When you say to a family that if you come, we're going to break you up, they don't come."*

- To counter the enormous rise in national debt incurred during Trump's tenure (+$7.8 trillion)[11], the former president is **advocating raising the debt ceiling**[12] to a level that would put the United States in default of payment to its global creditors and put the country at par with El Salvador, Sri Lanka, Pakistan, Egypt, Lebanon, Zambia, Malawi, and Ghana. It's a club that is not very consistent with *"Make America Great Again."*

- As far as his position on a Federal Abortion Ban, Trump has played the weathercock. One day for it, the next against it, and then back again. So take your pick.

---

[11] In part due to Trump massive tax cut for the rich.
[12] If the Democrats do not agree to massive spending cuts.

HOW DO PEOPLE WHO KNOW HIM BEST
SEE DONALD TRUMP

We had president *"Don't ask what your country can do for you,"* president *"I am not a crook,"* president *"Mission Accomplished,"* president *"Yes we can,"* and president *"Teflon,"* because nothing sticks to him. But.......

People who laud Teflon-Trump capability should know that Teflon eventually wears off and that it becomes toxic when heated, just like Trump.

Donald Trump's personality

Question:

Is Donald Trump faking to be stupid, or is he too stupid for faking it? Donald Trump is neither smart nor stupid. He simply gave the impression of being stupid because whatever comes out of his mouth is not filtered by his brain.

But he certainly does his best to prove the superiority of his intellect by rating himself:

"I'm a Genius" Donald Trump

If this is true, his schooling records, for one, do not reflect the self-evaluation of his intellect. And even though Donald Trump attended Wharton College from 1966 to 1968, he had his transcript sealed to prevent public access to his schooling records. However, public records show that he graduated with a C or worse, since he did not make the Dean's List. This information probably explains Trump's Marketing Professor William T. Kelly's comment:

"Dumbest G-damned student I've ever seen!"

And that was probably the kindest evaluation of Trump's intelligence since, according to former members of Trump's cabinet, those who have known him personally and worked with him regularly, everything went downhill from there.

- **"An idiot"** and that *"the president was "unhinged"* from White House Chief of Staff John Kelly.
- An **"idiot"** from Treasury Secretary Steven Mnuchin, former Chief of Staff Reince Priebus, and former advisor Sam Nunn.
- A **"dope"** and **"An idiot with the intelligence of a kindergartener"** from former National Security Advisor HR McMaster.
- **"Dumb as shit,"** and **"Less a person than a collection of terrible traits,"** from former chief economic adviser Gary Cohn.
- **"Like an 11-year-old child,"** and **"sick of being a wet nurse to a 71-year-old man."** from Steve Bannon.
- A **"fifth or sixth-grader"** understanding from Defense Secretary Jim Mattis.
- A **"moron."** from former Secretary of State Rex Tillerson.
- **"A stunning level of superficial knowledge and plain ignorance."** From Tony Schwartz, the ghostwriter of *"The Art of the Deal."*
- **"Like trying to figure out what a child wants,"** from former White House deputy chief of staff Katie Walsh.

Etc... etc.... So, there is probably some truth in the rumor that his father "*bought*" his degree by donating to the college since other teachers reported Trump as a poor student, lazy, and unable to comprehend even basic facts.

But all that does not prove Trump's stupidity. A lot of kids who do poorly at school turn out to be more intelligent than average. They were just bored, that's all. But since Trump claims to know more than anybody else, we could wonder where he got all his knowledge. Perhaps we should just take for granted his assertion:

"I read a lot. I read a lot. They like to say I don't read. I read a lot. I comprehend extraordinarily well. Probably better than anybody that you've interviewed in a long time. I read a lot".

This evaluation of himself must be true since he repeated it four times in case we did not get it the first time. But again, he repeated more than a thousand times that the election was stolen, which does not make it any more true. Although, according to Trump's own admission, he reads a lot..... of newspapers, not the fake news, but The Funny Section, the comics, and cartoons.

But seriously, if we are talking about books trying to decipher Trump's personality, perhaps we should start with his own book, "*The Art of the Deal*," which Trump considers not nearly as good as the Bible but comparable enough for wanted to be sworn in using a copy of his book, rather than the Bible[13]. That makes sense, considering that Trump said that his 1987 memoir

---

[13] According to Donald Trump's former adviser Omarosa Manigault Newman in the book "*Unhinged.*

The Art of the Deal is *"the No. 1 selling business book of all time."* But that is another truthful hyperbole line that gave him so **many Pinocchios and Pants on Fires** from the fact-checkers who estimated that the book sold about 177,000 copies in all its editions[14]. But even if we credit Trump's book with 1 million sales since 1987, the best-selling business book, by comparison, is the 1937 book *"Think and Grow Rich"* by Napoleon Hill, which sold 120 million copies worldwide.

All that being said, there is no denying that the Trump character has elicited more books from insiders than any other president in U.S. history. About 300 would be a rough estimate, not including journalists and other political talking heads. The first observation is that barely any of them paint Donald Trump in a positive light. In fact, many paint a reality of Donald Trump that is even worse than we can imagine.

From being inept at anything to being a complete moron with no redeeming qualities as a human being, we should interrogate ourselves for the reason we elected such an individual as our president to represent us.

In her 2020 book *"Too Much and Never Enough: How My Family Created the World's Most Dangerous Man,"* Mary L. Trump, a niece of Donald Trump, convincingly describes how their dysfunctional family primed Donald Trump into the man he is. What Mary Trump has over pundits and armchair psychologists, aside from being a trained psychologist, is being a firsthand witness of events that created the damaged man who once had his finger on the nuclear button of our country.

Among all those tell-all books about Trump are many former Trump enablers who tardily experienced an Epiphany of some

---

[14] Statistics from Nielsen data

sort after slavishly praising the man for being the greatest president ever. Of course, it would be easy to discount their narrative depicting Trump as a low-life character, devoid of any empathy, entirely absorbed by himself, and unfit for the highest post in the land as a pay-back from disgruntled former aides and associates of Donald Trump. Except that they are specific in detail, showing that reality is even worse than we could imagine.

In any event, all the books written about Trump seem to agree with Michael Cohen, Trump's former personal lawyer's latest book describing Trump as

"A cheat, a liar, a fraud, a bully, a racist, a predator, a con man."

Coming from Trump's lawyer, that is very telling.

"Calling me a liar, a cheat, and a con man does not insult me. I don't believe in truth." From D. Trump's little voice in his head.

There is, however, one book to counter all the bad things said about Trump. It is called *"Our Journey Together,"* published by Winning Team Publishing, founded in 2021 with Donald Trump as the co-founder. Which proves the saying that

"You are never better served than by yourself."
French proverb.

If Trump is not a genius, he is a genie. He can make all your wishes become a reality in exchange for your ability to think for yourself.

HOW WILL WE REMEMBER DONALD TRUMP?

Since nobody is immortal, the day will come when even Donald Trump will go to Heaven or Hell to meet his maker. Donald Trump will then enter the history book and the collective memories. Until then, and without wishing him ill, we can still joke about it.

In 2017, shortly after his election, Trump was invited to participate in the traditional Bastille Day military Parade in Paris. Trump was so impressed that upon his return, he immediately instructed the Pentagon with the following marching orders.

"I want a parade like the one in France."

A few days later, one of Trump's aid came back and said to him:

"Sir, I had a dream you got your parade. It was miles and miles long, winding through Washington, D.C.. Joyful Americans lined the route, literally in the millions. People were laughing, cheering, and playing in the street. You were riding in the most beautiful carriage."

Trump asks, "Was I happy?"[15]

The aide answered, "I don't know, sir. The casket was closed."

---

[15] Unknown author but cited by Elzanna Zapperlli on Quora.

On the more serious side, this is probably how people will remember Donald Trump:

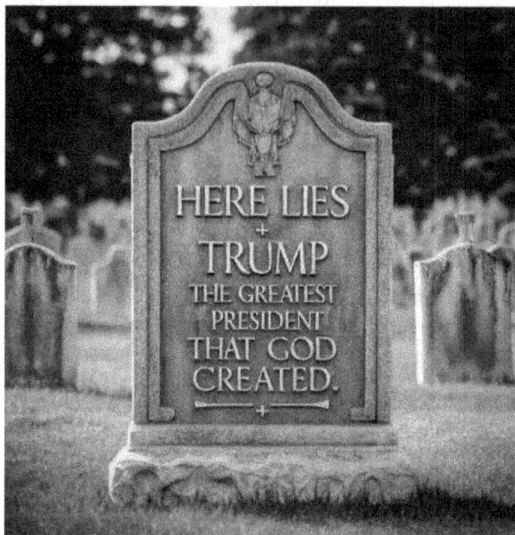

Tombstone designed by Donald Trump

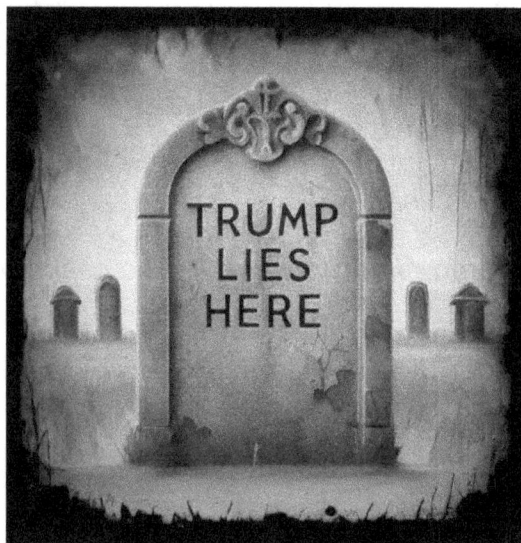

In the collective memory.

The takeaway

It would be incorrect to attribute Trump's success to any particular of his character trait. His success resides in the failure of our imagination to accept the possibility that there is anyone who can lie and cons as shamelessly and effectively as he does.

Not many modern-time politicians have been the subject of so much adulation from their supporters and loathing from their detractors than Donald Trump. If the man elicits so much visceral reaction, it is because he is a man of extremes, an exceptional person in the literal sense of the term, and not necessarily in a good way. Exceptional because he has set the political bar of morality and decency so low that now all other aspiring mini-Trump of the world will be judged on how well they compare to their inspirational model in the following areas:

A case of the pot calling the kettle black.

"*Worst President ever.*"

In a typical case of Gastrumping,[16] this is what Donald Trump called Joe Biden after he won the Iowa Caucuses in January 2024. Such a distinction would be funny if historians had not already determined who the worst President of the United States ever was. For historians, that distinction belongs to Donald Trump as the second last worst president ever. However, Trump has not said his last words yet, but he still has a chance if re-elected.

Donald J. Trump is undoubtedly the single most important reason why our country is on the edge of the abyss. Not that he

---

[16] See Glossary

is responsible for all the negative undercurrents that plague American society, but rather that his role acted as a catalyst to coalesce under his banner all those latent negative beliefs and behaviors that came to the surface today.

Regardless of his presidential rating, Donald J. Trump, as a person, deserves to enter the history books as the greatest illusionist, con man, and escape artist of all time.

As a con man, Trump has nothing to envy from another American swindler, Victor Lustig, one of the greatest con men of all time and the one who sold the Eiffel Tower, twice.

As a politician, Trump's major con coup was to convince voters that his presidency would benefit them. It is a great mystery how a self-proclaimed billionaire can understand them and muster an ascension to power by convincing the American working class to vote against their economic self-interest. Trump ultimately passed a 1.5 trillion tax cut that benefited mainly the rich like himself.

Trump's most profitable con is his scheme not to pay any tax. Trump's family empire operates like a tax evasion scheme, probably making him the greatest tax-dodging artist in IRS history. By artificially (and probably fraudulently) deflating his assets and inflating his expenses, he has managed to pay no tax by claiming a whopping $916 million loss on money that was not even his. Some will applaud this scheme as particularly clever, while the burden of running the country falls on the average American taxpayer. Trump also lost $3 billion in Atlantic City, which, along with his multiple business failures and bankruptcies, also made him the greatest loser in America. Perhaps his book "*The Art of the Deal*" should be rebranded "*The Art of the Steal.*"

As an escape artist, he should have his place in the Guinness Book of Records for being the only U.S. president to be impeached twice, escape unscathed as many times, dodge any consequences, and be emboldened to continue just doing the same thing.

But his most famous claim to fame is indubitably to have orchestrated a coup to overthrow our democracy without even being charged with a crime for which any other American citizen would have had to spend the rest of their life in solitary confinement.

But his master coup is yet to come.

Of all the criminal charges against him, Trump may succeed in facing little or no consequences. Thanks in part to his lawyers' ability to delay trials and The Supreme Court's refusal to rule on whether Trump as president has full immunity on anything he does, Trump is running the clock to the presidential election where, if he wins, he will simply make all cases against him disappear or just pardon himself. Isn't America Great?

As a cheat.

Donald Trump cheats all the time about anything, from his school record to golf. Who else but Donald Trump cheats at golfing?

But because Trump cheats all the time, he naturally believes that others do it as well.

As the master of illusions, he can make people believe in things that do not exist, like the claim that he won the 2020 presidential election and that the votes were rigged.

Not being an ideological person himself, he has nonetheless managed to inspire an ideology with millions of followers.

Who else than Donald Trump can succeed in creating the illusion that he is still the United States president when he is not?

He has managed to gain Messianic status while acting like the anti-Christ, meaning doing the opposite of Jesus' teaching.

As a tinhorn, he has given the illusion of being an acute businessman after multiple bankruptcies, business failures, and being the biggest money loser in American history.

As the most profitable snake oil salesman in history, Donald Trump managed to swindle for his sole profit, $495 million from suckers, in a massive haul allegedly to be used to contest election frauds.

But this magisterial sleight of hand that gave millions of Americans the illusion of an alternate reality was only the last attempt of a grand illusion scheme that Donald Trump had practiced all his life: the illusion of being a winner.

Finally, except for his unconditional fans, Donald Trump will be remembered by many by the adjective he fears the most:

As a felon

Tracking Trump's indictments and lawsuits is almost a full-time job. Forget the 88 felony charges for which he is so proud. Even if Trump manages to run the clock on all his trials, with all his delaying tactics and the assistance of the Supreme Court, with four Federal and State indictments, Trump will undoubtedly remain for a long time the NUMBER ONE in the crooked president category.

According to the bean counters, as of 2020, Trump had been involved in 3500 suits[17]. A boon for lawyers, or not, since he has a history of not paying them, as is the case for most of his bills. Still, it has been a boon for himself since millions of his supporters have contributed millions of dollars to fight his numerous indictments, thus giving a new meaning to the MAGA Acronym: **M**ilking **A**merica's **G**ullible **A**ssholes.

As one of the crassest presidents ever

Crass synonyms: vulgar, rude, crude, uncouth, insensitive, uncultivated, illiberal, clownish, tacky. All adjectives that fit Donald Trump to a T.

As a loser.

In a typical case of GASTRUMPING[18] , Trump relishes in calling others "*losers.*" but he himself will be remembered as the biggest loser of American business and politics, or to paraphrase the Great one as "*The biggest loser that God ever created.*" And now that Joe Biden is turning the label on him, that must "*piss him off*" to no end.

If "*Loser*" is a word in Trump's limited vocabulary that can be applied to others, not being perceived as one has been his lifelong obsession. In his universe, where everything is a transaction, there is no win-win situation. He is a winner, and everybody else is a loser. That simple fact is all anyone has to know to understand Trump's obsess insistence that he did not win the 2020 presidential election. Because, **since his younger age, Donald Trump had been wired to cheat, lie, and be**

---

[17] From James D. Zirin book "*Plaintiff in Chief*": A Portrait of Donald Trump in 3,500 Lawsuits.
[18] See Glossary

ruthless to be perceived as the cleverest and the most successful person in the room.

As not as wealthy as he pretends to be.

Right after becoming a presidential candidate, Trump promised to release his income tax returns, as it has been customary for all candidates to go to the Oval Office. But for the four years of his presidency, Trump fought tooth and nail to renege on his promise until he was finally forced to do so, having lost all legal attempts to keep his tax records concealed from the public. Six years after Trump promised to release his tax return, and on its last days of power, The Ways and Means Committee finally did it for him even though Trump went so far as to sue the committee to try to keep them private, but the U.S. high court ruled in the committee's favor.

The first takeaway from his tax returns shows that Donald Trump is the most prominent business money loser in all American history since losses are his contention for paying little or no tax. Legally, there is nothing wrong with evading tax dues through tax avoidance schemes. It is up to Congress to close all the tax loopholes that allow the wealthiest people to deprive our country of billions of revenues that could be used for our common wealth. But for that, we all know that it will never happen.

The second takeaway raises the question of the validity of all those business losses claimed by Trump since his company, the Trump Organization, was recently convicted of decades of tax fraud and schemes. In essence, The Trump Organization was essentially used as a front, like the Mafia.

The third takeaway is that contrary to custom, the Internal Revenue Service did not audit Trump during the first year of his presidency and did so only after the Democrats sought to gain access to his tax records. All along, Trump had claimed that the reason for not releasing his tax returns was because he was being audited. So Trump lied, so what?

Except that, the "*So what*" finally managed to reveal that the Emperor was half naked when it became obvious that Trump had difficulties coming up with the money, or Bonds to cover for all his legal woes. But there is hope: maybe Trump will manage to sell enough MAGA hats, T-shirts, mugs, and sneakers to avoid selling Trump Tower, Mar-a-Lago, or a golf club.

As a not-so-great business genius.

In his book "*The Art of the Deal*," Donald Trump purports to prove his business acumen in becoming a real estate mogul and becoming rich. Later on, his TV reality show The Apprentice perpetuated the well-founded 11 business principles of the book that guided him through all his business decisions.

For starters, it appears that Trump received a modern-day equivalent of at least $413 million from his father's real estate holdings[19]. So much for the self-made millionaire that Trump claims to be. So what has he done to prove that with all that money, he has been a successful entrepreneur?

To his credit, Donald Trump has had many real estate and business success stories, such as the Trump Tower, The Grand Hyatt Hotel, the Trump International Tower in Chicago, the Trump Place development along the Hudson River, the 40 Wall Street office building, The elite group of 17 golf courses, and of course, the very successful TV reality shows The Apprentice and its spinoff The Celebrity Apprentice, for which Trump with

---

[19] According to a 2018 New York Times published reports that claims that most of the money comes from "*tax dodges*" in the 1990s.

all his humility credits himself as *"The most successful man that ever lived"*

Notwithstanding those business success stories, Trump's most personal profitable venture has been his claim to a fraudulent election, yielding him his biggest financial score by raising $250 million mainly from small donors to contest the election results. Of course, very little of that money was used for any legal endeavor to achieve its intended purpose but ended up instead lining up the pockets of Trump's cronies and the pockets of one of the greater snake oil salesmen in America since Clark Stanley[20] was peddling his wares to an already gullible American public. No wonder Trump wanted to trademark the phrase *"rigged election."*[21] The catchphrase is a good business.

Trump's business failures are as resounding as his successes.

- **Trump Airlines**. When for roughly $365 million, Trump proudly put his name on a fleet of 17 Boeing 727s that never turned a profit, forcing Trump to default on his loans to acquire the planes.
- **Trump Mortgage**. Predicted to be the nation's No. 1 home-loan lender closed shop after a year and a half of existence.
- **Trump casinos**. Trump Entertainment Resorts Inc., which ran the three casinos, the Taj Mahal, the Trump Plaza, and the Trump Marina, all located in Atlantic City, filed for Chapter 11 bankruptcy in 2009. Bad bet.
- **Trump steak**. Dubbed what else as the *"world's greatest,"* it turned out to be a flop along the Trump Steakhouse in Las Vegas.

---

[20] Better known in the 1900s as the Rattle-Snake King which gave popularity to the term "snake oil" synonymous with a hoax.
[21] From the testimony of Jared Kushner to the Committee Investigating the January 6th Attack on the Capitol.

- **Trump Magazine**. Catering to the rich, it closed a year and a half after its launch.
- **Trump University**. Opened in 2005. In 2013, the New York Attorney General sued Trump and the *"university"* for $40 million for allegedly defrauding students. This is one of the rare cases where defrauded parties got their money back.
- **Go Trump.com**. A luxury travel search engine launched in 2006 and shut down a year later.
- **Trump the Game**. In which three to four players must buy and sell real estate and outsmart each other. Predicted 2 million units, it was a flop.
- **Trump vodka**. Predicted to outsell Grey Goose vodka and become the most popular cocktail in America when mixed with Tonic. Trump, who does not drink, should have known better. Another flop.
- **The Trump Network,** which was supposed to make people rich because of Trump's branding, filed for bankruptcy.
- **Trump Ice,** branded as "*one of the highest quality spring waters in the world*," was used as a publicity stunt when Trump delivered a pallet of his beautiful water on February 22, 2023, to the population of East Palestine, Ohio after a freight train derailed with cars carrying toxic chemicals. It turned out that the Trump-branded water he delivered was 13 years old and could be a health hazard.
- **The New Jersey Generals**. The United States Football League (USFL) bought for $9 million in 1983 and lost $30 million in the same year.
- **Truth Social,** branded as the source of truth where Trump's devotees go to receive their daily dose of Trump's Gospel, is, as of 2024, losing tens of millions of dollars. In March 2024, Media & Technology Group Corp, the parent company of Truth Social went public and hit $78 per share on its first day of trading.

But all of this does not even compare with his famous claim:

*"We're going to win so much.
You're going to be so sick and tired of winning."*

So what is the score?

- Donald Trump lost the popular vote in the 2020 presidential election.
- Donald Trump lost the Electoral College.
- Donald Trump lost multiple recounts in two states.
- Donald Trump paid $3 million in a state recount to find out that Joe Biden, in fact, gained votes.
- Donald Trump lost nearly 50 lawsuits that he or his allies claiming that the election should be overturned or votes should be tossed out because of widespread fraud, including two cases rejected by the U.S. Supreme Court.

But the worst humiliation is that Trump lost to "***Sleepy Joe,***"

The "*worst candidate in the history of presidential politics.*" D. Trump.

So yes, Mr. President, aren't you tired of losing?

A CAUTIONARY TALE

Unknown Russian origin

A scorpion wants to cross a river but cannot swim, so it asks a frog to carry it across.

The frog hesitates, afraid that the scorpion might sting it, but the scorpion argues that if it did that, they would both drown.

The frog considers this argument sensible and agrees to transport the scorpion.

The frog lets the scorpion climb onto its back and begins to swim. Midway across the river, the scorpion stings the frog anyway, dooming them both.

The dying frog asks the scorpion why it stung despite knowing the consequence, to which the scorpion replies,

"I couldn't help it. It's in my nature."[1]

This tale could be interpreted as a metaphor for psychopaths whose impulsive and vicious personalities lead them to keep doing bad things they cannot control, like compulsive lying or ruining the reputation of good men.

Contrary to Midas, who turned to gold anything he touched, Trump turns anybody he touches into a foul and stinky invertebrate creature he uses to restock the pond he was supposed to drain, like William Barr, Rudy Giuliani, and all the generals who served in his administration and ruined their reputation.

"The worst thing a son of a bitch can do Is to turn you into a son of a bitch."
Frank Oppenheimer.

DONALD TRUMP'S AUTOCRATIC POTENTIAL

"I have an Article II, where I have the right to do whatever I want as president."

A question that only The Trump Party does not ask because they already know the answer: yes, he can.

A question that the Supreme Court delayed answering because the Court's Republican majority could not openly rule: yes, he can.

So far, the answer suggests that there are no limits on what a re-elected Donald Trump could do. Which leads to the next logical question:

Does Donald Trump have what it takes to be an autocratic leader?

Donald Trump is a charismatic and ambitious leader in both business and politics, but he is not an ideological person. He only believes in two things:

1. In himself as the smartest, the most intelligent, the most knowledgeable person in the room and,

2. That truth is elastic and relative. For Donald Trump, the truth is whatever serves him at that moment. This is the reason why what he says to be true one moment becomes false the next.

It is not always easy to predict if a newly elected leader will betray his campaign promises and take a completely different direction once elected. By the same token, predicting which freshly elected leader will become an autocrat is not an exact science either. On many occasions, the person elected on the promise to be the nation's savior turned out to completely change the destiny of that country. Autocratic tendencies were not evident in Xi Jinping in 2012 when he was first elected to the posts of general secretary of the Communist Party and chairman of the Central Military Commission. Neither was Recep Erdoğan when he was first elected president and head of government of Turkey.

However, the opposite is not true. We still have to see a leader with autocratic tendencies becoming a democratic one or giving up power gracefully on his own accord.

This is not that Donald Trump never gave us a heads-up or a hint of his anti-democratic tendencies. There is one thing we could all give him credit for: Trump is very transparent in his intentions. All of this is old news. All we have to do is look in the rear-view mirror.

- Like Hitler, Trump believes he is on a messianic mission when he says, "*I am the chosen one.*" A delusion supported with religious fervor not only by more than 80 percent of white Evangelical Christians but by millions of his supporters. Even though white Evangelicals represent no more than 15% of the American population, they still account for one-third of Republicans and 15 percent of all voters. This is why Trump cannot afford to stop himself from some dog and pony shows embracing the Bible.

- Trump has made many attempts to use chaos to shred democratic safeguards and consolidate authoritarian power. The January 6th, 2021, assault on the Capitol was only his last-ditch effort to overturn democracy. A date that, like Pearl Harbor and 9/11, will forever be marked as a day of infamy in American history.

- Trump acts like he owns our government and can fire any official who defends the law. Of all presidents, Trump is the one who fired the most government officials that he replaced with an acting secretary of something. Not too shy about leading by example, Trump attempted and sometimes succeeded in convincing other officials to commit fraud or act against the law. We know that from the long list of people serving time for acting on his behalf and that he pardoned just before leaving office.

- Trump uses powerful media platforms like Fox News to propagate lies, misinformation, disinformation, and conspiracy theories, just like in any autocratic country where the state controls the media.

- Like Hitler and many after him, Trump subscribes to a doctrine of genetic and white superiority by supporting the proponents of *"the great replacement."* Taking a page from successful nationalist political opportunists, he incited racial hatred to scapegoat immigrants and gain power. For the next time around, Trump can always count on a myriad of white militias who stand *"willing, able, and ready"* to answer the call.

- As typical dictators do, Trump used the Department of Justice and any judicial power to circumvent the law and the Constitution and investigate his opponents and anyone who dares scrutinize him or his allies for crimes they may have committed.

- In another dictator's typical move, Trump tried to muzzle critics and opposition by attempting to use his power to outlaw speech critical of him. In a textbook move from *"How to Subvert Democracy for "A Dear Leader" Wannabe,"* Trump called the free press *"the enemy of the people."* The sad reality is that millions of Americans believe it, oblivious that this is the first step in how democracy dies.

- Trump used military power and federal law enforcement to suppress peaceful political protest. Here is a fact: Under the Trump administration, the FBI has charged and convicted more people who protested for *"Black Lives Matter"* than anybody involved in the Capitol riot under the Biden administration.

- Starting in 2016, Trump has persistently lied about voter fraud. As a favorite move from a wanna-be-dictator, this topic is more developed in the *"head I win, tail you lose"* chapter *"A slow-moving coup,"*

- Trump viciously attacks his critics, going as far as advocating the hanging for treason for the whistleblower and all those who testify against him at his impeachment trial. Always leading by example, Trump prompted his followers to do the same to Vice President Mike Pence for daring to do his democratic duty.

- Trump has repeatedly suggested that he might remain in office after a second term. So, nobody can pretend that they did not receive the memo, since this is precisely what Putin and other banana republic autocrats have done with success in the past.

- Trump believes that he has the power to do what he wants, regardless of Congress or the courts. And he is right. The two impeachment charades proved his point. More power to him for the next time.

- Trump finds common ground with the world's most ruthless dictators while denigrating America's democratic allies. *"Qui se resemble, s'assemble,"*[22] as the French would say.

If being a fascist means exalting nationalism, contempt for electoral democracy, and race over the individual while seeking personal power, then by all standards, Donald Trump is a fascist. If the definition of fascism is a political ideology that promotes a strong centralized one-party government devoted to a single political leader, then the TADPOLE-GOP is definitely fascist.

PUTIN WANNABE

You have to give it to Donald Trump for not being too subtle about his fondness for leaders with authoritarian tendencies. He even exchanged *"love letters"* with Dear Leader Kim Jong-un from North Korea. But his undying admiration is for *"President for Life"* Vladimir Vladimirovich Putin. Unless, of course, his submissive feigned adoration for this modern Tsar is dictated by fear. Fear of all the dirty laundry the former KGB strongman has on him. Because once a spook, always a spook. Old habits die hard.

---

[22] Birds of a feather flock together

DOES DONALD TRUMP PERSONIFY AMERICA, OR DOES AMERICA IDENTIFY ITSELF WITH TRUMP?

There is no point in identifying for you how many horrible character traits describe Donald Trump. But if you do not recognize that he does not possess any, it could mean that your identification with Donald Trump is the reason for your affinity with him and your inability to acknowledge that he is a reflection of you.[23]

The question begs an answer because if Trump is an authoritarian, so are millions of Americans who identify with him.

Since America has a history of flirting with fascism, it is not a stretch of the imagination to think that many of our citizens long for a strong leader, Putin style, who will deliver on the MAGA motto. Trump himself has mused several times about calling on the far-right militia to start an armed insurrection to overthrow our democracy. If there is no doubt that many of our compatriots saw the calling as their patriotic duty to answer the invitation, how many genuinely believe that ignoring the democratic will of the people would not be a bad thing after all? Hence, the FBI identification of homegrown violent extremists as the main terrorism threat to the Homeland.

Indeed, if totalism would not be the preference of choice for the many who drape themselves in The Star-Spangled Banner,

---

[23] This is a reference to a reported gathering of about 600 Republicans who, after Trump had been indicted for the third time, were asked if they could name one single thing Donald Trump did wrong, not a single one could find any.

many others are predisposed to consider it as an acceptable form of government. Far from being an oxymoron, *"American authoritarianism,"* which has always been a dormant ideology of the Republican Party, is in the process of becoming mainstream and openly assumed. Of course, few would express it out loud, but their actions speak louder than their words.

What is scary is that according to some polls, approximately four Americans out of ten would be okay with some form of totalism in America, [24] especially in periods of social and political uncertainty. This choice is why Trump and all the mini-Trumps make it their business to promote fear and insecurity while promising to secure law and order for voters.

"Chaos is my friend," from inside Trump's head.

If the weaponization of fear is a staple artifice for demagogues, to be effective, it has to find a fertile ground in order to flourish to a point when it becomes an existential threat to the people claiming to share the same worldviews. So, who is that part of America for whom the call for authoritarianism resonates the most? More specifically, if fear is the great motivator for the lure of an autocratic leader, on what fears would a demagogue surf in America?

One of the perceived strengths of America over other countries was its ability to be a melting pot of various ethnicities and creeds. Not anymore. Diversity has become the threat and the battle cry of the *"us against them."* The "Great R*eplacement*" is just one aspect of that perceived threat that feeds on the conspiracy theory that views immigration as a nefarious plot to replace the white population of Western countries. With the systemic problem of racism in America, it is no wonder this

---

[24] Source: Matthew C. MacWilliams writing in the Politico Magazin

particular aspect of diversity resonates particularly well among a vast segment of the U.S. population. The fact that neither the Trump Party nor the Democrats have managed to come up with a comprehensive immigration policy brings oxygen to the fire that fuels the "*Great Replacement*" conspiracy theory.

The next type of fear is one of the most common in the world: the fear of change. The status quo is reassuring, while change always has a part of the unknown. This fear is why authoritarian leaders mainly appeal to conservative-minded people who see progressive values as threatening their way of life, culture, and identity. A good example of this gut reaction can be seen in the Conservative war against the so-called "*Woke movement,*" which, according to them, is "*the belief there are systemic injustices in American society and the need to address them.*"[25] This means that for Conservatives, everything is just fine the way it is, and any attempt to change their worldview is pure anathema. That this way of thinking flies in the face of the majority of Americans who live in this reality and recognize that many things in America are broken and need to be fixed does not seem to faze them whatsoever.

Another big fear that gets people going is anything having to do with the safety of children. From the fear of high-ranking Democrats using pizza parlors (Pizzagate) as child sex rings to being involved in satanic rituals called Frazzledrip, where they drink the blood of children they are about to kill to achieve superpowers.

Last but most feared by true patriots is the imminent threat the elite poses from business, finance, entertainment, sport, politics, etc., Generally identified as the Illuminati, a secret society dating back to the 1800s whose goal is to impose a new

---

[25] As defined by the DeSantis administration

world order or a totalitarian one-world government to replace sovereign nations. The New World Order conspiracy finds credence with a large American audience, especially among fundamentalist Christians, as it relates to the End-time and the Anti-Christ. This worldview is also prevalent among right-wing populists as a backlash against secular government and liberalism.

The closest we came to establishing a New World Order in America was back in 2016 when a Republican neoconservative think-tank[26] published "*Project for the New American Century,*" a sort of manifesto focussing on foreign policy and advocating, among other things, the need for a **new Pearl Harbor** to kick-start the transformation of the United States with the stated goal "*to promote American global leadership.*" In other words, a New World Order dominated by America. President George W. Bush was openly a fierce advocate of a New World Order and used it explicitly as a pretext for his war in Iraq, invade Afghanistan, declare "*the war on terror,*" and curtail civil liberties with the enactment of the Patriot Act just weeks after 9/11.

Today, the Trump Party has not abandoned its goal of a New World Order. They simply got smarter about it. With wars being so messy and unpredictable, why not establish a new form of government right at home as a model that other-minded countries would join to form a new world order where America would be the leader? But before that, they have to get rid of democracy. Thank God, the Trump Party now has their man who could finally realize their long-time ambition for fascism.

---

[26] Which included Dick Cheney, Donald Rumsfeld, and Paul Wolfowitz who later served in the administration of President George W. Bush,

It is sort of ironic that some Americans are perfectly fine to stomp on the same principles they are pretending to uphold and curtail the fundamental rights of others, like voting in the name of liberty and patriotism.

When you do the sum of all fears, America is heading towards a perfect storm that will sink all our illusions. All mini-Trump of the world, unite. A New World order is coming!

THE TADPOLE aka GOP
ANTI-DEMOCRATIC PAST

The Republican Party has no morals, no integrity, no honesty, no balls, no shame, and is proud of it. That is why it has now become the Trump Party as a true reflection of Trump's personality.

The best way to con people into hiding the true motives of your activity is to call it something with a name that is the opposite of what you represent. Something like *"Democratic Republic,* of ......" for an autocratic country, *"Crisis Pregnancy Center"* for an anti-abortion advocacy Office, or Global Climate Coalition for a lobbying firm for Big Oil companies, or *"Research Institute"*[27] of ......" (Fill in the blanks), or for a political lobby consulting agency. The same goes for the TADPOLE-GOP, which promotes itself as the party that *"fights to keep our country free and democratic for the real America"* when all its actions demonstrate the contrary. If the TADPOLE-GOP represents the real America, we are in big shit! Nevertheless, that statement of purpose should be laughable if it was not believed by millions of Americans who know so little about the history of the Party they claim to represent them or simply just do not give a damn.

So, for those who need a refresher on when the Party they support departed from the values supported by its first

---

[27] Such as the George C Marshall Institute, an Exxon funded company dedicated to fight climate change science.

president, Abraham Lincoln, it all started during the 1964 Republican convention when Nelson Rockefeller, a Republican liberal progressist (if such a thing ever existed) attempted and failed to get the party to steer away and renounce its segregation and extremist goals. Even though the Party had until now been rather pro-civil rights, the Party instead embraced the right-wing views of the extremist Republican nominee for president, Barry Goldwater, and never looked back. When Lyndon Johnson won the nomination and became President, Goldwater went on to start the conservative revolution among the right-wing supporters of the Party.

In the '60s, America was engulfed in riots for Civil Rights and against the Vietnam War when Richard Nixon appeared as the savior of both the country and the Republican Party. By appealing to whiles voters in the Southern states and selling law and order, Nixon became the great hope of the Republican Party. But what a betrayal. Instead of expanding the Conservative Revolution, Nixon went on to produce more government and social programs. Worse, he protected the environment by creating the Environment Protection Agency. So, when Nixon had to resign because of the Watergate scandal for the Republicans, his departure appeared to be a blessing.

When the 80s rolled along, a cowboy actor riding on Barry Goldwater's horse rode to the White House: Ronald Reagan. Again, great expectations and a big letdown to the measure of the hopes. Reagan had all the credentials of a poster Republican hero: anti-communist, anti-social programs, anti-people of color, anti-immigrant, and anti-progressive policies fully resumed in his slogan "*Let's Make America Great Again.*" To his credit, Reagan sort of defeated the Soviet Union. Still, this accomplishment did not help the Republicans to swallow the rest of his domestic policies that exploded the debt and the deficit. The Republicans finally choked a final gasp when Reagan expanded Medicare, the ultimate sin.

At the beginning of the '90s, the President *"read my lips."* George H.W. Bush brought the first *"Neocons"* (neo-conservatives) to an American administration. That should have more than pleased the Republicans until they gave us the invasion of Panama, the first Gulf War as a prelude to the Second Gulf War, and the invasion of Iraq. So, from the conservative revolution supporter's point of view, George H.W. Bush's presidency was also a flop, since he did not bring to fruition what the base was expecting.

At the beginning of the 2000s, President *"Mission Accomplished"* George W. Bush started with a strong approval rating that elicited high hopes from the base after years of betrayal from preceding Republican Presidents. Bush faced significant challenges: an economic recession in the wake of the bursting of the dot-com bubble and the 9/11 terrorist attack on America. Against most Republican opposition, Bush passed many social, environmental, and energy policies that benefited the American people, not exactly in the TADPOLE-GOP cup of tea. However, what enraged the Conservatives the most was his bungled Iraq war and the bailout of Wall Street after they caused the subprime mortgage crisis.

Between 2009 and 2017, the two consecutive mandates of Barack Obama pushed the TADPOLE-GOP's desperation and rage for power to its paroxysm. A Negro at the White House!. Race had finally been pushed to the forefront of politics and the Republicans to the edge.

In 2016, enters Donald Trump. To the TADPOLE-GOP and other proponents of the long-awaited conservative revolution, Donald Trump is the *"Providence Men,"* the Messiah, and Barry

Goldwater reincarnated, all in one. Thank you, God! With this new Messiah, we will finally transform the TADPOLE-GOP and take and retain power forever. Then everything went downhill from there, or was it the dawn of "*Make America Great Again*," depending on your perspective?

After years of disappointments from previous Republican presidents who failed to implement the Party's conservative revolution agenda, The TADPOLE, aka GOP, is finally ready, willing, and able to trump democracy.

THE TRANSFORMATION OF THE TADPOLE, aka GOP

from a political party to a sect

How not to admire Pinocchio-Trump's capability to use his growing nose[28] to evolve from a puppet to a puppet master?

---

[28] A reference to Pinocchio's nose that grows longer every time he lies.

As far back as 1966[29], Republican Senator Thomas Kuchel already assessed the GOP as follows:

"A fanatical neo-fascist political cult in the GOP, driven by a strange mixture of corrosive hatred and sickening fear, who are recklessly determined to either control or destroy our party."

Fifty-eight years later, if the needle has moved, it is further to the extreme right. What makes Kuchel's assessment even more dangerous today since, for the first time, the Party has a charismatic political *"Dear Leader"*: Donald J. Trump, who unceremoniously and single-handedly destroyed the Republican Party.

Should we be comforted by the apologetic whine of old-fashioned Republicans? The party of Abraham Lincoln, Theodore Roosevelt, Dwight Eisenhower, Richard M. Nixon, and the two George Bush proclaiming:

"I do not recognize our Party. This is not us, this is not who we are, this is not what America is."

News flash! This assessment is precisely where the former Republican Party is and why it needed a new name: TADPOLE. But before making up your mind about the imminent danger that the TADPOLE represents to the Nation, you only have to consider the ultimate goal of the new Party. It has made no bone about it:

---

[29] Lyndon Baines Johnson was president

We, Republicans, don't care about democracy or the sharing of governance. Our only mission until we achieve complete power has three goals: obstruct, obstruct, and obstruct.

But how did we get there?

Right after the 2020 presidential election and before Donald Trump started his big lie that the election was stolen, only a handful of the TADPOLE-GOP questioned Joe Biden's presidential legitimacy. Today, those who have not fully embraced Trump's false claim can be counted on one hand. Since it would be too easy to think that they were all too stupid to believe it honestly, we are left to conclude that their political self-preservation gave them the rationale to convince themselves that it was true. Of course, it is better for our own sanity to believe in that explanation than to fall into the old stereotype of thinking that politicians never tell us things they do not believe in. But that, we will never know for sure since after each of Trump's saying or actions that would put to shame any mafia boss, the TADPOLE-GOP's reaction has always been consistent with a deafening silence.

"Doublethink means the power of holding two contradictory beliefs in one's mind simultaneously and accepting both of them."
George Orwell.

TRUMPISM

To say that half of Trump's supporters are complete idiots would not be politically correct, so let me rephrase my statement: half of Trump's supporters are not complete idiots.

"*Say nothing, See nothing, Hear nothing.*"[30]

Question with a disturbing answer: Can we live without a brain?

If the question begs an answer, it is because many have raised it regarding Trump's unconditional supporter's ability to think. That is true since it had been believed that nobody could live without a brain until recently, and those asking the question generally conceded that Trump's supporters had at least half a brain. But it turned out that this assumption was not even true.

---

[30] Brrowed from " *mizaru, kikazaru, iwazaru*" a 3 monkeys Japanese saying

It is quite possible to live a normal life with no brain at all[31]. This finding raises several disturbing questions:

- How many Americans are afflicted with this condition since it cannot be detected unless a person has a reason to receive a CAT scan?
- To what degree does this condition mentally impair a person?
- Is it genetic? (a scary thought).
- How do we know for certain that Donald Trump has a brain?

If the last question should be taken as a joke, the whole prospect that some of us could be classified as "*brain dead,*" either totally or partially, could explain the attraction that some have for seeking the leadership of someone who thinks for them.

Question with a disturbing possible answer

Is Trumpism a sect, a cult, or more?

America is in danger of being taken over by zealots, not the Islamist Radical style, but by a new kind of zealots, those belonging to a new cult/sect: Trumpism.

Cult: from the French word "*culte,*" which means a particular form of worship and devotion to a person or a thing. Trumpism is a sect or a cult if:

- **It tends to possess a monopoly on truth.**
  Trump always tells the truth. He is the truth and the law; everything else is fake news.
- **It has a charismatic leader, who is generally perceived to be mandated with a special mission**.

---

[31] CAT scans of several people in the UK, France and Japan revealed that some people had only 5% of a normal brain while other had none.

Trump will drain the pond, make America great again, and save children from pedophile Democrats.

- **It displays a zealous and unquestioning commitment to its leader**.
  Trump's followers' slavish obedience and devotion are typical of members of fundamentalist organizations like the Taliban or Al-Qaeda.

- **The leader does not allow questioning, doubt, or contradiction and punishes dissenters**.
  Fear for the TADPOLE-GOP of not being re-elected by the base if not anointed by the Great One.

- **The leader dictates how members should think, speak, and behave.**
  Trump has effectively drained the pond by replacing it with invertebrate bottom-feeder creatures who must ask permission to breathe.

- **It has a polarized, us-versus-them mentality, which may cause conflict, dissension, and division in the broader society.**
  Today, America is divided and fractured politically and intellectually, as ever since the Civil War. And we all owe it to one man.

- **The leader is not accountable to anybody and feels immune to any type of consequence.**
  Two impeachments without consequences have bolstered Trump's belief that he could shoot someone in the middle of Times Square and get away with it. That does not bode well for assuming he would not attempt an armed insurrection against our democracy.

- **The leader promotes the belief that the ends justify whatever means are deemed necessary to secure power and control. This belief may result in members participating in behaviors or activities they would have considered against the law, reprehensible, or unethical before.**

Unlike Midas, who was cursed with the ability to turn anything he touched into gold, Donald Trump is blessed with the ability to turn any good man he touches into a douchbag more than willing to do his bidding.

- **The leader is preoccupied with making money and even resorts to lies and deceits to persuade people to subscribe to his cause.**

    After losing the 2020 Presidential election, Trump managed to swindle $495 million from suckers in a massive haul allegedly to be used to contest election frauds, but more likely to line his personal coffer.

Considering the above characteristics and how well they describe Trumpism, it would be tempting to classify it as a sect/cult. There is, however, one characteristic that does not fit entirely with Trumpism. Pushed to their extremes, cult members are prepared to die for their beliefs. The 1978 mass murder-suicide of 900+ people in Jonestown in Guyana, the 39 members of the Heaven's Gate followers who committed suicide in the hope of getting picked up by UFO in order to escape the last days of the apocalypse, or the 7000+ German people who kill themselves in 1945 because they could not imagine a world without Hitler are only some example of people who died for their beliefs. But this is definitely not the case for the Trump worshipers. On the contrary, they would rather kill all those who do not adhere to their beliefs. To that effect, Trumpism is more than a sect/cult; it is a religion.

From the day Christianity ceased to be persecuted, it started persecuting others. That is when Christianity became a religion.

If "*Trumpster*" has become more than a cult or a sect, the real question is whether or not the number of adepts to Trumpism and their dedication makes this new ideology the greatest existential threat America has faced since the Civil War.

To answer this question, we must first answer another one.

How many world leaders would you describe as a version of Joe Biden and Donald Trump? If you drew a blank for Biden, finding at least half a dozen mini-Trump should not have been difficult. Leaders of Hungary, Poland, India, Turkey, the Philippines, Colombia, Mexico, Nigeria, Venezuela, and Brazil, until Jair Bolsonaro's own Capitol riot attempt, and another dozen leaders in the Americas, South East Asia, and Africa fit the bill. Of course, in this lot, we should also grant an honorific place to Boris Johnson, also dubbed a Mimi-Trump, who could be credited for fooling the most democratic of all countries, Great Britain, into voting against its own interest, Brexit, and accelerating its fall as a great nation. If we, Americans, do not draw any lesson from that example, then we genuinely deserve whatever happens to America.

Also, note that if Russia and China are not cited in this roaster of demagogue leaders, it is because, contrary to those aspiring to imitate their role model, it is Trump himself who is longing to emulate those two full-fledged autocrats and de facto dictators.

What all those Trump wannabes have in common, aside from their narcissist/psychopath traits, is their charismatic appeal to people with strong conspiracy theories and nationalistic or religious beliefs. It is almost certain that many of Trump's and mini-Trump's admirers do not care as much about their political policies as they do about their admiration for the sense of virility and machismo displayed by their outrageous rhetoric and behavior. This crowd appeal has not escaped in the U.S. the attention of politicians of the Conservative Left who compete to outdo each other as who would be the most extreme in wackiness and earn the most money for their re-election. Everywhere else on the planet, the same crowd psychology is at play.

This is why, to answer the earlier posited question, Trumpism is more than a sect/cult and should be considered a religion.

"I heard that some people consider me as the Second Coming of Christ. That is false. I have already created my own religion." From Trump's little voice in his head.

PART III

A SLOW-MOVING COUP[32]

Normally, people who have lived under an authoritarian regime fight for a more democratic one. America is the only country in the world where people fight to overthrow their democracy to live under an autocratic ruler.

---

[32] Coined by Bill Maher

Two MAGA astronauts on the moon

Trump said that the Earth is flat, and that is exactly what we will report

THE GREAT DELUSION
OF A GREATER DISILLUSION
CAUSED BY A GREAT ILLUSION

Delusion: *an idiosyncratic belief or impression that is firmly maintained despite being contradicted by what is generally accepted as reality or rational argument, typically a symptom of a mental disorder.* Example: The 2020 election was rigged with massive fraud.

Disillusion: *disappointment resulting from the discovery that something is not as good as one believed it to be.* Example: Never-lose Donald Trump lost the 2020 presidential election to what he called a loser, Joe Biden.

Illusion: something that deceives by producing a false or misleading impression of reality. Example: Donald Trump.

If you are still comforting yourself in the illusion that the refusal to concede the 2020 presidential election results was a grass-roots reaction to election frauds and not a well-planned and executed plan to subvert our democracy, the proof will come soon enough in the next 2024 presidential election. Everything that happens until that date has only one goal: to restore "*Dear Leader*" to his God-given mission to save America from the blood-sucking pedophile Democrats.

True, Donald Trump's attempt to subvert democracy did not start until he had a taste of power and discovered through trials and errors how far he could go to ignore the institutions,   the rule of law, and our democracy without consequences. Embolden by the weak responses and reactions to his increasingly authoritarian actions, Donald Trump correctly deduced that he could become like the many other authoritarian leaders he so admires.

It is also true that the "*conspiracy*" to subvert our democracy did not start until Trump lost his bid for a second mandate to the Oval Office. It is only then that the TADPOLE-GOP saw in Trump an opportunity to regain the only thing they truly care about: power. From that point on, lies, deceptions, moral bankruptcy, and obstruction to govern are fair game. But a conspiracy? Let's first examine the "*conspiracy*" premise.

Conspiracy: a secret plan by a group to do something unlawful, immoral, illegal, or harmful.

If this standard definition of the word is still part of the English language here in America, it has completely lost its initial meaning since The Trump Party has rendered it obsolete. When applied to the plot to subvert our democracy, the terms "*unlawful, illegal, and harmful*" have been replaced by the words "*legal, necessary, and patriotic.*"

As for the word "*secret,*" that attribute no longer applies since the TADPOLE-GOP, Donald Trump, and all his enablers, in both their words and actions, are not coy about their intention to subvert our democracy.

The Trump Party's claim is, therefore, correct; there is no plot, and everything is in the open for everyone to see, and a **4-point-plan to reinstate Donald Trump as president "*in days, not years*"** started in earnest at CPAC[33] hours after it was clear that Trump had lost the 2020 presidential election.

---

[33] Conservative Political Action Conference

As outlandish as it sounded, the plan, if it had actually been implemented, would have unraveled as follows:

1. Ousting House Speaker Nancy Pelosi.
2. Installing Donald Trump as Speaker of the House.
3. As the new speaker, Donald Trump would then call for a vote to impeach, charge, and remove *"imposters"* President Joe Biden and Vice President Kamala Harris.
4. As the Speaker of the House is third in the line of presidential succession, Trump would then take up the presidency.

And voila, with a caveat: the plan hinged upon The Trump Party regaining control of the House.

When someone tells you what reality is, that everything else is a lie, and you accept it, he has become your God. Your thoughts are no longer yours, and you are just an avatar being manipulated, just like in a video game.

A SLOW-MOVING COUP[34]

IN FIVE ACTS

It was a slow-moving coup in plain sight that few people took seriously until it was too late.

Greek tragedies were dramas played around the 6th century BCE in ancient Greece. Although not necessarily the case, they often end badly, not only for the hero who, despite admirable qualities, manages to fall with unforeseen consequences.

In this case, the hero allegory can be attributed to America, which, despite its superpower status and many economic, political, and military advantages, is on the brink of committing collective suicide by sleepwalking through its many social and democratic flaws instead of addressing them.

America's own tragedy is currently being played in five acts:

- **Act I** - The setup, in which the stage is set to lay the ground for future claims of voting fraud in the event Donald Trump is not re-elected president in 2020.
- **Act II** - The confrontation in which "*The Big Lie*" and "*Stop the Steal*" are orchestrated to challenge and reverse voting results.
- **Act III** - The climax, in which the playbook "*How to Subvert a Democracy for "A Dear Leader" Wannabe*" is implemented.

---

[34] First coined by Bill Maher.

- **Act IV** - The plot is revealed, in which a last-ditch effort to subvert our democracy culminated in the 2020 attack on the Capitol.
- **Act V** - The resolution, the last Act of this tragedy that has not been played yet and in which America's democracy may fall in the next 2024 presidential election. A real tragedy of monumental proportions for America and the world.

ACT I – The setup

TRAINING GROUNDS TO TEST THE
"HOW TO SUBVERT DEMOCRACY for "A DEAR LEADER" WANNABE" PLAYBOOK

Setting the stage

THE NEW MATH: ZERO + ZERO = MILLIONS

In the 2020 presidential election, 62 state and federal lawsuits were dismissed without merit and concluded without any ambiguity that there was ZERO evidence of widespread voting fraud.

On the contrary, all the private and State institutions whose job it is to monitor the fairness of the democratic process all agreed that the 2020 election was one of the fairest and most transparent election ever held in America. Still, two-thirds of Republicans, representing millions of citizens, firmly believe that the election was rigged. Their evidence: Donald Trump said so. In short, their belief is based on faith, exactly like religion; no proof is necessary, and all those doubting Trump's Gospel deserve to die.

All of this does not bode well for the next 2024 presidential election that pits the electorate of this country into two antagonistic camps: the keepers of the truth, according to Trump, and the heretics. Unfortunately for America, the outcome of this fratricide, *"radical divergence of belief,"* can only conclude, like any religious war, in the separation of the two antagonists.

Religion split up one great empire into two: the Roman and the Byzantine Empires. Differences in interpreting Christianity provoked the schism between Catholics and Reformers, which resulted in the separation of many people from the same country. Religion was also the root for the partition of India, resulting in up to 2 million deaths. When religion is involved, and Trumpism has all the allure of one, partition is the only way out because there is no common ground for people of divergent faiths.

For his presidential inauguration, DJT (Donald J. Trump) took the Oath of Office by swearing on the Bible to protect the United States of America:

"I do solemnly swear that I will support and defend the Constitution of the United States against all enemies, foreign and domestic; that I will bear true faith and allegiance to the same; that I take this obligation freely, without any mental reservation or purpose of evasion; and that I will well and faithfully discharge the duties of the office on which I am about to enter: So help me God."

During the course of his presidency, DJT (Donald J. Trump) has made it his mission to perjure himself at any possible occasion and do exactly the contrary to his Oath of Office. So, why was DJT never impeached for perjury? Aren't there severe penalties for any of us for lying under oath? If *"nothing but the truth, so help me God!"* means nothing, why bother with the charade of pretending anybody cares? Unless, of course, as Donald Trump would argue, justice standards or any moral considerations do not apply when you hold the highest Office of the Land. In his case, he is right and has proved it.

DJT drew the correct conclusion for being the only president that got impeached twice and got away with it scot-free without any consequences:

"I have demonstrated that I can do whatever I want. The next time, no more Mister Nice Guy," From Donald Trump's little voice in his head.

Bill Maher [35] had long before anybody predicted the inconceivable notion that Donald J. Trump would never leave office but would instead perpetuate a *"slow-moving coup"* to stay indefinitely in power as president.

In a typical *"Putin wannabe"* fashion, Trump has attempted to do just that. And because he failed the first time, you can bet your bottom dollar that he will try again and, this time, succeed.

---

[35] Bill Maher, political commentator, and television host of the HBO political talk show *"Real Time with Bill Maher"*.

THE ART OF THE STEAL

You're such a big whining baby. So cry me a river, build yourself a bridge, and jump![36]

This is what half of America would tell Donald Trump's non-stop whining about losing the election and making it the leitmotiv of his current election campaign.

Even before running for the presidency was a little voice in Donald Trump's head, the way he cheated to get his book "The Art of the Deal" in which he glorifies his "I win you lose" transactional, zero-sum way to doing business on the New York Times Bestseller List, should have been a warning into Trump's character. Trump's bragging that his book only comes second to the Bible is nothing compared to how he cheated his way to make it a bestseller. His plan was simple, straightforward, and not against the law: he simply asked his then-wife Ivana to order 4,000 books and pitted his top executives to out-compete themselves to match Ivana's purchase[37]. The incentive? The threat of facing the unforeseen unpleasant consequences of a vindictive, unpredictable man.

Those familiar with the life of Trump and those who know him personally will attest that lying and cheating have always been the modus operandi of his life. Based on a well-recognized

---

[36] *"You're such a big BABY. So cry me a river, build yourself a bridge, and GET OVER IT."* Rachel Renée Russell.

[37] As reported by ex-Trump executive Jack O'Donnell in his 1991 tell-all book *"Trumped!" in which he revealed that* the Trump organization bought tens of thousands of copies of Trump's book to give the appearance that it was a bestseller.

psychological diagnostic that people tend to attribute their own character traits to others, it is natural that Trump truly believes that everybody lies and cheats. Thus, his firm belief that the only explanation for the Democrats to win the 2020 presidential election is that they **cheated better than he did.**

Consequently, Trump had no problem adopting for himself the precepts outlined in **Rule number eight: make people cynical of democracy of the "HOW TO SUBVERT DEMOCRACY for "A Dear Leader" Wannabe"** playbook.

In that respect, credit should be given to Donald Trump for executing a perfect textbook case of how to apply perfectly the three steps of the "*Heads, I win, and Tails, you lose*" strategy, which, as a reminder, are as follows:

1. Well ahead of an election, you make it known that the only way you might lose is if your opponent cheats.

2. Keep repeating it often enough until it becomes evidence.

3. If you win, nobody will remember that you accused the other party of cheating, but if you lose, many will take it for granted that the other party cheated. You now have grounds for contesting the results and calling yourself the winner.

This strategy is second nature for Trump, who often boasts, "*I never lose*," even when he does, and which goes in pair like two bookends with another one of his boasts: "*I never lie.*"

How to recognize the ultimate con artist?

You cannot blame Trump for using every trick in the con book he himself wrote.

There have been several famous con artists throughout history. Although we may not condone such predatory behavior on people less intellectually equipped, we may allow ourselves to admire their duplicity in the way they can deceive so-called intelligent people multiple times over a long period of time. Of course, it is also possible that the play does not dupe the so-called intelligent people who decide to go along with the con because they find in it some personal benefit.

What is different with Donald Trump is that not only do people not recognize his deceits as a con, but his capacity to con them increases with time as they demand more.

In *"How to Subvert a Democracy for "A Dear Leader" Wannabes,"* lying is a significant factor for success.

In social media, interviews, and speeches, Trump has made numerous pre-emptive claims of massive election frauds to come. Who at the time would have suspected that his claims were nothing more than a scheming and dishonest plot aimed at stealing the election himself? As the events eventually proved, claims are easier to make than to prove.

Enter Trump's enablers, such as Sen. Mike Lee (R-Utah) and Rep. Chip Roy (R-Tex.), who were tasked to find voting frauds in any manner possible. As Roy put it to Meadows, *"We need ammo, "* evidently because the White House will need a strong evidentiary argument to compel senators to challenge the election. Thus came about the accusations of ballots being found in the garbage, burned up in mail trucks, or that voting machines made by Dominion Voting Systems were programmed to switch votes from Trump to Biden, etc. When such accusations were debunked, from his insistences before the election that fraud would happen, Trump rapidly pivoted to *"fraud would be proved and that they are coming soon."* As we now know, "*soon*" meant "*never*," which left Trump with no other choice but to double and triple down with his allegations.

MyPillow C.E.O. Mike Lindell was over-optimistic when he claimed that there was also rampant fraud and that they were not weeks, not days, but hours away from proving it.

Trump even tried to overbid him by stating that "*new evidence of fraud will emerge, showing millions of illegal votes.*"

Unfortunately for him, as for Trump's insistence that his tax returns will be coming, as far as proofs of voting frauds are concerned, we are still in the expectation of "*Anne, sister Anne, do you see nothing coming?*".[38]

For a while, as announced by Mark Meadow in a tweet, there was hope that such evidence was coming.

"*BIG news in Nevada: a judge has allowed NV Republicans to present findings of widespread voter fraud in a Dec. 3rd hearing. Americans will now hear evidence from those who saw firsthand what happened, a critical step for transparency and remedying illegal ballots. Stay tuned.*"

In case you did not stay tuned, here is what happened to that case. The court gutted the pro-Trump challenge as baseless.

" *In a detailed, 35-page decision, Judge James T. Russell of the Nevada District Court in Carson City vetted each claim of fraud and wrongdoing made by the Trump campaign in the state and found that none was supported by convincing proof,*" [39]

---

[38] From the Blue Beard fairy tale by Charles Perrault

[39] As related in an article of the Guardian

The judge dismissed the challenge with prejudice, ruling that the campaign failed to offer any basis for annulling more than 1.3 million votes cast in the state's presidential race.

Far from being an exception, this case exemplifies all the 66 other cases that Trump and his enablers filled in States and the Supreme Court to prove Trump's claims of voting fraud.

Having been unable to prove widespread voting frauds, Trump then pivoted again from "*frauds*" to "*rigged.*" Thus, the TADPOLE-GOP battle cry that the election was rigged.

And here we are, and the charade is still going on strong and ready for the next presidential election.

This begs the obvious question: What makes people believe in something for which there is no evidence?

Except for the TADPOLE-GOP that pretends to believe and religious people for which belief is a matter of faith, without going into the psychology of beliefs, sometimes the answer is simple. Some people are just plain stupid.

"It is always more difficult to fight against faith than against knowledge," Adolf Hitler.

Case in point

On a dull weekend day in 2017, Peter McIndoe, a student in psychology at the University of Arkansas, was visiting friends in Memphis, Tennessee, and watching a group of older white men counter-protesters to a Women's March and carrying provoking signs with the apparent intent to create chaos to a peaceful freedom of expression.

As a prank, McIndoe decided to make a placard that had absolutely nothing to do with what was going on, and went out to join the march and stand with the counter-protestors. The sign simply read, "*Birds aren't real.*"

To the people who asked what the sign meant, McIndoe decided to give legs to his joke by declaring that he was part of a movement that had been around for 50 years and was initially started to save American birds but had failed. The "*deep state*" had destroyed them all and replaced them with surveillance drones. Every bird you see is actually a tiny feathered robot watching you.[40]

If you are laughing your head off, good for you because you got the joke and proved to yourself that you do not easily fall for insane B.S. Unfortunately, as someone was filming the scene, the comment was immediately posted on Facebook and became viral before becoming a conspiracy movement.

Conspiracy theorists were quick to jump on the bandwagon until, faced with the stupidity of their beliefs, they decided that "*Birds aren't real*" was a CIA plot to discredit them.

In other words, they tried to explain their stupidity with more stupidity. In Trump's parlor, this is called doubling down.

The takeaway: Something doesn't have to make sense for people to believe it to be true. But millions of Americans firmly believe that if Trump does not win the next presidential election, it will be because the Democrats will cheat, like the last time.

So, how are the Democrats planning to "*Steal*" the 2024 election?

---

[40] As related in an article of the Guardian.

Since there will be a rematch between "*Sleepy Jo*"[41] and that "*Whiny Little Bitch*"[42] The Democrats are planning to "*Steal*" the next election the same way they did in 2020: by voting at the polls. Albeit that this time, Democratic voters, like the Ukrainians, will have to cross several lines of minefields laid down by The Trump Party. Indeed, like the Russians, the Republicans had ample time to prepare several lines of defense by installing State voting suppressions regulations, packing voting stations with officials devoted to their cause, and garnering countless battalions of Trump "*soldiers*" ready to die to allow the Second Coming of Donald Trump. If all that fails, Trump can always count on the Supreme Court as the last arbitrator of who won the election.

---

[41] Trump's derogatory name for Joe Biden.
[42] Bill Maher's derogatory name for Donald Trump.

.THE STOP THE STEAL CONSPIRACY

TO SUBVERT AMERICAN DEMOCRACY

"There's none as blind as those who will not see,"
Proverb

First, a question: *"How many angels can dance on the head of a pin?"* Thomas Aquinas

Answer: About the same number as the number of potentially fraudulent votes found in battleground States won by Biden.

Second question: Is someone lying if he genuinely believes what he is saying?

White House staff and members who testified under oath at the January 6/20 Committee had made it clear that Donald Trump conceded the fact that he had lost the election. Thus, his childish temper tantrum outburst in the Oval Office when he realized he had lost.

Then Trump remembered that way before the election, he predicted that the only way he would lose was if his opponent cheated. So, he applied rule # 10[43] of *"How to subvert a democracy for "A Dear Leader" Wannabe"* by crying fool and saying that the election was stolen. But first, he had to devise a clever and catchy slogan to rally the troop. That is how *"Stop the Steal!"* was born.

---

[43] Rule # 10 ten: Make lying and deceit the principal means to achieve your goals

But if Trump is a liar since he knows the truth, what about those who keep repeating it? Obviously, members of the TADPOLE-GOP who keep repeating it, not by conviction but for self-interest in saving their political career, are liars too, but what to expect from people with no moral compass?

As for all those MAGA supporters who have found validation in social media echo chambers that support their belief, the verdict is more nuanced. Were all the Germans who adhered to Hitler's big lie that they lost WWI because of the Jews liars? The same could apply to the majority of Russians who believed that Ukraine was about to invade Russia and had to be "*Denazified.*" So, we could be tempted to absolve MAGA supporters for succumbing to the same mass intoxication as in the preceding two examples. Except that the equivalence would not be entirely accurate. Both Germans and Russians were subjected to the same state propaganda with little opportunity to head discordant information. But Americans, for their part, have access to all sorts of information before reaching a judgment. That they lack critical thinking and are ready to accept conspiracy theories without any proof is just a matter of belief, just like believing in God or UFOs.

Because what are the proofs that the election was stolen?

Some States have been recounting votes once, twice, three, and even four times as if Jesus would change the math and miraculously make $1+1+1 = 5$.

- Other States, like Arizona, engaged private firms such as Cyber Ninjas, whose owner, Doug Logan, is a Trump supporter who advanced conspiracy theories about fraud.
  In a typical case of "*be careful what you wish for,*" the audit delivered the ultimate humiliation when the

recounting gave more votes to Biden[44] after Trump proclaimed, *"We won on the Arizona forensic audit yesterday at a level that you wouldn't believe."*. That was the only truth he said. Don't believe it.

- In a show of how desperate Trump supporters are, some States were still recounting votes one year after the election with the following results:
  In Ohio, over 5.9 million registered voters cast ballots. The number of potential fraud cases was 27, or just **0.0005 percent. A massive fraud by Trump's standard.**

In some respect, we should be Christian and feel sorry and even pity for all those poor Trump unconditional true believers. It must be utterly frustrating to experience the same letdown every time your hopes are up. Think about those people still waiting for flying saucers to come and rescue them from a zombie apocalypse or those fundamentalist Christians disappointed that the Rapture[45] did not happen as predicted.

Since there is no point in reminding anybody that despite bringing some 60 lawsuits of voting frauds, the Courts have failed to see a single[46] case of an undocumented immigrant casting a ballot, a citizen double voting, nor any evidence that legions of the voting dead voted for Biden, we should all follow

---

[44] The recount found three hundred and sixty more votes than was previously known for Biden.

[45] The transporting of believers to heaven at the Second Coming of Christ.

[46] In the single case that Trump won, his campaign challenged a state-ordered deadline extension in Pennsylvania for the submission of personal identification for mailed ballots, affecting a small number of votes.

the advice of former president Donald Trump when he alleged without evidence, that the 2020 election was rigged.

"Look at the numbers." Donald Trump.

So here they are:

- Over 20 years (from 2000 to 2019), recounts occurred **31 times (0.54 percent).**
- The average shift across all recounts was 430 votes, which accounted for **0.024 percent** of the statewide ballot.
- For the 2020 election, the Trump campaign filed 10 *"election contests"* in Arizona, Georgia, and Nevada. None of these lawsuits or contests succeeded, and none of the recounts or audits changed the election results.

- Arizona: three separate election contests were filed under Arizona law, but none succeeded.

- Georgia: four separate election contests were filed, but none succeeded.

- Nevada: three separate election contests were filled by Trump-supporting voters, and two were filed by Republican candidates alleging that the electronic voting machines counted illegal votes. None of these contests were successful.
- Pennsylvania: Trump filed lawsuits to try to block the vote certification but failed.

That Trump's own Department of Homeland Security declared the 2020 election "the most secure in history." That it was also the fairest and the most thoroughly scrutinized election in U.S. recent history that found Zero, zilch, nada, rien, walou, nichts, niente, nashi, widespread voting fraud means absolutely nothing to those who are still sleepwalking through reality. They are waiting for their revenge when they will wake up in 2024 for Donald Trump's Second Coming.

However, not finding voting fraud is not entirely true.

Dozens of local and state Republican leaders who cast fake electoral votes for Donald Trump are now facing the music and real prison time in return for their devotion to him.

State prosecutors in Michigan announced criminal charges against the 16 Republicans who served as fake electors in 2020, a watershed moment in the still-ongoing federal and state investigations into the 2020 election aftermath. In addition, at least seven other States are following suit to prosecute numerous cases of fake Trump voters. In August 2023, Trump himself was indicted on four counts for masterminding a well-orchestrated plan to steal the 2020 presidential election.

Finally, here is the big one:

FROM 2000 TO 2014, THERE HAVE BEEN 1 BILLION VOTES CAST AND ONLY 31 CASES OF VOTER PERSONIFICATION FRAUD.

Don't bother to do the math; there are too many zeroes after the decimal point. So, yes, Donald Trump, America followed your advice and looked at the numbers. The result is without appeal; **you lost**.

"What good fortune for those in power that people who do not think." Adolf Hitler.

THE BIG LIE

"The election was stolen" Donald Trump

or

The Easter Bunny Who Stole Christmas

rigged · rigged · vote dumps · landslide · landslide · fraud · rigged · rigged · We won. · vote dumps · fake · fake · We won. · landslide · stolen · stolen · vote dumps · We won. · We won. · stolen · stolen · We won. · fraud · landslide · We won. · fake · We won. · rigged · vote dumps · rigged · fraud · rigged · rigged · rigged · fake · fake · We won. · fake · fraud · stolen · landslide · fraud · fake · fraud · fake · fake · vote dumps

If you are gullible enough to think that the Big Lie is about democracy, you are so naive. It is about the only things that drive American politics: money and power.

If one day, for any reason, you have to cancel Christmas and are looking for an excuse to tell your 3-year-old daughter, blaming the Easter Bunny for not having a Christmas seems like a plausible reason. She is a child, after all, and believes in both. But what do you tell grown-ups who still believe in fairy tales?

The prevalent response to that question among Democrats would be not to tell them they are stupid. That could hurt their self-esteem and further entrench their belief of having been despoiled from their presumed presidential election victory.

Others, not necessarily Democrats, would call a cat a cat and affirm that, yes, indeed, those people are complete morons because how can you believe in something for which there is no proof whatsoever.

The third group of people, the most tolerant, would simply say that it is all a matter of belief, like the Irish, who believe in fairies and think they are lucky. After all, millions of people believe in God, although they have never seen him/her/it. The final analysis has no satisfactory answer to why people believe what they believe. Some people believe that the earth is flat, others that we live in a Matrix controlled by super-intelligent beings, and millions more genuinely believe that the election was stolen. There is nothing to argue about; it is what it is because nothing in the world will make them change their mind.

There is, however, one simple explanation of why Donald Trump could not accept that he had lost the election.

"I'm the most successful person ever to run for the presidency, by far. Nobody's ever been more successful than me. I'm the most successful person ever to run."

Donald Trump cannot lose. Losing to him is as incomprehensible as a woman doing anything better than him.

Thus, there is a visceral need to alter reality, pretend otherwise, and make everybody believe in his fantasy.

But if you are going to lie, make it big.

The bigger the lie, the more believable it becomes

One day, when the history books will do the post-mortem of America's democracy demise, it is pretty much assured that the "**Stop the steal**" Trumpster slogan will come on top of the reasons for such an unfortunate outcome.

It won't be the first time a big lie would be responsible for many global consequences. Trump and Hitler's[47] big lies will be placed side-by-side for comparison purposes on how they were able to fool millions of supposedly intelligent people.

The first thing that historians will point out is that they both built their support on racist and anti-democratic agendas and will most likely cite Ted Cruz of Texas arguing that *"America should rely on white nationalist precedent"* to choose their president to prove their point.

Historians will also undoubtedly point to the importance of packing the judicial system in your favor if you wish to give your claims a semblance of credibility. This is also one of the first things would-be dictators do before F&%$ing democracy.

"An election free from strong evidence of systemic fraud is not alone sufficient for election confidence." Supreme Court Justice Clarence Thomas.

---

[47] Hitler's assertion that their country had been defeated in World War I because they were betrayed by a secret coalition of Jews and socialists.

Today, as nearly half of the country believes that the 2020 presidential election was rigged, the parallel between the two big lies becomes even more ominous. Not because the Trumpsters do not have a chance to win the next presidential election, on the contrary. They are determined, focused, ruthless, and deprived of any morality. But because, like in 1933, when the Nazis could leverage their minority to seize power, their opposing democratically minded opponents were in great denial that such an aberration could ever happen. What are you talking about? The country of Goethe, Schiller, and Beethoven? Never, we are civilized people!

Well said, in theory! But it is to forget the adage that

"Those who believe in bullshit will commit incredible crimes in its name."

Officially, Donald Trump is no longer the President of the United States. The problem is that nobody in his party has dared to give him the heads up that there is a new tenant in the White House. How else can we explain his juvenile delusion? In his head and the head of millions of his supporters, "*Dear Leader*" is simply in exile, like a monarch temporarily forced to leave town in the dead of night to avoid a rowdy crowd of peasants to depart him of his head.

Since Trump left office, myriads of political analysts, pundits, and other talking heads from the left have been pondering ad nauseam the reasons why elected TADPOLE-GOP officials have been so keen on perpetuating the lie that the 2020 presidential election was stolen. Are Republicans simply stupid or lying not to irritate "*dear leader*" or jeopardize their re-election chances by going against the Republican base?

The answer to this persistent question is as obvious as it is simple. Apart from those morally bankrupt politicians who know the truth but pretend to go along with the lie for political reasons, the great majority of Trump's supporters genuinely believe that he won the 2020 Presidential election[48] and that for a very simple reason: Way before the election, Trump had repeatedly told them that the only way he would lose the presidential election is if the Democrats cheat.

Saying or naming something exactly the opposite of what it purported to be is very common. Many countries that officially call themselves *"republic democratic"* of something are nothing but. So-called *"Pregnancy resource centers"* are, in fact, anti-abortion centers in disguise operated by activists. Many *"independent research institutes"* of something are run by lobbyists with a specific agenda.

So. When Donald Trump tells the world well in advance how the presidential election will be won or lost, he is applying exactly the same strategy of saying the opposite of what he certainly thinks: that the only way for him to win is to cheat.

This is not particularly an innovative strategy, but it is very effective. Numerous dictators have used it with success, and it works like this:

Imagine that there are two front runners to win the horse race at the Kentucky Derby. If one of the contestants is not sure about winning the race, he will not say, *"The only way I can win this race is by cheating."* Being smart, he would apply rule 8 of *"HOW TO SUBVERT DEMOCRACY for A "Dear Leader" Wannabe"* and instead proclaim well in advance, *"The only way I can lose is if my main contender cheats."* With this kind of

---

[48] According to a recent poll, and only a few months before the next presidential election, 69% of Republicans still believe that Trump won the 2020 election.

subliminal message, if you win, nobody will remember that your opponent did not cheat, but if you lose, it gives you the ground for contesting the results. A win-win strategy.

D. Trump is a pathological liar. Citing the obvious is not a revelation to anybody. You would think that Democrats would not have failed to point out his particular compulsive trait every time Trump opens his mouth, but you would be mistaken. It is not in the Democrats' DNA to call a cat a cat. It is true that having to do so nearly 30,000 times during Trump's presidency would have been exhausting, But at least the label of "*Pinocchio Trump*" would have stuck, making it more difficult for him to peddle his big lie.

If it is given that D. Trump cannot help himself from lying, the big question remains: why so many people are so readily eager to believe him? Apart from QAnon believers living in an alternate reality, Christians already conditioned to have faith, and TADPOLE-GOP politicians pretending to believe him, why does your next-door neighbor believe in B.S.?

Could Goebbels's motto, "*If you tell a lie big enough and keep repeating it, people will eventually come to believe it,*" in fact be true?

The "*Big Lie*" peddled by Trump that the election was stolen is a page directly borrowed from Adolph Hitler's 1925 book Mein Kampf. In his book, Hitler called his "*große Lüge*" (big lie in German) his assertion that Germany lost WWI because the Jews stabbed the country in the back and commented that the lie is so "colossal that no one would believe that someone could have the impudence to distort the truth so infamously."

If Hitler did not believe that the German people would be gullible enough to swallow such a snake oil potion, D. Trump was quite confident that the American people would not find his lie so colossal after all.

The takeaway

This state of the Nation brings us to the pivotal question: Now that the nation is almost equally divided between those who live in this reality and those who live in an alternate one, where do we go from here?

From the Republicans' perspective, the ideal would be that a big "rapture" transports miraculously all Democrats from Earth to Hell.

For the Democrats, the ideal would be that TADPOLE-GOP miraculously grows a spine. But given the time natural selection takes to turn a jellyfish into an ordinary fish, we might have gone through several zombie apocalypses by then.

All those improbable scenarios leave us with only one alternative: "THE NUCLEAR OPTION that will be explained later. In the meantime, the main agenda is how to implement the BIG LIE.

Enters "*The Art of the Steal.*"

"Men are so simple of mind, and so much dominated by their immediate needs, that a deceitful man will always find plenty who are ready to be deceived." Niccolò Machiavelli.

Annotation on the Big Lie

In America, we believe in three things: God, money, and bullshit, and not necessarily in that order

Donald Trump's main claims, for which there was no proof, are only mentioned here for the record for which Donald Trump will go down as one of the most imaginative and prolific liars of American political history and for having single-handedly flushed American democracy down the toilet.

"THE OBSERVERS WERE NOT ALLOWED INTO THE COUNTING ROOMS. I WON THE ELECTION AND GOT 71,000,000 LEGAL VOTES. BAD THINGS HAPPENED WHICH OUR OBSERVERS WERE NOT ALLOWED TO SEE. NEVER HAPPENED BEFORE. MILLIONS OF MAIL-IN BALLOTS WERE SENT TO PEOPLE WHO NEVER ASKED FOR THEM!"

However, no violations of election laws were reported, and Trump offered no proof of "illegal ballots."

"REPORT: DOMINION DELETED 2.7 MILLION TRUMP VOTES NATIONWIDE. DATA ANALYSIS FINDS 221,000 PENNSYLVANIA VOTES SWITCHED FROM PRESIDENT TRUMP TO BIDEN. 941,000 TRUMP VOTES DELETED. STATES USING DOMINION VOTING SYSTEMS SWITCHED 435,000 VOTES FROM TRUMP TO BIDEN."

Trump's own Cybersecurity and Infrastructure Security Agency — part of the Department of Homeland Security — debunked the story.

"STOP THE COUNT! .....ANY VOTE THAT CAME IN AFTER ELECTION DAY WILL NOT BE COUNTED!"
A president does not have the authority to halt vote counting. Besides, all mailed-in ballots that came after Election Day have always been counted,

"RIGGED 2020 ELECTION," he tweeted. *"MILLIONS OF MAIL-IN BALLOTS WILL BE PRINTED BY FOREIGN COUNTRIES AND OTHERS. IT WILL BE THE SCANDAL OF OUR TIMES!"*
There has been no evidence of significant fraud aided by mail-in ballots.

"This is a fraud on the American public....This is an embarrassment to our country. We were getting ready to win this election. Frankly, we did win this election.".

"We have claimed, for Electoral Vote purposes, the Commonwealth of Pennsylvania, the State of Georgia, and the State of North Carolina, each of which has a BIG Trump lead......Additionally, we hereby claim the State of Michigan if, in fact, ... there was a large number of secretly dumped ballots as has been widely reported!"

A president has no legal right to claim Electoral College votes. Nor has there been any credible evidence of illegal dumping of ballots.

"We believe these people are thieves. The big city machines are corrupt. This was a stolen election... We have a history in this country of election problems."

"We won't let a RIGGED ELECTION steal our country! .... how badly shattered and violated our great Constitution has been in the 2020 Election. It was attacked, perhaps like never before!"
"These two countries were selected because they are the locations of the worst irregularities,....illegally altered absentee ballots, illegally issued absentee ballots, and illegal advice given by government officials allowing Wisconsin's Voter ID laws to be circumvented."

"So now the Democrats are using mail, which is a voter security disaster. Among other things, they make it possible for a person to vote multiple times. Also, who controls them, are they placed in Republican or Democrat areas? They are not COVID sanitized. A big fraud!"

It would be unfair to label all of Trump's supporters as morons and complete idiots. After all, we do not judge the people that a hypnotist makes flap their arms, thinking they are chickens.

ACT III - The climax

How to subvert democracy for *"A Dear Leader"* Wannabe[49]
In twelve easy steps (annotated for D.J. Trump).

Subverting a democracy by democratic means is relatively easy. Countless charismatic politicians, military men, or your average Joe Blow have surfed on the nationalist wave of their country to do just that. It is, therefore, a well-defined and time-tested playbook that Donald Trump, who has never been coy about his admiration for dictators, is following to the letter.

- **Rule number one**: **Assess your potential.**

For aspiring autocratic leaders, the first thing to consider is your personality traits. You must be a psychopath or, at the very minimum, a narcissist, and preferably both. You must be able to lie easily, think that you have a Messianic mission, and have a complete lack of empathy. Those basic character traits are essential for any chance of success.

In addition, all great dictators have one more character trait they must possess to be successful: they must be paranoid or have some mental illness.

Hitler and Stalin are perfect examples; nobody managed to take them out despite being the devil incarnated. The first one took himself out, and the second died in his bed. Of all the notorious

---

[49] This self-help guide does not exist. It has only elaborated specifically for this book.

dictators, only Mussolini, Gaddafi of Libya, and Saddam Hussein had an unpleasant demise.

It is unclear that Trump has shown signs of worrying about his safety and for good reasons. America has only a history of taking out the good ones, Abraham. Lincoln, Kennedy, Martin Luther King, and John Lennon, just to name a few. But a case could be made for some other signs of mental illness concerning Trump.

In 2017, during a conference at Yale University, a group of psychiatrists and Mental health experts claimed the President was *"paranoid and delusional"* and was not fit to lead the U.S. Other Mental Health specialists have even gone further, labeling Trump as *"A paranoid, psychopathic, narcissist"* requesting that he be removed from office, according to article 3 of the 25th amendment to the Constitution, which states that the president will be replaced if he is *"unable to discharge the powers and duties of his office."*

- **Rule number two: Become a Messiah of some cause.**

It would help to be imbued with a messianic mission that makes you special or even unique. You alone have the ability to save the people from a looming catastrophe or the reality of their social condition. Better still, find a cause that would appeal to everybody's desire to protect, especially women. Anything with the words "save the children" is a guaranteed winner.

In this department, to Donald Trump's credit, he has outdone himself in being a Mafia boss, guru, Jesus Christ, Jules

Caesar[50], and cult leader with God-like status, all at the same time.

Most incredibly, that a self-proclaimed billionaire can manage to convince the middle class and people earning $10 an hour that he is the only one who can understand them and work to improve their lot is both a testament to people's gullibility and a tribute to Donald Trump's power of persuasion. Unless that says more about ourselves and our willingness to believe anything as long as it fits our worldviews.

- **Rule number three**: **thrive on chaos.**

Chaos is your friend. Your goal is to make people angry and frustrated about something. Try to make them economically insecure and anxious. Provoke their anger, incite civil disobedience, protests, riots, and even armed conflicts. You must act like a firefighter pouring gasoline on a fire while pretending to be the only one who can extinguish it.

Donald Trump has no lesson to learn from anybody in this department

- **Rule number four**: **Invoke internal and external enemies.**

You must portray yourself as the only strong man who can protect the country and fix anything. If you can't rely on the traditional scapegoats, the Jews, fall back to alternative choices, like the blacks, the yellows, the browns, in short, anybody who does not look like you. Capitalize on people's fear of differences,

---

[50] Julius Caesar was assassinated because he wanted to be king, overthrow the Senate and the republic and rule as a tyrant. The irony is that his assassination became the pretext of internal wars that led despots to power and turned a republic into an empire.

social or religious. Your goal is to sow divisions, discord, and distrust of the other who does not belong to your tribe.

Another area where D. Trump excels. For external enemies, think of the hordes of migrants ready to overrun the borders. All thieves, rapists, drug addicts, prostitutes, and drug dealers. All "*bad hombres,*" for sure. Let us not forget the Muslims, all potential terrorists, except for Saudi Arabia, who had already reached its quota by providing 15 of the 19 terrorists of 9/11. No need either to mention all the asylum seekers from war-torn "*shithole countries*" who, on top of that, are all black. And who needs more blacks? Hasn't America already done its part by importing more than its quota of slaves from Africa two centuries ago?[51]

As far as internal enemies are concerned, it is easy; you must first eradicate "the enemy of the people": the free press. Controlling the narrative and the news cycle 24/7 is a must.

In this area, "*the great communicator*" is a pro; he wrote the book.

- **Rule number five: Undermine the institutions.**

If you want to control any facet of government, you must first dismantle all existing institutions controlled by the State.

This is an area where D. Trump did not waste time. According to the Center for American Progress, for his first 100 days in office, the President has slashed or canceled more than one hundred measures and regulations to the detriment of the

---

[51] Only a fraction of the Trans-Altlantic slave trade landed in America, Most were destined to the Caribbeans and Brazil.

average American and the benefit of corporations, the wealthiest, and to enrich himself.[52]

During the four years of his presidency, Donald Trump has done a great job to eviscerate or corrupt Federal Agencies whose mission did not meet his world views. To this end, he appointed cronies with no experience in the field they were supposed to lead.

At the EPA (*Environmental Protection Agency*), Trump's appointees set about to dismantle all the climate policies put in place under former President Barack Obama. Donald Trump could be particularly proud in this area since he has outdone himself by weakening or wiping out more than 125 rules and policies protecting Americans. The EPA may never recover.

For the *United States Postal Service, Donald Trump slashed their operating budget, forcing it to diminish its operational capability to deal with mail voting.*

*Donald Trump politicized the CDC (*United States Centers for Disease Control), a world-renowned agency to control the message of COVID-19.

When they were not wholly gutted, Donald Trump politicized the agencies to dedicate them for his benefit. FOR INSTANCE, the FBI and the Justice Department were weaponized and tasked to go primarily after his political opponents. So when Donald Trump and the TADPOLE-GOP accuse Biden's Administration of weaponizing the Department of Justice for going after his conspiracy to steal an election, it is pure. "*Trumpgassing*" of accusing others of the things you do.

---

[52]

https://www.americanprogress.org/issues/general/news/2017/04/26/431299/100-ways-100-days-trump-hurt-americans/

In addition, the Trump administration has slashed tens of thousands of civil servant employees to administrations not deemed important. Some of the most impacted were the Agriculture Department, The Health and Human Services Department, and the Education Department.

Finally, in order to protect Russia's involvement in the 2016 presidential election, Trump made it his personal mission to discredit the CIA.

- **Rule number six: secure the allegiance of an army of thugs.**

From the smallest to the biggest countries, any well-respected dictator ought to be able to count on his personal Praetorian Guards who only swear allegiance to him.

In the smallest of those countries, you had Haitian dictator François Duvalier's "Tonton Macoute" army of thugs to assassinate, torture, and intimidate anybody perceived as an opponent.

For the most renowned army of thugs, the precursor was, without a doubt, Hitler's SA Sturmabteilung (Storm Detachment). In 1933, Hitler could count on an army of close to 3,000,000 of those thugs to which we owe the infamous "Kristallnacht," the Night of Crystal. Unfortunately, as was often the case, Hitler soon became wary of such a force and initiated a purge where many were massacred and replaced by a more reliable army of thugs, the Schutzstaffel S.S.

Fortunately, officially, Trump does not yet have an army of men who only swore allegiance to him (although many did in their heads). But in case of needs, Trump believes that he can rely on an army of bikers, far-right paramilitary militias, and who knows how many "*Proud Boys*" or "*Patriots*" who are watching and interpreting any signals from "*Dear Leader.*"

Signal: Donald Trump scratches his nose with his pinky finger.

Interpretation: Stand by, be ready!

Signal: Donald Trump boards Air Force One and salutes the guards with two fingers.

Interpretation: Action is imminent. Rally the troops. Something is about to happen.

For those finding any armed coup banana republic style too farfetched, just consider the statement of retired United States Army lieutenant general and former Trump's National Security Advisor, Michael Flynn, who endorsed a Myanmar-style coup to reinstate Trump as president.

You may think what you want of Trump, but the rule of law is not his forte, so beware, you have been warned.

- **Rule number seven** (this is a great one): **Pack the Courts with like-minded judges.**

Military coups could be hazardous and not guaranteed to succeed (for example, in Turkey). Packing the Courts is less obvious, bloodless, perfectly democratic, and so much more efficient. Today, as the number of autocratic countries worldwide outnumbers the democratic ones, we should be more than alarmed that many of them were fully democratic countries. We should indeed be wary that a good number of countries run by de facto dictators had a Constitution mirroring the United States. Many of those who were too complacent in believing that such a thing could happen to them are either in prison, dead, or in a clandestine opposition.

Donald Trump understands this process too well. Personally or through his party, Donald Trump has succeeded in packing state and federal courts with judges who are more inclined to rule in his favor in case he wants to overturn presidential election results that he does not like. Ultimately, Donald Trump could have recourse to the nuclear option of using the Supreme Court to change the Constitution to remove the two-term limit a U.S. president can stay in office. Many recent dictators have done just that.

Some people, mostly Democrats, would point out that for the 2020 presidential election, Donald Trump did not succeed (except one) in his nefarious 62 Court lawsuits to challenge and overturn voting results. This result was essentially due to the probity and integrity of the Judges, some Republicans, whose moral ethics outweighed political considerations. To be blunt, the judicial system saved democracy. But do not count on this miracle to be duplicated the next time around; The Trump Party is making sure of it.

One thing for sure: Donald Trump may be out of Office for the time being, but make no mistake, he has not abandoned his goal of becoming president for life, like China's Xi Jinping, the dictator he is in love with, Kim Jong-un of North Korea, or better still, his mentor, Vladimir Vladimirovich Putin, President for life (almost) of the Russian Federation.

- **Rule number eight: Make people cynical about democracy.**

Subverting democracy is relatively easy. It is much easier, in fact, than in an established dictatorship or when only one party rules, where it is difficult to identify friends from foes, and where the slightest miscalculation can send you directly to the firing squad. In a democracy, however, the parties to beat are clearly identified and are no threat to your health.

However, the main element that runs in your favor is the fickleness of voters and the corruptibility of the people you run against.

Voters are not rational but emotional. Find the chord that makes them vibrate, and you can play them like a violin.

Plato was right; people are too easily manipulated to be trusted to have a say in governing the city. This is why your main job is to convince them that you are the only one who knows what is good for them and that you alone can deliver.

Democracy's weak point: the voters

To achieve your goal, your first order of business is to make people cynical about democracy. In a democratic country, military coups would be too obvious and counterproductive. Therefore, the best approach would be to use democracy against itself and democratic elections to achieve your goal. If this had been the royal road to many dictators, starting with Hitler, it would not have been as straightforward as a military coup. It would have required patience, preparation, and commitment, especially if you were not certain of winning. In this case, a new, more efficient strategy must be used. It is called the:

"Heads, I win. Tails, you lose."
or how to win either way
Three steps:

1. Well ahead of an election, you make it known that the only way you might lose is if your opponent cheats.

2. *Keep repeating it often enough until it becomes evidence.*

3. *If you win, nobody will remember that you accused the other party of cheating, but if you lose, many will take it for granted that the other party cheated. You now have grounds for contesting the results and calling yourself the winner. It's a win-win for you.*

Of course, that strategy does not preclude you from cheating yourself, but this old strategy does not guarantee you a victory like the new one.

Taking power by force

This strategy is so passé, so try to avoid it as much as possible, but if you do, refer to **rule # 6: secure the allegiance of an army of thugs.**

If your goal is to change your country's government from a democracy to an autocracy, your second order of business is to make people believe that less civil liberty and more police state are good for them. On the surface, this goal seems unlikely to be embraced with enthusiasm by the majority of people, especially in a country that views itself as a model of liberty for the world. But in actuality, with the right incentive, coercion, or a perceived threat, people will learn to accept it willingly. The main reason? Apathy, like in 1933 Germany.

It took only six years between the fall of the Weimar Republic and the start of WWI. It was the same time as Trump's presidential term, plus the two years before the Senate and the House of Representatives midterm elections of 2022.

Why compare the rise of Nazism in Germany with today's America, you may ask? Undoubtedly, many patriots would raise the alarm if such a thing happened here. But that is exactly what many Americans thought in 1933 when some pro-Nazi groups were contemplating the American Government and replacing it with a dictator, Hitler's style. However, the real difference between Germany then and America now is that instead of an openly assumed goal to overthrow the Weimar Republic, the same process is happening in a much slower fashion. It is democracy death by thousands of little cuts that nobody notices.

- **Rule number nine: Set up your own propaganda apparatus** dedicated to disseminating your vision to the broadest audience possible.

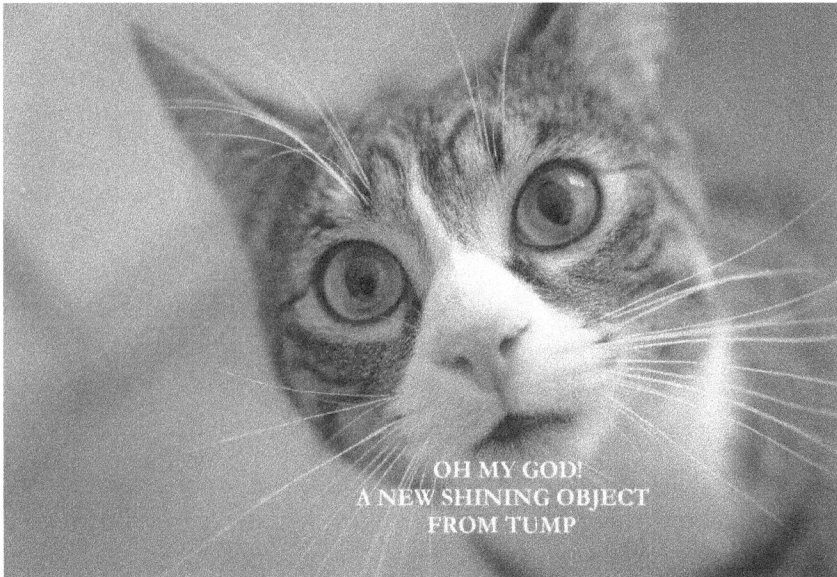

OH MY GOD!
A NEW SHINING OBJECT
FROM TUMP

What shining object can I throw to the media today to stay on top of the news cycle? From Trump's little voice in his head.

No need to mention how D. Trump used social media, especially Twitter, as his bullhorn to propagate to the Universe anything that came out of his ass to control the news cycle 24/7.

You must also have noticed that things with a word in their name to describe them are often the contrary to what they purport to be. For example, "Democratic Republic of something," like "The Democratic People's Republic of Korea" (North Korea), "the Democratic Republic of Congo," or "of Afghanistan" are either a dictator or a failed state. The same goes for "institutes" or "research centers" for lobby companies or "Planned Parenthood centers" masquerading as abortion clinics.

Enters "*Truth*," Trump's new social media platform dedicated to spewing the Gospel according to Trump, propaganda, and lies.

- **Rule number ten: Make lying and deceit the principal means to achieve your goals.**

"*If you tell a lie big enough and keep repeating it, people will eventually come to believe it*[53]. *Remember, people are so easily manipulated that the challenge to make them believe anything is almost boring.* But it is a must.

All great dictators are master manipulators of the truth. It does not matter if the lie is benign or enormous. In fact, the more preposterous, the better because the more people question and repeat it, the more plausible it becomes.

If you are still questioning Donald Trump's affinity for becoming a dictator, one only has to notice his facility for lying. It comes to him naturally, like second nature. Trump lies, even when he does not have to, or for trivial and benign matters.

For the bean counters who make it their business to fact-check anything Trump said or wrote, they came up with an almost laughable tally. **During the span of his presidency, Trump lied 30,000 times, that is more than 20 times a day**. He truly

---

[53] Attributed to Joseph Goebbels , Hitler's Propaganda Reich Minister

deserves his nickname of "*Pinocchio Trump.*" That number, of course, does not consider the number of times he doubles or triples down on his lies because "*the more you repeat it, the more…*etc,*" you know the rest.

If you are not a Donald Trump supporter, you might be tempted to laugh it all, especially when Trump denied having said something that you can see or hear him saying on video or tape. But for his supporters, this is no laughing matter. This proves there is a conspiracy to misinterpret his sayings to discredit him.

- **Rule number eleven: Use the Justice system as your personal "*special* op"** striking force to go after whoever opposes you.

If your autocratic rule has not yet reached full maturity to the point where you can arbitrarily arrest, torture, make disappear, or execute by firing squad people you don't like, you can always fall back onto your "independent" justice system.

The beauty of this approach is that you do not even have to control the entire justice system. All you need is to have the person in charge of it in your pocket. In addition, as a bonus, it gives the whole process the veneer of legitimacy and deniability if something goes wrong.

If you cannot openly take out your critics (political opponents, journalists, minorities, religious leaders, etc.), at least ensure they cannot muster an opposition that could challenge your power. Use your "independent" justice system to vigorously investigate your political opponents on trumped-up charges if necessary. You do not even have to go through the trouble of setting up kangaroo courts to prove anything. In the mind of most people, the simple fact of investigating someone is sufficient to ruin a person's reputation and create enough doubts about his lack of guilt.

Short of a military coup, controlling the justice system is the modus operandi of choice to subvert democracy.

Donald Trump understood that very well by getting rid of an Attorney General who would not do his bidding (Jeff Sessions) to replace him with a more agreeable one (William Barr). But when Trump asked his until then submissive Attorney General *"just announce that the election was rigged and leave the rest to me,"* Barr, to his credit, declined.

In a textbook wannabe dictator's move, Trump also instructed his DOJ (Department of Justice) to use federal prosecutorial powers to go on a fishing expedition by issuing hundreds of subpoenas to seize the communications data of Democrats in the U.S. House of Representatives for potential wrongdoings.

When Trump approached Volodymyr Zelenskyy, the President of Ukraine, to offer a quid pro quo in exchange for digging up dirt on political rival Joe Biden and his son Hunter, it was made clear to the Ukrainians that they did not literally have to investigate anything. All they had to do was simply announce their intention to do so. Unfortunately for Trump, despite a reputation for corruption, Ukraine's leadership opted to pass.

If the corruption request did not bear fruit this time, it nevertheless led Trump into hot water with the U.S. Congress that impeached him for abuse of power and obstruction of Congress. Fortunately for Trump, his minions at the Senate handed him a *"get out of jail"* free card. Morality: Donald Trump, who, contrary to what Democrats think, is not as stupid as he appears to be, learned a valuable lesson: Impeachment is a joke; I can do what I want regardless of Congress or the courts.

- **Rule number twelve**: **be ruthless.**
  Ban empathy and the rule of law from your vocabulary. You are strong, and you have a mission: power. Be prepared to do anything necessary to achieve your goal. You are, above all, a winner.
- Finally, here is the most important rule: **never give up. If you don't succeed the first time, try again.**

Hitler's first attempt at a coup landed him in jail. The second time around, his party did not win a majority to govern. It was only after the Nazis managed the set the Reichstag (lower house of Germany's parliament) on fire and blame the communists and the Jews that he finally obtained the power to take emergency measures to protect public safety and order, that he could start implementing his divine mission as outlined in Mein Kampf.

In Hitler's own words: "*At the risk of appearing to talk nonsense, I tell you that the National Socialist movement will go on for 1,000 years! ... Don't forget how people laughed at me 15 years ago when I declared that I would govern Germany one day. They laugh now, just as foolishly, when I declare that I shall remain in power.*" *Adolf Hitler to a British correspondent in Berlin in June 1934.*

No convincing is necessary here. "*Donald Trump The First*" How does that sound for someone who has outsmarted the self-proclaimed greatest democracy on earth?

Remember how we laughed when Donald Trump first declared his candidacy to become President of the United States? Rupert Murdoch, the great media mogul, even called him "*a fucking idiot.*" No one is laughing today. A " *fucking idiot.*" may very well represent all of us to the rest of the world, again.

The Road to a Day of Infamy

DRESSED REHEARSAL
TO A DEMOCRACY TAKEDOWN

- **first attempt: a shot across the bow - false assertions,**

Spring 2020. Trump, emulating Napoleon, who believed that the best defense is to attack, launched a series of pre-emptive attacks on the integrity of our democracy by concentrating on its weaker point: the country's voting system.

"Elections are rigged." D. Trump.

In case you did not get the memo while he was in office, Trump used his battle cry *"rigged"* 157 times in his tweets. Of course, that does not include the times when he literally said it, but the beans counters whose job it is to keep track of those things lost track of it, overwhelmed by the numbers. No wonder that faced with such an onslaught of assertions, many people now believe it as fact. Mission accomplished!

This was not the first time that Trump claimed the election was rigged. According to Trump, at least six elections were rigged, and most famously in 2006, when **Sen. Ted Cruz, R-Texas,** defeated Trump in the Iowa caucuses, the latter tweeted:

"Ted Cruz didn't win Iowa, he stole it. That is why all of the polls were so wrong and why he got far more votes than anticipated. Bad!" to finally add what would become his leitmotiv in 2020:

"Either a new election should take place or ... results nullified."

At least no one can accuse Trump of not being consistent.

- ### second attempt: cannon ball volleys - Legal challenges,

Trump's cronies and enablers had filed 62 lawsuits in state and federal courts seeking to overturn election results in states Trump lost.

In State Supreme Courts, with both Democratic-appointed and Republican-appointed judges and Federal judges appointed by Trump, 61 cases were dismissed for either lack of standing or on the merits of the voter fraud allegations.

On the winning side for Trump, he racked up hundreds of millions of dollars from his supporters to fund legal challenges that the Republicans lost. Since most of that money ended in Trump's pocket, who said that crime does not pay?

- ### third attempt: carpet bombing - Attempt to enlist federal and state officials to do his bidding for overturning voting results,

Trump tried to pressure Secretaries of State not to certify the results or *"find"* fraudulent ballots.

Georgia's secretary of state, Brad Raffensperger, a conservative Republican, will probably never get re-elected to a second term as Georgia's top election administrator. Still, he will enter the history book as one of the few good men who saved our democracy by refusing Donald Trump's direct pleas to find him 14,000 votes.

Attention, this call might be recorded: Dictator in training

The fact that Trump's call to Brad Raffensperger was recorded and that Trump probably knew it shows without any ambiguity his complete disregard for the rule of law or even gives the appearance of caring about openly asking an election official to suppress or falsify votes.

The same scenario was repeated in the states of Pennsylvania, Michigan, and Arizona, where Trump publicly urged Republican-controlled statehouses to declare him the winner.

"Hopefully, the Courts and/or Legislatures will have the COURAGE to do what has to be done to maintain the integrity of our elections and the United States of America itself."

Trump also attempted to apply **Rule number eleven** of *"HOW TO SUBVERT DEMOCRACY for "A Dear Leader" Wannabe,"* **use the Justice system as your personal *"special op"*** when he said:

"I have the absolute right to do what I want with the Justice Department."

Ken Paxton, Attorney General of Texas, supported by 20 Republican state attorneys general and 126 Republicans in Congress, filed a lawsuit to a Conservative-controlled Supreme Court to overturn and void the 2020 election results in Wisconsin, Georgia, Michigan, and Pennsylvania. Trump, who had packed the Supreme Court with Republican judges sympathetic to his political agenda just in case a presidential election was going to be decided by them, like for George W. Bush and Al Gore in 2000, had high hopes. Fortunately for our democracy, the Supreme Court threw out the case and declined to be Trump's puppets.

Undeterred by this rebuke from the highest court of the land, Trump attempted to coerce the Justice Department into providing him with a pretext to overturn the Presidential voting results. In a last and rare struggle with his conscience, Bill Barr, his attorney general, refused to do so.

"*Just say that the election was corrupt [and] leave the rest to me.*" D. Trump. [54]

Many will say that it was a little too late for Bill Barr to try to redeem himself and enter the history books as one of the many mindlessly corrupt Trump enablers. The fact is that if Barr had acquiesced to Trump's demand, this would have lent more credibility to Trump's baseless accusations that the votes were rigged.

Right after Bill Barr passed on doing Trump biddings, he announced his intention to resign. Not missing one beat, Trump put pressure on Jeffrey Rosen, his replacement, to:

- file legal briefs supporting lawsuits against the election results,
- announce Justice Department investigations of alleged serious election fraud,
- appoint special prosecutors to investigate Trump's unfounded allegations of voter fraud,
- go to the Supreme Court directly to invalidate the election results,

However, Rosen and acting Solicitor General Jeffrey Wall refused, saying there was no basis for the filings as there was no evidence of fraud. A few good men indeed.

---

[54] Reported by acting attorney general, Jeffrey Rosen

- **fourth attempt: torpedo launch to pressure Mike Pence to overturn voting results,**

If Trump had read the Constitution, he would have known that insisting that the vice president has the power to unilaterally decide who won an election was not in his power. Trump could just as well have asked Pence to part the Red Sea and menaced him with having his head on a pike for not complying. This leads to the hypothetical question:

What would have happened if the mob storming the Capitol had indeed caught up with Mike Pence and hanged him like they intended to? Would Trump have been impeached or sent to a donjon with no door for an invitation to murder? We can all venture guesses, but the most probable answer is probably not because his lawyers would have argued that it was impossible to prove that Trump truly wanted Pence to be hanged.

The most disturbing fact is that Mike Pence took Trump's request seriously enough to investigate the possibility that he could refuse to certify the results in particular States and turn to Congress to decide the election. Because each state has one vote and the Republicans had the majority, the election results would have been overturned, and Trump would have been declared the winner.

Nobody will ever know what dilemma went into Pence's head before the *"you know what hit the fan,"* but to his credit and curse, Pence chose to do his democratic duty as his conscience commanded him to uphold the Constitution.

When every legal and illegal shenanigan in the book failed, at the last resort, Donald Trump unleashed a mob to do his bidding on the Capitol.

- **fifth attempt: going nuclear - Attack on the Capitol to prevent votes certification.**

January 6th, 2021, a day of infamy

Assault on the Capitol

"Normal tourist visit" by just *"Friendly Guys and Gals Taking a Tourist Trip through the Capitol"* Republicans' assertion.

To echo Franklin D. Roosevelt's speech after the attack on Pearl Harbor by the Japanese Imperial Navy on December 8, 1941, the January 6th, 2021, attack on the Capitol was a day of infamy.

As for Pearl Harbor, the term *"Infamy,"* which describes a bad, notoriously shocking, brutal event or incident that became famous, applies equally well to the assault on the temple of our democracy.

As for the attack on Pearl Harbor, the one on the Capitol was nothing but spontaneous, but rather the result of a well-planned last-ditch effort to subvert our democracy. That the attempt failed that day is only due to the moral integrity of a few good men, even if some subsequently turned their coats to go to the dark side. After all, even Benedict Arnold, who served with distinction in a blue coat of the American Continental Army before becoming a Red Coat, fulfilled his duties well before becoming a traitor. So, good job, Mike Pence, for doing your Constitutional duty under the threat of swinging at the end of a rope.

But if the comparison between the Pearl Harbor and the Capitol attack is more than coincidental or anecdotal, both show uncanny parallels between the two events.

To be honest, there is still a debate among historians to settle the issue of whether or not the Pearl Harbor Japanese attack was a false flag pretext on the part of FD Roosevelt to switch public opinion to enter the war against Nazi Germany on the side of Great Britain.

Documents released under the Freedom of Information Act Files may prove that FDR had foreknowledge of the Pearl Harbor attack, put in doubt numerous coincidences, alleged bureaucratic failures, and intelligence shortcomings to explain why the U.S. was taken flat-footed.

Historians, like scientists, have a big problem admitting evidence contradicting their hypothesis. That is contrary to the scientific approach that consists of having an open mind, investigating, following the evidence wherever it leads them, and drawing a reasonable conclusion as close to the facts as possible.

History is littered with examples of inventions and discoveries made by individuals initially dismissed as lunatics and crackpots by their time's so-called experts and luminaries. For historians, the impossibility of having access to all the facts obliges them to wander into conjunctures and hypotheses to interpret events as they occur. This crucial task becomes even more daunting when the information that could reveal the truth is subject to misinformation campaigns, evidence destruction, or withheld under some state secret regulations, like UFOs, Kennedy Assassination, or 9/11 investigations that lead to wild conspiracy theories.

Sometimes, conspiracy theories, like the CIA and government attempts to mind control, false flags wars, Watergate, Operation Snow White involving The Church of Scientology, Abraham Lincoln's Assassination conspiracy, Bayer Medicine Causing AIDS, the CIA having a special gun that shoots dissolvable darts that leave no trace and cause people to get a heart attack, your phone that is listening to you even when you aren't using it, the NSA who is basically storing and spying on everything sent across the internet, all FIFA World Cups being purchased from 1998 through 2014, the CIA putting LSD in the water supply, that Jeffrey Epstein was killed, and that the CIA kick-started the crack epidemic, and financed military groups and dictators in all South America, etc. all that.

Turned out to be true.

Those considerations lead us to the January 6th, 2021, assault on the Capitol.

Sometimes, the evidence of the truth is too unbelievable to comprehend and accept that we have to dismiss it as a conspiracy theory for the good of the country.

PRECEDENTS

Jamais deux sans trois

This French saying, "*never two without three,*" to mean that bad things usually come in threes, should raise some alarms about what is going to happen on November 5th, 2024, because the January 6th, 2021, attack on the Capitol was not the first time Americans tried a coup to overthrow their democracy.

First attempt.

Most Americans would be shocked to discover that in 1934, a fascist coup cooked up by some of the most prominent U.S. capitalists, industry captains, and Wall Street financiers had formed a group called *"The Liberty League"*[55] to overthrow democracy and replace it with a dictatorship, Hitler's style. Among the principal conspiracy members, you could find heads and executives of major U.S. companies such as General Motors, Phillips Petroleum, General Foods, Sun Oil, JP Morgan, the multimillionaire Irénée du Pont, and Prescott Bush (George W. Bush's grandfather). More telling is that the manpower for the coup was alleged to be the American Legion led by General Douglas MacArthur, which shows that back then, overthrowing our democracy was already a patriot thing.

On Nov. 20, 1934, readers of the *New York Post* were startled by a headline:

"Gen. Butler Accuses N.Y. Brokers of Plotting Dictatorship in U.S.; $3,000,000 Bid for Fascist Army Bared; Says He Was Asked to Lead 500,000 for Capital 'Putsch'; U.S. Probing Charge."

A two-man panel of the Special House Committee did indeed investigate the allegation, which, in view of the importance of the conspirators, was promptly buried for the sake of the Nation. This is why no American will ever learn the time when America almost became a fascist country in our history books.

The scariest part is that The Liberty League was all the time claiming that its goal was to *"Combat radicalism, preserve property rights, uphold and preserve the Constitution."* In short,

---

[55] Please notice again the irony of calling something totally opposed to the goal it pretends to defend.

basically the same thing that the Trump Party is claiming to uphold.

Second attempt

In August 2020, as a harbinger of the attack on the U.S. Capitol, hundreds of right-winged extremists stormed the Reichstag, the seat of the German Parliament in Berlin, to protest against the country's coronavirus policies. It appears that the motive given was just an excuse, as many were waving the pre-1918 German Empire and Nazi flag as a clear attack on German democracy. Contrary to us Americans, the great majority of German did not support this assault on their temple of democracy, which for them was reminiscent of the Nazi's false flag burning of the Reichstag in 1933.

This event probably gave some ideas to Trump for encouraging supporters to gather at statehouses in Washington, Arizona, Georgia, Kansas, Ohio, Michigan, California, Colorado, Utah, New Mexico, Wyoming, and Texas to protest the presidential voting results and demand recounts.

When everything failed at the state level, a last-ditch effort to subvert our democracy was planned and executed at the federal level in our state capital. Washington.

Next attempt

The next time a coup will attempt to overthrow our democracy may happen on November 6, 2024, in the event Joe Biden wins the presidential election.

Commentary

ATTACK ON PEARL HARBOR

Provocation

The United States had an eight-action plan known as The *McCollum* Memo to provoke Japan into war, including:

- Keep the main strength of the U.S. fleet now in the Pacific in the vicinity of the Hawaiian Islands.
- Insist that the Dutch refuse to grant Japanese demands for economic concessions, particularly oil.
- Completely embargo all U.S. trade with Japan, in collaboration with a similar embargo imposed by the British Empire.

"Sooner or later, the Japanese will commit an overt act against the United States, and the nation will be willing to enter the war." FD Roosevelt

Was the United States well aware of the incoming attack on Hawaii?

It is now an open secret that the U.S. had cracked the Japanese Navy code and was aware of an imminent attack on Hawaii. According to newly released naval records, nearly three weeks before December 7, 1941, the United States Navy had already intercepted eighty-three messages that Yamamoto sent to his carriers moving into Hawaiian waters.

Incompetence or deliberate attempts to ignore warnings?

- On December 6th, 1941, the U.S. intercepted messages sent to the Japanese ambassador in Washington to break negotiations with the Americans and declare war. The date and time for the declaration were to be the exact hour when Pearl Harbor was attacked. When the last intercept was shown to Roosevelt, he decided not to warn Hawaii of the impending attack.

- General Marshall also sat on the message for about fifteen hours, but then decided to send it to Honolulu only after the attack had occurred. It is now a fact that Admiral Kimmel and General Short, who headed up the army in Hawaii were, deliberately cut off any information concerning the Japanese attack on Pearl Harbor, with a notable exception. A week before the attack, Admiral Kimmel received this message: **"Stand aside and let Japan commit the first overt act,"** and in case he did not understand the message he received, it was repeated twice.

- A few hours before the attack, Japanese submarines were attacked at the harbor's entrance, and one was sunk. That did not alert the authorities, who did not see any reason to put the fleet on alert.

- The day before the attack, Washington had sent warnings that aircrafts were heading toward the islands from the north. On the day of the attack, a large number of planes were effectively picked up by radar. Still, the information was dismissed by the duty officer at Pearl Harbor, who was expecting a group of B-17 Flying Fortresses to arrive from California that same morning.

ATTACK ON THE CAPITOL

It is a mistake to think that the Trump Party goes off the rails pretending that the January 6, 2021 *Capitol insurrection was an FBI plot and that Joe Biden is the biggest threat to American democracy. On the contrary, their rhetoric keeps them well on track to achieving their long-time aspiration: authoritarian rule.*

The attack on the Capitol was our own Reichstag Fire planned as a setting stage to use emergency powers to seize control of the election, just like Hitler did.

Incompetence or deliberate attempts to ignore warnings?

Law enforcement agencies and the FBI had picked up ample information and noise about a possible attack on the Capitol. Social media, in particular, were flooded with warnings on Jan. 6, but federal agencies, for whatever reasons, did not show much interest in its information. More puzzling is why the FBI decided to classify so many of the threatening social media posts.

Why didn't law enforcement heed the scores of security warnings gathered by the Department of Homeland Security? Apparently, nearly 80 nation's regional homeland security offices, known as fusion centers, reported alarming threats for January 6th at the Capitol. And still, government authorities sat on their hands, apparently unconcerned, as if they were just buying their time for "the shit to hit the fan," exactly like Pearl Harbor.

The Pentagon was also aware of the potential threat to the Capitol and even feared that Trump would call up the National Guard to remain in power. However, instead of yielding to this potential threat by maintaining the troops on standby in case of need, the decision was made to keep them away instead. Worse, when Chief Steven Sund of the U.S. Capitol Police made a last-minute request to bring in the National Guard, the request was swiftly rejected.

Donald Trump can claim all he wants for not having previous knowledge of the attack on the Capitol. Still, on January 6, 2021, he was the one who urged the mob to take action into their own hands and waited 3 hours standing by before telling his supporters to go home. The implication is clear. The attack on the Capitol was not a surprise. All the people who could have done something to prevent or control it did nothing. As for Pearl Harbor, some people at the highest level of the State wanted it to happen, and it did, as expected.

ACT V – The Resolution

If the last days of the Trump presidency culminated with a dress rehearsal of a slow-moving coup to overthrow our democracy, what followed is a clear demonstration of a well-too-often reoccurring scenario:

Once an authoritarian leader has tasted the addictive thrills of power, he will never leave voluntarily.

This perspective leads us to the corollary proposition that if Donald Trump is re-elected in 2024, this could very well be the last time that a fair and free presidential election takes place in America.

And as things stand today, everything is in place to make that possibility a reality.

Shit never happens at random.
It is just a failure of the imagination
to forecast the future and accept the
possibility that the worst may happen

TRUMPOCRACY[56] , HERE WE COME

Our democracy is going down the toilet, and Donald Trump is the one flushing it. The tragedy is that nearly half of America is cheering him on while draping themselves in the patriot flag of the Star-Spangled Banner.

"**Trumpocracy**": A form of government that isn't completely a *dictatorship* and isn't completely a democracy where a single political party controls all levels of government and where voting is routinely rigged to favor one candidate. It's sort of a hybrid between a banana republic and a capitalist dictatorship, Russian or Chinese style.

Because we were the first, with the French, to create the first modern democratic form of government, we Americans wrongly believe that it will last forever. We have faith in our institutions and our three branches of government. **However, democracy is like anything else; it is only when it is no longer there that we realize what a good thing we had.**

In this case, the premiums are the attention you must constantly pay for not doing anything that would render it void.

Look around you; democracy is under siege in places you would least expect it, like in our own backyard. On every continent, autocracies pop up everywhere, like mushrooms after the rain. What a letdown! We had so much hope after China opened up to world trade and the fall of the Soviet Union. Unfortunately, the latter two have since embraced authoritarian regimes and are doing their best to export them as a model of governance worldwide, and it is catching on.

Donald Trump's vision to emulate the autocratic leaders he admires cannot hope to fully turn "*the Land of the Free and the Home of the Brave*" into a full-fledged dictatorship.

That would take time, if ever[57]. But to turn America into a Trumpocracy is entirely within his possibilities. At least as long as he can count on the support of his morally bankrupt enablers that used to be known as the Republican Party. They tried it once but failed. But this time, they are more than ready.

---

[57] Although, with the help of the Supreme Court, Donald Trump could very well extend his time in office over the two consecutive terms allowed by the Constitution. Alternatively, he could copy his mentor Vladimir Putin, have a puppet to replace him for one term, and come back for another two terms.

2024 PRESIDENTIAL ELECTION

WHO TO ELECT?

When you let yourself be robbed of your rights, your moral compass, and your democracy by electing corrupt, liars and self-centered politicians, you are not a victim; you are complicit.

We Americans do not have a very good record of electing good presidents. Since it is still too soon for historians to decide on Joe Biden's presidential legacy, of all the 45 presidents who came before him, only a selected few did not turn out to be badasses, sons of bitches, outright incompetent, or with a mixed record such as Lyndon Johnson, George Bush Sr, and Barack Obama.

Indeed, according to those who make it their business to rank presidents, only a paltry four make the cut as best presidents: Abraham Lincoln, Martin Van Buren, Jimmy Carter, and Ulysses Grant. That is it!

A path commonly traveled

Authoritarian rulers are very conservative. When it comes to sizing power, they know what worked well before and are not going to take unnecessary risks by deviating too much from a time-proven path to power that goes like this:

- Present yourself as the defender of traditional moral values and the ordinary people.
- Appeal to patriotism against existential threats, foreign or domestic (migrants and Jews always work).

151

- Portrait yourself as the only one who can fix whatever goes wrong in your country. It is you or the chaos.
- Promise to re-establish order, security, pride, and prosperity to the country that has become the laughingstock of the world. MAKE (fill in the blanks) GREAT AGAIN or MAKE (fill in the blanks) FIRST, always work.
- Promise to fight against crime, corruption, and the elite.
- Do not bother to have an economic, social, or foreign policy program. People don't care.

This road map to authoritarian rule is so constant and obvious that we may wonder why people always fall for it. And when they finally wake up, it is too late because authoritarian rulers never leave voluntarily.

For his supporters, D. Trump was the best American president ever living, period. For his detractors, he was the worst, a calamity for our country, democracy, and the world at large.

For historians who we expect to be impartial and only judge on the record of a person to determine his place in history, their judgment is radical, even among conservative scholars: as president, Donald Trump was not the worst, but the worst of the worst. Number One, like Donald Trump, loves to be, but in the wrong way.

For Donald Trump, who deemed himself the greatest of all presidents, including Abraham Lincoln, to be placed in the 40th place must have put a dent in his self-esteem. Or maybe not, because as for all experts, according to Trump, historians don't know what they are talking about.

But all this was in the past. The main question for America now is who will we elect as president in 2024?

For the forever Trumpsters, the answer is obvious. But for the rest of the voters, the never-Trumpsters, the sitting-on-the-fence voters, and those determined to select the best person for the task and the country, how do you decide?

The best way to answer this question is first to find out what we are looking for in selecting a new president. Although the type of characters and qualities sought after for the job would vary among people, certain character traits are certainly more desirable than others. Assuming that personality and character traits are a good gauge to predict presidential performance, the following are those that should help us who to elect as our next president.

In a democracy, whoever you elect to represent you is, at the subconscious level, a reflection of who you truly are. Your character, your moral values, and your worldviews.

A MUST READ FOR ANYBODY WHO STILL HAS NOT MADE UP THEIR MIND ABOUT WHOM TO ELECT

Must have Presidential character traits

Must have character traits sought for a president are the bare minimum we should expect from the person representing us for the next four years. Seriously, would you want someone with no principles, who is dishonest, and who has no integrity to be our president? Although millions of Americans would say "*yes*," for others.

Here are some of the character traits they should seek.

1. A person with principles

A person without principles is a person who lacks a moral compass for his actions. Asking for a politician with principles is like going to the fish market and asking for an oyster with a pearl. So, instead, we should be asking our president to have at least some principles when it counts the most.

2. Honesty and integrity

If honesty covers all the character traits that we wish our president to have, another one is paramount to all others: telling the truth. Contrary to what many believe, there is no alternative truth any more than being half-pregnant.

3. Ability to summon the citizens to a sense of common purpose

Been the Civil War, the Great Depression, or the two World Wars, U.S. Presidents had to lead the country through great challenges, division, social unrest, and dire tribulations.

Franklin Roosevelt inspired the country to fight itself out of the Great Depression. Reagan wanted to make the country great again (like you know who), and Kennedy challenged us to reach for the moon. Today, in the face of unprecedented global challenges, our country cries out for such a leader more than ever.

4. Communication and public persuasion

To get elected to represent all of us, a presidential candidate must be able to sell his message to the masses. Not all presidents were great communicators or even charismatic enough to move crowds on their vision alone. But at the very minimum, they had to be articulate enough to persuade voters that at least they were not as bad as the next guy. And sometimes, that was enough.

5. Ability to fulfill campaign promises

Obviously, this characteristic only applies to a candidate seeking a second term since the first time around, we can only be hopeful that the promises made will be kept. Since it is assumed that first-time candidates will promise anything to everybody, nobody truly believes that once elected, the new president will fulfill all the promises for which he was elected in the first place.

Good to have Presidential character traits

Good to have presidential characteristics is like the cherry on the cake. Those characteristics are not essential for being a good president, but those who had them were outstanding presidents. If we are only aiming for mediocrity, "*must-have*" characteristics would suffice.

1. Transparency

If transparency in government, like army intelligence, sounds like an oxymoron, sharing with the public in the decision-making process is a must in democracy. Its lacking breeds public distrust in both the government and the institutions.

2. Empathy

As the first civil servant of the people, it is certainly not too much of a quality to expect from a president. You could always fake it, but it is the actions rather than words that determine whether or not the person in charge is in it for himself or others.

3. Thoughtfulness

Thoughtful in the sense of being cautious or careful, as the opposite of being impulsive or acting on emotion without considering all the facts. After all, we don't want someone who starts bombing the shit out of some country as a diversion for his own misdeeds or under pretenses out of personal vendetta like the Iraq war. In short, we want someone with some crisis management skills and not someone who acts on impulse by tweets or otherwise.

4. Taking the blame

Taking responsibility and the blame when things go south is not only the sign of great leaders but the sign of a strong person who is confident in himself, whatever the results. The opposite would be a president who always seeks scapegoats to cover up his own weaknesses and shortcomings and play the blaming game.

5. Ability to work, listen, and empower others

Napoleon Bonaparte was a great leader of men, but one of his major shortcomings was not listening to the advice and expertise of others. Had it done so, he would have never ventured into the vastness of Russia expecting a quick victory. So did Hitler, with the same outcome: near annihilation of their armies.

6. Stubbornness and disagreeableness

As surprising as this may seem, according to the American Psychological Association that researches the personality traits that make great presidents, the traits you would hate from your next-door neighbor are a plus for presidents. Apparently, being a dominator is also a good thing, although they did not specify in what way.

7. The ability to make unpopular but necessary decisions

Another rare pearl to find since it runs contrary to any politician's instinct to be popular and get re-elected. Finding one would be the hallmark of a great president, as proven by those who in American history had the guts to do it.

8. Respect for others

The American presidency used to elicit a certain level of decorum in both its demeanor and communication with the public. As one branch of government, you would expect that the Oval Office works in tandem and supports the other governmental institutions that make up the backbone of our democracy. Still, judging from the last administration, it has been anything but.

9. Foreign standing

Foreign policies have traditionally never been a determining factor in any presidential election. However, global challenges like climate change, the war on terrorism, and trade globalization have become important enough to affect our society at home. For instance, the successive failures of all our military adventures since WWII have contributed significantly to the fall of our global standing. Especially since Donald Trump, America is no longer regarded as the beacon of democracy nor a model of governance to emulate.

Character traits in a president to avoid at all costs

Any of those character traits in a president would be a red flag that the person at the top is more concerned about his own welfare than ours. We had a few presidents who filled that description. Do we want another one?

1. Disrespect for the law and the institutions

You must be wondering why disrespect for the law and the institutions comes on top of all the characteristics to be avoided when selecting a president. Respect for the law and the institutions is more important than honesty, integrity, and transparency because it is paramount to the guarantee and protection of the Constitution and the three branches of government that are the hallmarks of our democracy. If the president, who is the guardian of our Constitution, does not respect and protect it as his inaugural oath of allegiance to the Constitution commands it, we are in big trouble.

It has been demonstrated that the weakening and control of institutions, like the judiciary, voting, and everything that protects the environment and the citizens, is one of the first things rulers with authoritarian tendencies try to achieve.

2. Personal ego

In theory, personal ego is incompatible with the Office of the Presidency, which is supposed to put the good of the country before yourself. However, having a big ego is not always a bad thing. Ego is defined as a person's sense of self-importance and can give you confidence when faced with challenging situations. The ego can also feed your willpower and resilience to accomplish things others would easily give up on pursuing. The only problem is when your ego is inflated to the point of becoming arrogant and believing that only you can accomplish something.

For Donald Trump, the ego is a double-sided blade. It could be good when applied correctly and look foolish or stupid when overplayed.

3. Dishonesty

It is quite natural to hate everything you are not. Like liars if you seek the truth, and the truth if you are a liar.

Trump's willful perversion of truth in order to deceive, cheat, mislead, swindle, or defraud for personal or political gain had been unprecedented in U.S. politics. The bar for the office of the Presidency is now so low that it has become the norm that could allow Donald Trump to get re-elected in 2024.

4. Search for personal power and financial gain

Contrary to banana republics and failed states, personal power, and financial gain had never been an obvious goal or ambition of any of our past presidents. But again, that was then, the good old days.

5. Cronyism

Cronyism, which consists of appointing your friends and associates to positions of authority without proper regard for their qualifications, used to be the hallmark of authoritarian countries and banana republics. We are getting there.

Now you have it. All you now have to do is to match the "*must-have, good to have, and characteristics to avoid at all costs*" character traits with the ones of your presidential candidate.

Of course, if your choice is already made, regardless of your candidate's moral standing and competence, you may as well skip the next section entirely and jump directly to the 2024 presidential election aftermath predictions section.

Character traits and characteristics required for a president are not in the eye of the beholder. They are the common denominator that everybody should agree upon.

A MUST READ FOR ANYONE WHO IS STILL CONSIDERING D.J. TRUMP AS THE BEST PERSON SUITED TO BE OUR PRESIDENT

"He is the most flawed person I know.
The depths of his dishonesty are astounding."
John Kelly, Four-Star General and Trump's former Chief of Staff

Does D. Trump have the Presidential character traits listed on pages 154-160 above?

A person with principles

To label Donald Trump as a person without principles would be incorrect. He has no ideology, which is different. If a principle is a kind of rule, belief, or idea that guides you, then Donald Trump has a few. Ten exactly, like the Ten Commandments:

1. He believes that he is the greatest in anything,
2. Truth is elastic and is only what serves him most,
3. Winning is the most essential thing in life,
4. He never lies,
5. He never apologizes,
6. Empathy is for the weak,
7. If you are not with him, you are against him,
8. Money defines who you are,
9. Paying tax is for losers, and,
10. A pussy from any bab is a pussy to grab.

Honesty and integrity

If we give the word "*Honesty*" its primary sense of being truthful: not lying, stealing, or cheating, and free of fraud, then a new word should be entered in the dictionaries as its antonym: Trump.

It is irrelevant that Trump supporters would consider this proposition ludicrous, because Donald Trump has already secured his place in the history books as the most dishonest U.S. president ever, and we had a few. But Donald Trump should cherish this notoriety: he is number one.

Ability to summon the citizens to a sense of common purpose

We must give Donald Trump credit when it is due. His ability to summon people to a common purpose is more than a quality. It is a gift. Based on that ability alone, Donald Trump could have been the best president since the foundation of our republic instead of being the worst. At least he has the same ability as Churchill and Hitler. The difference is what you do with it. For Donald Trump, the only common purpose he is fighting tooth and nail to instill in his supporters is to keep him in power no matter what.

Communication and persuasion

Here again, a great quality common to all great leaders. As a show-business animal, we did not expect less from Trump. But his most outstanding achievement is to have been able to convey his message to millions of Americans with the vocabulary of a 4th grader. Thank you, Twitter, for not overloading the attention span of most of us by limiting the size of a tweet to 289 characters.

Ability to fulfill campaign promises

How big were Trump's campaign promises? 282 items, to be exact

"I didn't back down from my promises. I kept every single one," Donald Trump.

Reality check: Trump promised his supporters *"Everything."* But what did he, in reality, deliver?

According to his supporters: *"Almost everything he said he would do, he has done."*

In a typical glass *"half-full"* versus glass *"half-empty,"* both Trump's detractors and supporters are right because Trump effectively delivered on about half of his promises, which in itself is an accomplishment given the low credibility attached to politicians' campaign promises.

Good to have Presidential characteristics

"Good to have" is like the cherry on the cake; it is nice but not necessary.

Empathy

- In 2018, Trump canceled a visit to an American World War I cemetery in France where more than 1,800 U.S. Marines died, arguing, *"Why should I go to that cemetery? It's filled with losers."* Then added that the Marines were *"suckers"* for getting killed.

- The Trump administration will have executed more inmates than any other president in over 130 years.

- A federal judge rejected a Trump policy cutting billions of dollars in food aid to low-income Americans during the pandemic, but the administration appealed the order.

- Trump's Agriculture Department also eliminated roughly $480 million in nutrition assistance for people in the state of Pennsylvania alone.

- Under the Trump administration's *"zero tolerance"* immigration policy, the parents of 545 children, including roughly 60, were under the age of 5 and were separated at the Mexican cannot be found. These children are now essentially orphaned, and most live in privately run detention centers in the United States.

- The Trump administration secretly withheld roughly $4 million from a program that helps New York City firefighters, emergency medical technicians, and paramedics who suffer from illnesses related to the Sept. 11, 2001, terrorist attacks.

- On the anniversary of the 2016 massacre at a gay nightclub in Orlando, Florida, the Trump administration eliminated health care protections for transgender patients. The rule was announced during Pride Month.

- Breaking from more than 160 countries that agreed to the Mine Ban Treaty, Trump canceled a policy that prohibited using anti-personnel landmines outside the Korean peninsula. Most landmine casualties have been civilians.

Thoughtfulness

If thoughtfulness is a consideration for the needs of other people, this goes utterly against Trump's principles of thinking about anybody else but himself.

Taking the blame

Just from the horse's mouth, *"I never take the blame"* Donald Trump.

Ability to work and empower others

"My way or the highway" is Trump's way to work and empower others. He fired all the people who had some sort of experience or expertise in their job to replace them with *"yes men."* In a sense, Trump applied his experience from *"The Apprentice"* TV reality show and used it to run the government.

Stubbornness and disagreeableness

Not according to Bill Maher, who defined him as *"Irrational, pouty, vain, thin-skinned, hysterical and just not that bright, does that sound like anyone we know today?"* and summarized it all up by calling him *"a whiny little bitch"*.

Ability to make unpopular but necessary decisions

We cannot blame Trump for not making any, since that goes against the DNA of any politician.

Respect for others

Ok, that is a silly thought.

Foreign standing

- By executive orders, Donald Trump dismantled or disrupted many multilateral pacts where America was the initiator or the leading participant. If the 2015 Paris Accords on Climate change and the non-proliferation nuclear treaty with Iran were the most publicized, others, such as withdrawing from the World Health Organization and the UN Human Rights Council, were just as detrimental to U.S. interests.

- Trump alienated his European allies and the NATO alliance while at the same time indulging in his admiration and even his love for some autocratic leaders.
- Trump partially delivered on a campaign promise to bring troops home from "*endless wars*," particularly in Afghanistan. Too bad that Joe Biden fucked up its execution.

- Despite Trump's love for North Korean leader Kim Jong Un, he did not succeed in persuading him to give up on his nuclear ambitions.

- On the plus side, if Trump's decision to relocate the U.S. Embassy in Israel to divided Jerusalem was a self-serving, politically motivated move, he also helped broker historic deals between Israel and the United Arab Emirates, Bahrain, and Sudan to normalize relations.

- But by far, Trump's most far-reaching foreign policy blunder for the planet has been the cancellation of the 2015 Iran nuclear deal. Although Iran abode to all the terms of the Agreement, with one pen stroke, Trump sent to the garbage bin an agreement sanctioned by the five permanent powers of the United Nations that had put limits on uranium enrichment and reprocessing as well as rules on monitoring the respect of the agreement.

Today, Iran has become a de facto nuclear power with ballistic missiles capable of ensuring the country the nuclear security enjoyed by other rogue countries like North Korea.

In the final analysis, Donald Trump's more enduring legacy will be to have found in China a new "*enemy for America*" that will have the potential to end badly for the world.

The character traits of a president to avoid at all costs

"*Based on the president's moral deficiencies, President Trump should be removed from office,* "Mark Galli, editor-in-chief of *Christianity Today.*

Well said for a Christian!

Disrespect for the law and the institutions

- Based on his actions while in Office, Trump made it abundantly clear that rules, laws, and norms were not his thing. Although his preference leans towards inciting other people to break the law for him, Trump has, on occasion, never shied away from testing the limits of how far he can go without consequences. Judging from the unbelievable way he got away from being impeached twice and surviving an insurrection attempt against our democracy without even being charged for the highest crime outlined in our Constitution, force is to recognize his talent for being an outstanding escape artist.

- When Trump indeed flirts with the law, it is tough to determine if he broke any in the first place since, like in

StarTreck , he went where nobody has gone before. Case in point:

When Trump took with him boxes of confidential documents to Mar-a-Lago, some classified and marked "*Top Secret*," destroyed others destined for the National Archives, or clogged the Oval Office toilet with wads of paper, did he violate the Presidential Records Act? Nobody knows because the creators of Norms never envisioned a president actually doing that.

- In 2021, the House Oversight Committee released a report on the coronavirus crisis showing that Trump administration officials made "*deliberate efforts to undermine the nation's coronavirus response for political purposes*," More specifically, the report made it clear that the administration worked to undermine the public health response to the coronavirus pandemic by blocking officials from speaking publicly, watering down testing guidance and attempting to interfere with other public health guidance.

- Even the CDC, the World-renowned Centers for Disease Control and Prevention, suffered from the hires of Donald Trump, who blocked it from conducting public briefings for three months.

"Trump Administration officials engaged in a staggering pattern of political interference in the pandemic response and failed to heed early warnings about the looming crisis."

"These decisions placed countless American lives at risk, undermined the nation's public health institutions, and contributed to one of the worst failures of leadership in American history." [58]

- The Trump administration removed Michael Kuperberg, the head of the program that produces the National Climate Assessment, to be replaced by David Legates, a climate-change skeptic who wrote in June that "carbon dioxide is plant food and is not a pollutant.

- Trump issued an Executive Order to take away job security from tens of thousands and possibly hundreds of thousands of civil servants. The Order allows policymaking employees to be removed from their jobs with little cause at Trump's pleasure.

- Perchlorate, a toxic chemical compound used in rocket fuel, has been found to contaminate water, causing fetal and infant brain damage. The Obama administration planned to regulate the chemical. Still, the Environmental Protection Agency, led by Trump's appointee Andrew Wheeler, went against the decision, saying that the regulation was "not in the public interest."

- The White House issued new guidance that banned members of its pandemic task force from testifying before Congress. The decision was made shortly after infectious disease expert Dr. Anthony Fauci, whose views often

---

[58] As reported by Deborah Leah Birx who served as the White House Coronavirus Response Coordinator under President Donald Trump and who specializes in HIV/AIDS immunology, vaccine research, and global health

diverged from Trump's, was prohibited from testifying before a House committee.

- The Trump administration eliminated an Obama-era rule that required oil and gas companies to repair methane leaks. The EPA said the companies will no longer pay roughly $100 million a year for repairs, resulting in the release of 850,000 tons of planet-warming methane by the end of the decade.

- The Trump administration announced it would begin selling oil and gas drilling leases in the Arctic National Wildlife Refuge, a vast area of undisturbed wilderness in Alaska. The Center for American Progress said that the drilling sought by Republican lawmakers for decades would release more than 4.3 billion metric tons of carbon dioxide.

- Congress approved $1 billion for the Pentagon to *"prevent, prepare for, and respond to coronavirus,"* including making more masks and medical equipment available. Instead, the Defense Department gave most of the money to defense contractors for jet engine parts and other military supplies.

- The Trump administration auctioned off the rights to allow oil and gas companies to drill in the vast and pristine Arctic National Wildlife Refuge in Alaska — before President-elect Joe Biden could block the move.

- The Trump administration_helped wealthy companies benefit from the Treasury Department's coronavirus emergency fund_that was intended for small businesses.

More than half of the $522 billion for small businesses went to larger companies.

- Two months before his term was set to end, Trump fired Defense Secretary Mark Esper, the latest on a long list of political appointees who have resigned or been dismissed. The firing created instability atop the military chain of command at an uncertain time when the president refused to concede his loss in the election.

- The Trump administration removed Michael Kuperberg, the head of the program that produces the National Climate Assessment, the government's most important report on climate change. Kuperberg was expected to be replaced by David Legates, a climate change.

- The coronavirus stabilization law that Congress passed included money for public education institutions hurt by the pandemic. Still, Trump's Education Secretary, Betsy DeVos, directed $180 million of it to private and religious schools.

- Trump ousted the chairman of a watchdog panel that oversaw how the Trump administration managed $2 trillion in coronavirus relief. Glenn Fine, the acting Pentagon inspector general, was chosen to head the Pandemic Response Accountability Committee. Fine was the second inspector general in a week to be fired by the president after the firing of whistleblower Michael Atkinson.

- The Environmental Protection Agency finalized its revised Navigable Waters Protection Rule. Under Trump, protections for many rivers, streams, and wetlands were officially removed.

Too much personal ego

You cannot deny Trump of his obsessive use of superlatives about himself. Everything he does is always the best, the greatest, something you have never seen before in America, the world, or ever. However, this flattering assessment of himself is one of the rare areas where you cannot accuse him of lying because he indeed believes it.

If the ego is defined as a person's sense of self-importance, everybody will agree that Trump is not lacking in that department. It would be no exaggeration to explain Donald Trump as egocentric: someone who only thinks of himself without regard for the feelings or desires of others.

- Trump boasted at least six times about winning the Michigan state's "*Man of the Year*" award. There is no such award.

- At some of the Trump golf clubs, there was a mocked-up cover of Time Magazine's "*Man of the Year*" where Trump appeared with arms crossed beneath a banner that reads, "*TRUMP IS HITTING ON ALL FRONTS … EVEN TV!* ". This was a fake that Time Magazine asked to be taken down from the walls of several of Trump's golf clubs.

- Trump boasted of receiving a *"highly honored Bay of Pigs Award"* from Cuban Americans. There is no such award named after the failed 1961 invasion of Cuba.

- When a reporter asked Trump why he repeatedly took over 150 times credit for a veterans' health care bill that was signed into law by President Obama, Trump replied, "*Why do you keep saying that you passed Veterans Choice?*" Trump answered, "*OK. Thank you very much, everybody.*" Then, he abruptly walked away.

- In 2018, Trump told future Governor Kristi Noem, "*Do you know it's my dream to have my face on Mount Rushmore?*".

- As a candidate, Trump made it clear that he believed himself to be more knowledgeable than the military's leadership. *"I know more about ISIS than the generals do, believe me."* He must have been on to something because once elected, there was an exodus of generals from the Trump administration.

- The Treasury Department ordered that Trump's name appear on the $1,200 stimulus checks that millions of Americans were to receive.

- Commenting on his impeachment, "*I think I'm getting A-pluses for the way I handled myself during a phony impeachment. Okay? It was a hoax. But certainly, I guess, I thought of it.*"

- "*As I have stated strongly before, and just to reiterate, if Turkey does anything that I, in my great and unmatched wisdom, consider to be off-limits, I will totally destroy and obliterate the Economy of Turkey* (I've done before!)."

Search for personal power and financial gain.

- During his campaign, Trump always proclaimed that he would release his financial records as customary for all presidents. However, since being elected, Trump has fought nails and teeth to prevent his promise from happening. On August 20, 2020, a federal judge rejected Trump's most recent attempt to block the release of his returns. To which Trump replied.

"This is a continuation of the witch hunt, the greatest witch hunt in history. There's never been anything like it."

Perhaps the President has never heard of the Salem witch hunt.

- Trump said he would *"completely isolate"* himself from the Trump Organization. Except for the first two years of his presidency alone, scores of events at his properties netted roughly $12 million of business to his company.

- Just by visiting his properties 274 times, Trump's Organization netted close to one million dollars by charging the Secret Service for his protection while also bringing at least $3.8 million in fees associated with 37 political events held at Trump's properties.

- Claiming that he needed money for an Official Election Defense Fund (an account that does not exist), Trump begged, *"I need you now more than ever."* Read the fine print. Most of the $179 million raised will go to a new political action committee to fund future political activities, which is an euphemism for Trump's pockets.

- During his presidency, Trump's campaign has spent $6.7 million in donations at his businesses.

- Peter Navarro is an economist and author whom Trump nominated as Director of the White House National Trade Council. As the president's trade adviser, Navarro negotiated a coronavirus-related deal to buy ventilators from Royal Philips N.V. in a $646.7 million contract. After a congressional investigation that found "*evidence of fraud, waste, and abuse*" in the acquisition of the Philips ventilators, the deal was canceled after it appeared that the price for the ventilators jumped from $3,280 each under the Obama administration deal to $15,000 under the Trump administration. It is unclear who was profiteering from this deal that scammed the government, but somebody close to Trump was planning to fill his pockets.

- A New York judge ordered Trump to pay $2 million to settle claims that the Trump Foundation misused money raised for charitable donations during his 2016 campaign. Trump had raised the money during a televised fundraiser for veterans.

- According to the *Washington Post*, the Trump Organization earned at least $238,000 in taxpayer money by charging the government every time Trump's children visited his properties. The charges were for the Secret Service agents who stayed with them. The same thing happened every time Ivanka Trump visited the golf club in Bedminster, N.J.

- New York fraud investigators were looking into tax write-offs on roughly $26 million in consulting fees. Of that money, the president's daughter, Ivanka Trump, was paid $747,622 in consulting fees in 2017 while she was an executive officer of Trump's companies.

- During his re-election campaign, Trump accused Joe Biden of being too soft on China because of his son Hunter's business dealings in that country. That was before it was revealed that Trump maintains a secret bank account in China.

- Between 2016 and 2017, Trump paid only $750 in federal income taxes. However, between 2013 and 2015, he paid $188,561 in taxes in China. At the same time, Trump received an income tax refund of $72.9 million after declaring large losses.

- According to a *New York Times* investigation, Trump is $421 million in debt. He once boasted that his tax returns were *"very big"* and *"beautiful,"* but he has refused to release his returns for years.

Disregard for the law and the institutions

- Trump seriously considered pardoning himself. That would have been a first. It is not even sure if such a move would have been legal because nobody in the world before Trump would even think such a thing was possible. Although, for Trump, having the Department of Justice in your pocket would help.

- Trump urged Georgia's Secretary of State Brad Raffensperger, a Republican, to commit a felony by asking him to "*find*" votes to overturn Joe Biden's victory in the state. The angry one-hour telephone bidding was even recorded and could have landed Raffensperger in a lot of trouble as Trump insisted, "*All I want to do is this. I just want to find 11,780 votes, which is one more than we have. Because we won the state.*"

- After threatening Brad Raffensperger, Trump desperately concluded, "*So what are we going to do here, folks? I only need 11,000 votes. Fellas, I need 11,000 votes. Give me a break.*"

- Trump encouraged people to vote twice in the Presidential Election. Voting once in an absentee ballot, then voting in person on Election Day. Voting more than once in an election is illegal under federal law.

- On January 6, Trump attempted to have Vice President Pence not certify the votes when Congress meets to certify election results. He claimed that his vice president "*has the power to reject fraudulently chosen electors*" and, therefore, overturn the election. That power is not a matter of law; it is in the Constitution, which says no such thing.

- Trump said that he would order law enforcement to the polls for the Presidential election. "*We're going to have sheriffs, and we're going to have law enforcement. And we're going to have hopefully U.S. attorneys, and we're going to have everybody and attorney generals,*" Law enforcement is barred at polling places in several states because of concerns over voter intimidation.

- Trump fired Christopher Krebs, the director of the Cybersecurity and Infrastructure Security Agency, five days after the agency released a statement about the election that said there was no evidence that any voting system was "in any way compromised.".

- Trump signed an Executive Order that allowed him to expedite infrastructure projects by working around environmental reviews.

- "When somebody is the President of the United States," he said, "the authority is total, and that's the way it's got to be.".

- Trump said that if Iran retaliated for the airstrike that killed Suleimani, the U.S. would target 52 sites "important to Iran & the Iranian culture" and "HIT [them] VERY FAST AND VERY HARD." Targeting sites of cultural significance is in direct opposition to the 1954 Hague Convention and the Department of Defense's Law of War manual.
- An appeals court allowed Trump to divert $3.6 billion from Defense spending to construct his border wall. Declaring a national emergency along the southern border in February 2019 allowed Trump to have the money reallocated.

Cronyism

- Trump is asking the Food and Drug Administration to approve Oleandrin as a coronavirus cure without any evidence that it is beneficial against COVID. Oleandrin had been touted by MyPillow C.E.O. Mike Lindell, a prominent Trump donor who has invested in the company that makes the extract.

- DeJoy was allegedly appointed by Trump as Postmaster General to slow mailing in an absentee ballot mail-voting delivery to favor Trump. Deloy earned millions of dollars from a company that does business with the Postal Service. He donated $1.2 million to Trump's election campaign.

- In one of his last acts as president, Trump issued pardons to Steve Bannon, who was charged with cheating donors who thought their money was going toward constructing a border wall. Trump also granted clemency to 143 people, including Elliott Broidy, Rick Renzi, and Robert Hayes, both former House Republicans.

- Trump granted clemency to loyalists who committed fraud and lied to investigators to help the president. Charles Kushner, a real estate developer and the father of Trump's son-in-law, pleaded guilty to witness tampering and tax evasion. Paul Manafort, his former campaign chairman, was convicted of tax fraud, bank fraud, and conspiracy. Roger Stone, his long-time friend, was convicted of witness tampering, lying to Congress, and obstructing the investigation into Russian interference in the 2016 election.

- Trump pardoned his former national security adviser Michael Flynn, who was convicted in the investigation into Russian meddling in the 2016 election.

- Companies linked to Trump's family and friends applied for $21 million in Small Business Administration funding meant to help businesses hurt by the pandemic. Those positioned to benefit from the bailout money included companies owned or backed by the family of Trump's son-in-law, White House adviser Jared Kushner, and the president's son, Donald Jr. The government refused to share details of the loans until pressed by watchdog groups.

- More than 40 lobbyists connected to Trump obtained at least $10 billion in federal coronavirus aid for their clients.

- Trump commuted the sentence of former Illinois Governor Rod Blagojevich, who was convicted of corruption charges.

.FOOL ME ONCE, SHAME ON YOU.
FOOL ME TWICE, SHAME ON ME.

Comparing presidential eligibility criteria
With Donald Trump's record

I did not do anything wrong; the Devil made me do it

"I did not do anything wrong; I just told others to break the law. They are the ones who should go to jail." From D. Trump's little voice in his head.

From "I am not a crook." to "I am not a fraud."

Do not expect Donald Trump to use the same infamous self-assessment tirade uttered in 1973 by Richard Nixon in his defense for being accused of being the Mastermind behind the Watergate break-in of the Democratic National Committee headquarters in Washington, D.C. That is not in Trump's M.O. (Modus Operandi), and he would be right. Because "*Crook*" is too feeble a word to define someone indicted on 37 felony counts, including racketeering, a criminal offense under RICO, an anti-organized crime law in the State of Georgia.

So, putting aside his "*criminal*" accusations, on what other factors should we assess Trump's fitness to be re-elected president?

In evaluating candidates for our decision to select the most suitable person for the highest office of the land, we have only two things to rely on: what they tell us about themselves and what we can assess from their records.

As far as Donald Trump is concerned, that exercise is straightforward: we just have to look in the rear-view mirror to compare our previously identified presidential eligibility criteria (pages 831-385) to see how well they match Donald Trump's record.

But if there is one thing that won't change for sure, it is Donald Trump's character.

FROM THE PEOPLE WHO WORKED WITH TRUMP AND KNOW HIM BEST

From the most intelligent people who worked with him and knew him at close range: John Kelly, Reince Priebus, HR MacMaster, Gary Cohn, Jim Mattis, Katie Walsh, Tony Schwartz, and even Steve Banon.

"An idiot, a dope, Dumb as shit, an idiot with the intelligence of a kindergartener, Like an 11-year-old child, a fifth or sixth-grader, a moron, a stunning level of superficial knowledge and plain ignorance, like trying to figure out what a child wants."

Trump First Secretary of State, Rex Tillerson: *"Trump's understanding of global events, his understanding of global history, his understanding of U.S. history was really limited. It's really hard to have a conversation with someone who doesn't even understand the concept for why we're talking about this."*

Trump's third National Security Adviser, John Bolton: *"I believe (foreign leaders) think he is a laughing fool."*

Trump's final Chief of staff aide, Cassidy Hutchinson: *"I think that Donald Trump is the most grave threat we will face to our democracy in our lifetime, and potentially in American history."*

Trump's Chairman of the Joint Chiefs, retired Gen. Mark Milley: *"We don't take an oath to a wannabe dictator. We take an oath to the Constitution and we take an* oath to the idea that is America – and we're willing to die to protect it."

Trump's White House lawyer, Ty Cobb: *"Trump relentlessly puts forth claims that are not true."*

Trump's first homeland security adviser, Tom Bossert: *"The President undermined American democracy baselessly for months. As a result, he's guilty of this siege and an utter disgrace."*

Trump's former Communications Director, Stephanie Grisham: *"I am terrified of him running in 2024."*

Trump's second National Security Adviser, HR McMaster: *"We saw the absence of leadership, really anti-leadership, and what that can do to our country."*

Trump's Vice President, Mike Pence: *"The American people deserve to know that President Trump asked me to put him over my oath to the Constitution. ... Anyone who puts himself over the Constitution should never be President of the United States."*

Trump's former White House counsel Ty Cobb: *"He has never cared about America, its citizens, its future or anything but himself. In fact, as history well shows from his divisive lies, as well as from his unrestrained contempt for the rule of law and his related crimes, his conduct and mere existence have hastened the demise of democracy and of the nation."*

Trump's former White House communications director Alyssa Farah Griffin: *"Trump is a threat to democracy, and I will never support him."*

Trump's former national security adviser John Bolton: *"The only thing that's left is Trump's not fit to be president. He doesn't have a conservative philosophy. He follows his own personal interest, and that's not what you need in a president."*

Trump's Former White House Chief of Staff Mick Mulvaney: *"I am working hard to make sure that someone else is the nominee," Mulvaney said. "I think he's the Republican who is most likely to lose in a general election, of all our leading candidates. If anyone can lose to Joe Biden, it would be him."*

Trump's second Attorney General, Bill Barr: *"Someone who engaged in that kind of bullying about a process that is fundamental to our system and to our self-government shouldn't be anywhere near the Oval Office."*

One of Trump's many former communications directors, Anthony Scaramucci: *"He is the domestic terrorist of the 21st century."*

Trump's second Chief of Staff, John Kelly: *"A person that has nothing but contempt for our democratic institutions, our Constitution, and the rule of law. There is nothing more that can be said. God help us."*

"What's going on in the country that a single person thinks this guy would still be a good president when he's said the things he's said and done the things he's done? It's beyond my comprehension he has the support he has."

Trump's second Secretary of Defense, Mark Esper: *"I think he's unfit for office. ... He puts himself before country. His actions are all about him and not about the country. And then, of course, I believe he has integrity and character issues as well."*

Trump's first Secretary of Defense, James Mattis: *"Donald Trump is the first president in my lifetime who does not try to unite the American people – does not even pretend to try. Instead, he tries to divide us."*

From a member of Trump's own family, **Mary Trump.**

"A petty, pathetic little man ignorant, incapable, out of his depth, and lost to his own delusional spin."

So, yes, indeed

FOOL ME ONCE, SHAME ON YOU.
FOOL ME TWICE, SHAME ON ME.

A MUST READ FOR ANYBODY AFFLICTED BY THE SHORT-TERM MEMORY SYNDROME OF *"IT WAS MUCH BETTER WITH TRUMP."*

Collective amnesia is the only rational explanation for voters who keep re-electing politicians and leaders who only care about themselves..

"I have accomplished more than most previous U.S. presidents." D. Trump.

Much has been said about the disconnect between feelings and reality when it comes to polls' approval ratings between Donald Trump and Joe Biden.

If the approval rating between both contenders in the presidential race is almost neck to neck[59], the difference between the two seems fuelled by a feeling of nostalgia for the Trump's years, forgetting that by the end of his administration, Trump only had an approval rating of 34 percent.

Now for a closer look:

What Trump did right

- He did not start any new wars. A low bar that most of his predecessors failed to clear. But that was a close call considering that U.S. General Mark Milley, chairman of the Joint Chiefs of Staff in the Trump Administration, called China's counterparts, promising to warn them first if he were ordered to attack.

---

[59] 42% for D. Trump vs 41% for Joe Biden. Source 2024 Gallop Poll.

- Trump made a deal with the Taliban to start withdrawing from America's longest war in Afghanistan. A deal that Biden got blamed for when The Taliban reneged on their agreement and literally waltzed into Kabul when they met no opposition from the Afgan forces we spent billions training and equipping with our latest military material.

- Trump initiated Operation Warp Speed to coordinate the development, manufacturing, and deployment of vaccines against the COVID-19 coronavirus.

- Trump tried to address the enormous trade imbalance with China with mixed results since the American consumers ended up paying the cost of the tax import tariffs he imposed on imported products from China as well as the cost of subsidies he gave to farmers in compensation for lost export markets.

- In an effort to make the tax system more efficient and equitable, Trump significantly reduced the importance of the mortgage interest deduction for owner-occupied housing. However, the deduction has mainly benefited the rich since, in 2018, nearly 80 percent of the benefit went to households earning in the top 20 percent.

- Trump didn't repeal Obamacare, but that was not for the lack of trying since he came into office vowing to repeal it. So why give him credit for this failure? Because his repeated attempts to repeal the Affordable Care Act ironically had the opposing effect of forcing the Federal Government into pouring billions of extra federal dollars to subsidize the higher cost of Americans' coverage.

- It is hard to keep crediting Trump for something he did not do. Still, contrary to his anti-cannabis rhetoric for its legalization, the Trump Administration did not move to counter the 18 states that passed legislation to liberalize their marijuana laws. Cannabis is now legal in some form in 36 states, and more Americans now live in states with full legalization. Bill Maher[60] should be proud.

- Trump made it easier to prosecute financial crimes. Now, the new law would require millions of business entities to report the actual owners of shell companies, making it more difficult to hide behind the anonymity of shell companies that engage in money laundering or tax evasion, which is sort of ironic considering that New York prosecutors are treating the Trump Organization like it's the mob and his businesses organized like the Mafia.

Other Trump achievements

With regard to other Trump's achievements, it all depends on the eyes of the beholder. Should Trump be lauded for his attempts to deregulate a bloated bureaucracy or vilified for gutting Federal Agencies to assert his autocratic tendencies? Indeed, replacing the heads of such agencies with cronies dedicated to emasculating their powers does not leave much room for imagination regarding the real purpose of such moves. But that is exactly what Trump did: filling high-level jobs by Executive Orders to avoid Senate confirmation.

---

[60] Bill Maher, host of the acerbic TV show "*Real Time with Bill Maher*" on HBO

You can value a man by the quality of the persons he associates with.

Trump has often said he likes installing *"acting"* officials because it gives him more flexibility. By that, he meant *"more control,"* especially if it is for acting against the law.[61]

Trump's disdain for expertise is well-documented. In many ways, Trump knows more than any of them, so appointing neophytes to jobs they don't have a clue about is a good way to keep it that way. In Trump's eyes, political loyalty trumps knowledge or professional competence. So, filling the civil service with political hacks and cronies makes perfect sense. It is too bad that it does not make sense for the country.

Besides being a decent golf player with a handicap as low as 2.8, Trump's major achievements have been his ability to undo, dismantle, or repeal most of his predecessor's accomplishments, especially in the area of consumers' and workers' protection or regulations affecting Big Business.

From his track record, there is ample evidence that when it came to choosing between big business and the average American, the former was always the winner.

- Trump Administration **dismantled Obama-era policies that were designed to curb abuses by for-profit colleges**, including rules designed to make it easier for borrowers to obtain loan forgiveness if they were cheated or duped by their college. What is an **attempt to overturn a federal court judgment approving a $25 million settlement for students who said they were duped by Donald Trump and his now-defunct Trump**

[61] Trump's administration has been sued and lost when a federal judge found that it hired a top immigration official unlawfully.

University, which promised to teach them the "*secrets of success*" in the real estate industry? We'll never know.

- Under Trump, the Agriculture Department **scaled back the $60 billion Supplemental Nutrition Assistance Program, the food support program for low-income Americans** formerly known as food stamps. The administration said it wanted to cut back on waste and save money, probably by giving more to big business.

- Obama's Labor Department had finalized a rule that would raise the salary threshold for overtime eligibility from around $24,000 to some $47,000 a year, with triennial increases. The Trump Administration trashed it and re-wrote the rule to **cut the number of workers that would be eligible by half, resulting in wages lost at around $1 billion annually.**

- The Trump administration rolled **back environmental regulations to loosen the standards oil and gas companies** had to meet for how much methane they could emit into the atmosphere. Trump's stance was the polar opposite of what China and European countries pledged to do to rein in emissions of a gas considered one of the leading causes of climate change.

- The Trump administration **eliminated an Obama-era rule that required oil and gas companies to repair methane leaks.** The EPA said the companies will no longer pay roughly $100 million yearly for repairs. That will result in the release of 850,000 tons of planet-warming methane by the end of the decade.

- The Trump administration **repealed transparency safeguards enacted under Obama designed to protect hundreds of thousands of people working for companies bidding for federal contracts from sexual harassment**. Maybe it was because Trump saw nothing wrong with sexual harassment since he himself said.
"I don't even wait. And when you're a star, they let you do it, you can do anything… grab them by the pussy.".

- The Trump administration announced it was **selling leases for oil and gas drilling in the Arctic National Wildlife Refuge**, a vast area of undisturbed wilderness in Alaska. That could lead to the release of more than 4.3 billion metric tons of carbon dioxide.

- Vehicle emissions represent the largest source of greenhouse gas emissions in the U.S. The Obama administration had negotiated with automakers a plan requiring them to improve fuel efficiency by 5 percent per year. Still, the **Trump administration rolled those targets back to just a 1.5 percent improvement each year and attacked California's special regulatory authority for brokering a deal with five major auto manufacturers to meet standards similar to the Obama-era ones**.

- When Congress approved $1 billion for the Pentagon to *"prevent, prepare for, and respond to coronavirus,"* including making more masks and medical equipment available, **the Defense Department gave most of the money to defense contractors for jet engine parts and other military supplies**.

- Trump **auctioned off the rights to allow oil and gas companies to drill in the vast and pristine Arctic National Wildlife Refuge in Alaska.**

- Trump helped wealthy companies benefit from the Treasury Department's coronavirus emergency fund that was intended for small businesses. **More than half of the $522 billion for small businesses went to larger companies.**

- Trump **eliminated Clinton-era protections that banned logging and development on 9.3 million acres of Alaska's Tongass National Forest**. His action will allow logging companies to cut down trees and build roads in one of the largest temperate rainforests on Earth.

- Reversing Obama's approach to tackling climate change, **Trump completely gutted the EPA to replace it instead with a group of chemicals industry experts to run and advise** the program that regulates toxic and dangerous chemicals, like asbestos and methylene chloride, that Americans are exposed to daily.

- Next time the world faces a new financial crisis, don't forget to thank Trump. His administration **rolled back rules set by Obama to regulate banks designed to prevent another financial crisis after the Wall Street meltdown that caused the 2008 financial crisis.**

- The Trump administration **rolled back Obama's efforts to combat racial segregation** in housing by scrapping the Affirmatively Furthering Fair Housing rule. It also made it harder for plaintiffs to bring claims of unintentional discrimination, dramatically cut back on enforcing fair lending laws, and exempted small banks from data collection requirements that help track racial discrimination in the mortgage market.

Taking care of all the "*left behind*" of the global economy. Promise not kept - widening the gap between the have-too-much and the have-not-enough.

Trump campaigned on his promises to take care of all the left behind of the global economy: the little guys, the farmers, the factory workers, the mineworkers, and the middle class. Big commitment for a self-proclaimed billionaire who pretends he alone can understand the "*little man.*"

To that end, the Trump administration had proposed new work requirements that could have prevented almost 700,000 adults from receiving Supplemental Nutrition Assistance Program benefits.

Remaking the judiciary - Promise kept, to Trump's exclusive benefit.

In his four-year term, Trump confirmed three Supreme Court justices. Thank you to Justice Ruth Bader Ginsberg, who had the good taste to die at the right time.

In addition, The Trump Party has managed to pack the State Courts with judicial appointments that could come in handy come a 2024 voting challenge.

Finally, in a typical GASTRUMPING example of accusing others of what he does: weaponizing the Department of Justice, and promising to do it again on a greater scale if re-elected.

Tax cuts - Promise kept, for big business. For the average American, not so much.

"A vote for me is a vote for massive, middle-class tax cuts, regulation cuts, fair trade." Donald Trump.

The Tax Cuts and Jobs Act, signed by Trump in December 2017, was the most significant restructuring of the U.S. tax system since the 1980s. It slashed the rate companies pay in the United States from 35% to 21%, **resulting in a $1.5 trillion tax cut for U.S. corporations.** With all that money, U.S. corporations elected to boost stock buybacks instead of hiring or increasing their capital investment. As a result of the tax cut and because of lower tax revenues, the reform caused the U.S. deficit to swell to over $1 trillion at the end of Trump's presidency.

Overall, Trump's tax-cutting was expected to save an estimated $1.5 trillion over ten years for big business versus a mere $2000 for a family of four earning less than $70,000.

Draining the swamp - Fulfilled, but not in the way you think.

Another of Trump's big campaign promises to root out political corruption and criminal behavior so prevalent in both the U.S. Congress and the Senate. Yes, Trump has drained the swamp, but to restock it with his own low-life creatures, of whom, with 91 criminal charges, he has become the alpha shark to reign at the top of the food chain.

Deregulation - Promise kept - American citizens are not less protected than ever before

Regarding deregulation, Trump has concentrated his efforts on gutting much of the administration dealing with the environment. Over 100 policies regarding clean air, water, wildlife, and toxic chemicals have been rolled back or reversed under Trump. These include weakening rules for emissions from vehicles and power plants and removing protections from wetlands.

It was a big win for the global-warming deniers, who could now watch Americans suffocating in the scorching heat of drowning in floods attributed to a Global Warming that does not exist.

Trade – Promise not kept - with unexpected consequences.

On his third day in office in 2017, Trump quit the Trans-Pacific Partnership, a 12-country Pacific Rim trade deal negotiated under Obama. Needless to say, China did not miss the opportunity to pick up the slack left by America to become the prime partner in a region where most of the world trade is already taking place.

Trump initiated a tit-for-tat tariff war with China, which was supposed to address the enormous trade deficit with China. Contrary to Trump's claim that his moves benefited the U.S. economy, American companies and consumers were left to pay higher duties on about $370 billion in annual Chinese imports. At the same time, U.S. farmers and other exporters watched sales to China crumble.

To compensate for the trade war, Trump's USDA (United States Department of Agriculture) steered billions in subsidies to farmers suffering from tariffs imposed by foreign countries. The subsidies far outpaced the massive auto bailout in 2008 by Obama.

On the plus side, Trump's administration re-negotiated the 1994 North American Free Trade Agreement with Canada and Mexico, adding more substantial environmental and labor standards.

Overall, under Trump, **the trade deficit jumped to its highest level in 14 years, and U.S. government subsidies now make up one-third of farmers' income.**

Economy - Mixed results

Trump's presidential campaign boasting that he would produce the "*best economy in history*" has not come to pass.

Trump's claim that he has delivered a growth rate better than his predecessor is also inaccurate. Obama, who was coming out of one of the worst economic crises the U.S. had ever faced, still managed to produce a greater GDP than Trump's pre-COVID first three years.

National debt - Abysmal

Despite his promise to reduce the national debt, Trump raised it by almost $7.8 trillion to reach 28 trillion.

Health care – Promise not met, thank God!

Since the beginning of his presidential candidacy, Trump made a big promise: to overhaul America's healthcare system and replace it with his beautiful, less expensive version. This meant repealing the Affordable Care Act, known as Obamacare. All that Trump has managed to achieve was to remove one section of the law as part of a sizeable tax-cut package.

"Maybe this COVID thing is a good thing. I don't like shaking hands with people. I don't have to shake hands with these disgusting people." Trump.

Then came the COVID-19 pandemic, which Trump and other mini-Trumps in Brazil and Great Britain dismissed as benign as the flu. With a death toll of 400,000[62] COVID-19 deaths attributed to the Trump administration's lack of proper response, America has lost its enviable reputation as having one of the best medical systems in the world while at the same time ruining the reputation of the CDC by politicizing it.

On the positive side, Trump's Operation Warp Speed can be credited for the rapid development of COVID-19 vaccines. Too bad that this positive fact does not square well with Trump anti-vaxxers who have a problem in conciliating the Trump-anti-science with the Trump-pro-vaccine.

Securing the borders - Not secured by a long shot.

This was Donald Trump's big campaign promise. Not only did Mexico not pay for the *"Big, beautiful, gorgeous wall"* meant to stem the flow of illegal migrants, but he is dead wrong when claiming about having the *" Most Secure Border in History"* as President.

The number of migrants arriving at the border increased every single year of the Trump administration until the pandemic year of 2020: 516,000 in 2017, 686,000 in 2018, and 1,147,000 in 2019.

---

[62] According to a Lancet report

The Biden administration has deported more than the U.S. average of 290,394 deportations per year during the four years of the Trump administration.

Trump's border wall to keep the bad "*hombres*" out was the signature promise of candidate Trump in 2016. **It is also a case study that illustrates perfectly the difference between promises and reality.**

First of all, there was no way that Mexico would pay for it. That Trump and his supporters truthfully believed it explains a lot of the amount of B.S. they would later take as Gospel from Dear Leader.

"My administration has done more than any administration in history to secure our southern border," so boasted Trump. But here are the facts:

- The U.S. border with Mexico is 1,954 miles.
- In total, only 452 miles of the wall were completed under the Trump administration.
- Out of that number, only 80 miles of new barriers have been built where there were none before.
- The rest was a replacement for existing dilapidated or inadequate fencing.
-
- Most of the wall is not a wall at all but barriers or fencing of various high and materials.
- So far, out of the 15 billion estimated cost, 10 billion was funded by diverting funds already allocated to the Defense Department. 6.3B from counter-drug and 3.6B from military construction. Mexico" zero.
- The wall does nothing to reduce the smuggling of illegal drugs (heroin, cocaine, and methamphetamine) into the

U.S. because 90% of it goes through regular points of entry.

- A significant part of the wall is now a big pile of rusting steel.
- *Biden did halt the construction of new border barriers immediately upon taking office.*
- *As of January 2021. The U.S. Army Corps of Engineers suspended all work on border infrastructure.*

Walls rarely keep people in or out, so ask the Chinese who built the Great Wall. Rather than building a wall, the U.S. should finally get to work on enacting a comprehensive and fair immigration policy.

And finally, the big one: **Make America great again**

Make Germany, Russia, Brazil, China, and Turkey great again! This slogan is a calling that resonates particularly well with autocratic leaders, since it appeals to the lowest common denominator of nationalist identity. Ronald Regan and Bill Clinton had already used the same slogan for their respective presidential campaign. This type of slogan works particularly well in America, where everybody considers themselves patriots. Never mind if being a patriot entails F%&#ing our democracy at the same time.

In Trump's mind, "*Make America Great Again*" is a synonym for his "*America First*" slogan, which, in a way, was sort of old news; America has always thought of itself first. This time, however, the "*America First*" resulted in America being alone, which is never a good thing in a global economy.

When France tried to impose a digital service tax on technology companies like Google, Facebook, etc., who pay no tax whatsoever on all the business they do in France, Trump retaliated by threatening to impose a 100 percent tax on French wine, arguing

"I've always said American wine is better than French wine!"

How would he know that since it is notoriously known that Trump does not drink alcohol?

So, what is the point of this example, you may ask?

The point comes in Trump's rationale for initiating such a move:

"We want to tax American companies. That's important. We want to tax them, not somebody else."

Translation: Even if we cannot tax our own companies doing business overseas, the countries they do business in cannot either. The only problem is that France belongs to the European Union, and if it decides to retaliate, it would be the E.U. that would impose a retaliatory tax on many American products and piss even more American exporting companies and consumers. In the end, *"American First"* means America alone.

The bottom line: Trump's *"America First"* isolationist approach to foreign policy and trade may sound good to Americans who feel like they've lost their jobs to workers overseas, but how many have seen their old jobs returning, and how many have been created as a consequence of *"America First"*?

Trump's overall approval rating never exceeded 50% and fell to a low of just 29% in his final weeks in office, the lowest approval rating of his presidency.

Considering Donald Trump's previous campaign promises, what can we expect for the new 2024 presidential election?

Based on Donald Trump's new 2024 presidential campaign slogan,

MAGAA *"Make America great again, again."*

Unless this new slogan is an admission by Donald Trump that he did not succeed in making America great the first time around, it appears that for his second rodeo ride, we can expect much of the same thing.

Donald Trump's most notorious failures and blunders

Foreign policies

Iran: On January 16, 2016, the International Atomic Energy Agency verified that Iran has completed the necessary steps under the Iran deal that will ensure Iran's nuclear program is and remains exclusively peaceful. Despite all the evidence that Iran was abiding by the agreement and all the monitoring in place to prevent Iran from developing a covert nuclear program, Trump decided to unilaterally withdraw the U.S. from the 2015 nuclear deal in May 2018. This could turn out to be the most consequential decision affecting not only the Middle East but the world since now all the experts agree that Iran has the capability to produce several nuclear bombs once it masters the technology of fitting the weapon on the long-range missiles it already possesses.

Syria: One of Trump's most disastrous foreign policy moves was his decision to withdraw U.S. troops from northern Syria, creating a huge humanitarian problem when he abandoned the U.S.-allied Kurdish forces who bore the brunt of the U.S.-led campaign against ISIS to a Turkish military invasion. This proves one more time that you cannot count on the U.S. not betraying its allies once they are no longer useful.

Afghanistan withdrawal

Much has been said about the way our forces hastily withdrew from Afghanistan, especially about whom to blame. The Republicans even tried to impeach Biden by making him the sole responsible for an exit reminiscing of the Vietnam debacle. However, a U.S. review led by the National Security Council of the chaotic 2021 withdrawal of U.S. troops from Afghanistan largely lays the blame on former President Donald Trump, saying President Biden was *"severely constrained"* by the decisions of his predecessor. To be fair, Biden should be credited for running the largest airborne evacuation of noncombatants in history, something that did not happen in Vietnam. But the Republicans instead are blaming Biden by focusing on the deaths of 13 service members in a suicide bombing at Kabul's airport, which, let's be realistic, would have happened regardless of who was president at the time.

In its search for finding an explanation for the chaotic withdrawal of Afghanistan, the Report produced by the National Security Council outlines that much blame should be placed on *"The February 2020 agreement Trump reached with the Taliban in Doha, Qatar, saying it boxed the U.S. into leaving the country. The agreement gave the Taliban significant legitimacy and has been blamed by analysts for undercutting the U.S.-backed government, which would collapse so quickly a year later."*

Covid-19 Pandemic

With 24.3 million confirmed COVID-19 cases in the U.S. and over 405,000[63] reported fatalities by the time Trump left office, his handling of the pandemic deserves to enter the history book as one of the biggest disasters in U.S. history and the worst response to the pandemic in the world.

Trump repeatedly downplayed the threat of the virus, and his deliberate misleading of the public on the dangers of the virus, as well as his natural tendency to reject science, was only matched by his insistence to blame China after first parroting their propaganda to cover their initial response to the virus. However, once the deadly consequences of the virus became evident, Trump bungled testing and delayed national measures such as invoking the Defense Production Act to mobilize our economy to fight the epidemic. Worst, Trump even undermined his administration's own efforts to fight the coronavirus outbreak, probably on the assumption that the virus will simply "*disappear.*"

The U.S. economy

This is the area where Trump, along with his supporters nostalgic for the Trump era, usually takes credit for a better economy than under Biden. Those with a short-term memory should be reminded that during the Trump administration, the U.S. faced one of the worst economic crises in its history. When Trump left office, the U.S. national debt was at the highest levels since World War II. And U.S. economic growth was set to average just above 0% for Trump's first term. Under Trump, the

---

[63] Almost surpassing the total number of American service members killed during World War II.

U.S. national debt increased by 39%, reaching $27.75 trillion by the end of his term.

No doubt that the COVID epidemic was somehow responsible, but this was the economy that Biden inherited and had since reversed to make the United States the fastest country to recover its economy in the world.

Trump's economic record by numbers[64]

Trump's economic legacy is closely related to his failure of leadership and his response to the COVID-19 epidemic.

"I'll be the greatest jobs president that God ever created." D. Trump.

- **The economy lost 2.9 million jobs**. The unemployment rate increased by 1.6 percentage points to 6.3%.
- **Paychecks grew faster than inflation**. Average weekly earnings for all workers were up 8.7% after inflation.
- After-tax corporate profits went up, and the stock market set new records. **The S&P 500 index rose 67.8%.**
- The international trade deficit Trump promised to reduce went up. **The U.S. trade deficit in goods and services** in 2020 was the highest since 2008 and **increased 40.5% from 2016.**
- The number of **people lacking health insurance rose by 3 million**.
- The federal debt held by the public went up, from **$14.4 trillion to $21.6 trillion.**
- **Home prices rose 27.5%,** and the homeownership rate increased 2.1 percentage points to 65.8%.

---

[64] Source https://www.factcheck.org/2021/10/trumps-final-numbers/

- **Illegal immigration increased**. Apprehensions at the Southwest border rose 14.7% last year compared with 2016.
- **Coal production declined 26.5%,** and coal-mining jobs dropped by 16.7%. Carbon emissions from energy consumption dropped 11.5%.
- **Handgun production rose 12.5%** last year compared with 2016, setting a new record.
- **The murder rate last year rose to the highest level since 1997**.
- Trump filled one-third of the Supreme Court, nearly 30% of the appellate court seats, and a quarter of District Court seats.

Trump's economic policies favored the wealthy -- and left the poor and middle class behind and were the major culprits contributing to the deficits that went up by **more than $7 trillion.**

Trump reduced the corporate income tax rate from 35% to 21% and increased inequality.

Disaster Trade War with China

At the beginning of Trump's term, with 555.59 billion in trade, china was the U.S.'s third trading partner after Canada and Mexico. One of Trump's presidential campaign promises was to reduce or eliminate the 342.65 billion trade imbalance in China's favor.

In 2017, unhappy with the way that trade negotiations with China were going, Trump started to impose tariffs as high as 25% on a variety of Chinese goods, from solar panels and washing machines to aluminum. In retaliation, China imposed a 25% tariff on hundreds of U.S. products, from soybeans to airplanes. This tit-for-tat trade war dragged on with one clear loser: the U.S..

If certain farmers even today recall with nostalgia the good old days when they were receiving tens of billions of Federal subsidies to make up for their products they could no longer sell to China, it did cost the U.S. economy and the taxpayers dearly with consequences that still can be felt to this day.

- By the end of Trump's term, the trade deficit was larger in absolute terms than it was when he came to office.
- The trade war had cost the U.S. economy some 300,000 jobs.
- U.S. firms lost some $1.7 trillion in stock value as a result of the trade war with China.
- Trump's steel and aluminum tariffs raised the cost of U.S.-based auto manufacturing by $1 billion.
- Sales of U.S. aircraft, engines, and parts to China amounted to just 18 percent of their 2020 target.
- U.S. companies primarily paid for U.S. tariffs, with the cost estimated at $46 billion.
- Farmers have lost most of what was once a $24 billion market in China.
- In most sectors, U.S. tariffs have been passed on entirely to U.S. importers and consumers.
- Tariffs on China diverted trade flows from China, causing the U.S. trade deficit with Europe, Mexico, Japan, South Korea, and Taiwan to increase as a result.
- U.S. exports of manufactured goods to China have not recovered from the trade war, and now, they are even showing signs of getting worse.
- Export of services to China, the largest component of pre-trade war has fallen to 41 percent.
- The tariffs imposed by Trump on imports from China caused a stiff price increase on many goods as manufacturers passed the added cost to consumers.

As of 2024, it appears that the true winners of Trump's trade war with China benefited other countries like Mexico and Vietnam.

2024 Trump campaign update.

Having apparently not learned anything from his past tenure at the White House, Trump vowed to repeat what had not worked before by ratcheting up the trade war and imposing more severe tariffs on China.

When Fox News asked whether Trump would consider implementing a 60% tariff on Chinese goods, Trump said: "*No, I would say maybe it's going to be more than t*hat."

Considering that Biden has kept most of the tariffs imposed on China by Trump without making any dent in the U.S. trade deficit with China, Trump's renewed rhetoric, if implemented, could only mean three things: The increased decoupling of the U.S. and Chinese economy, the re-alignment of former economic and political blocks, and the end of globalization as we know it.

TRUMP MIDNIGHT REGULATIONS

In his last days in office, the Trump Administration passed a slew of policy changes that will have a long-lasting effect, and the new Administration may have difficulties unwinding.

This exhaustive list is given here in its entirety to underline that right to the end, **the Trump Administration has passed more legislation that favors business to the detriment of the American people**. In that list, only **TWO policies marked with an * and underlined out of 40 benefit the people.** So much about Trump's claim of putting people ahead of business.

- Excluding scientific studies from environmental policy-making.
- Tightening eligibility for disabled veterans' access to medical devices.
- Ending Medicare Drug Rebates.
- Excluding secondary environmental and health benefits from evaluating regulations on air pollution.
- Allowing the Forest Service to bypass some environmental reviews.
- Making It easier for appliance manufacturers to get exceptions to efficiency standards.
- Exempting refineries, chemical plants, and other Polluters from EPA's Greenhouse Gas Regulations.
- Reverses Obama-era decision to require polluters to ensure cleanup funds.
- Broadening the definition of independent contractor benefits the "*gig economy*" by restricting workers to benefits and labor laws.
- Loosening rules on National Bank.
- Rolling back some Obama-era changes and insulating religious groups from non-discrimination requirements.

- Eliminating the ability of immigration judges to "*administratively close*" an immigrant's case to stop deportation orders.
- Lowering wages for immigrant farmworkers.
- Bolstering the position of faith-based organizations in government grants.
- Loosening safety standards for gas pipeline construction and maintenance.
- Excising 3.4 million acres in the Pacific Northwest from protections.
- Making it harder to raise energy efficiency standards for gas water heaters.
- Stripping down environmental reviews for LNG (liquefied natural gas) exports.
- Weakening anti-corruption laws by exempting disclosure requirements for oil and gas industry payments to foreign governments (bribes).
- Increasing scrutiny of continuing eligibility for disability benefits.
- Exempting Investment Advisors from conflict of Interest Rules.
- Loosening restrictions on overfishing.
- Preventing banks from withholding credit to finance carbon-intensive projects such as oil pipelines and fracking or companies like payday lenders and firearms dealers.
- Loosening the rules preventing massive processing companies from using their market power to exploit small farmers.
- Loosening the Clean Water Act enforcement by allowing them to depart from the federal standard for establishing criminal violations.

- Loosening permits to develop Near Waterways and Wetlands.
- Removing about 3 million individuals from food stamp rolls by changing eligibility so that recipients of other types of benefits do not automatically qualify.
- Pegging Drug Prices to an International Index *
- Easing Environmental and Safety Requirements for Oil Exploration in the Arctic.
- Repealing protections for editorial independence to protect the integrity and objectivity of journalists.
- Decreasing the amount of disaster aid for States when they declare a major disaster.
- Preventing the use of fetal tissue obtained from elective abortions in federally funded research effectively cutting down research on diseases like Parkinson's and diabetes.
- Removing the prohibition on lending to businesses primarily engaged in religious instruction or indoctrination.
- Relaxing nutritional requirements for school lunches, allowing more salt, white flour, and flavored milk.
- Making it more difficult to protect land for wildlife preservation and endangered species habitats against development.
- For the benefit of airlines, this rule will raise the bar for regulators to challenge unfair and deceptive business practices.
- Making it more difficult for people to qualify for disability benefits for musculoskeletal disorders like spine injuries or amputations.
- Making it very difficult, if not impossible, to make gas furnaces and water heaters more efficient in the future.

- Setting standards that don't require airplanes to reduce greenhouse gases.
- Creating a Pilot Program for Underage Truck Drivers.*

Now that, based on his record, we know what characterized Donald Trump's presidency in the past, we can now predict with near certainty his presidential style in the future should we choose to re-elect him to represent us again.

NOVEMBER 5TH 2024

US PRESIDENTIAL ELECTION DAY

If there is one single thing that all Americans should learn from their history, it is that fascism has been a long-time aspiration of the Republican Party. Now that the Second Coming of their Messiah is about to fulfill the **rapture**[65] *of our democracy, the Trump Party is in hypothetical Heaven anticipating with ecstasy the coronation in all his glory of Dear Leader who will make the new America great again, again.*

*People get the character they inherit
and the government they merit*

---

[65] **Rapture**: *from Medieval French, "Rapture," means "taking away, rape, kidnapping or extreme pleasure."*

2024, THE YEAR WHEN THE SUM OF ALL FEARS COULD BRING DEMOCRACY APOCALYPSE TO AMERICA AND THE WORLD

The year 2024 of the Common Era will remain unique in the modern history of the world.

This year, over four billion people, close to half of the world's population across 64 countries, will go to the polls to elect who will govern them, including countries with bogus elections, such as Belarus and Russia,[66] where opposition parties are running in name only.

What makes all those elections particularly troubling for the well-being of the planet is that many of the countries electing their leaders are non-democratic, making the transfer of power to a more democratic leader problematic. In other countries, such as India, the world's largest democracy, the right-wing Hindu nationalist Party of autocratic Prime Minister Narendra Modi will probably continue to bring India closer to the club of illiberal democracies.

In addition, not a country per se, the 27 countries of the second largest economic market in the world, the European Union will elect a new Parliament that may be impacted by the rise of right-wing populism in Hungary, Italy, Sweden, the Netherlands, and France.

Of lesser importance by their population size but still potentially important in their capacity of nuisance to the general world order are a score of Trump's shithole countries, mainly African, where

---

[66] Others are countries like Bangladesh, Iran and Tunisia.

the local dictator or junta in power will without a doubt be "*re-elected*" to consolidate their power for the "*good*" of the people. This will also be the year where AI deep-fakes, misinformation, and poll manipulations will be in full swing to influence the minds of voters. Among all the countries in the world, the most watched, anticipated, and with the most global impact will be, by far, the one taking place in the United States of America.

When you do the sum of all fears, only three pose an existential threat to America. Donald Trump, stupid people and AI. And if we do not eliminate the first two, the third one will eliminate us.

A HINT OF THINGS TO COME

Trump's candidacy is so toxic that we have to start to outweigh which outcome represents the greater danger for the Republic and the world: If Trump wins or if he loses the election?

Based on Donald Trump's promises

To be fair, many of Trump's campaign promises are pretty good. Although since most of his promises were made via teleprompter-Trump, it is almost guaranteed that none were made from his own initiative but were rather a presentation of policies elaborated by Project 2025 of the Heritage Foundation, a thinktank of Conservative policymakers who we should assume have the benefit of the greater good in mind. However, it remains to be seen how many of those promises will be implemented should Donald Trump regain the Oval Office, assuming they pass the test of *"What's in it for me."*

But one thing is certain: the sum of all good policies promised by Trump will never outweigh the threat of fascism that Trump's return would pose to our democracy, and this is for one single reason: Once an autocrat has tasted power, he will never leave. And Trump has certainly already proved that.

In the meantime, why should we worry about Trump's promises?

You should always pay attention to what narcissist/ psychopath leaders say. Because contrary to politicians, they usually do what they say.

If, during his 2016 campaign, Donald Trump labeled migrants as *"drug dealers," "criminals,"* and *"rapists,"* this is nothing to what he intends to do to the children of undocumented parents born on U.S. soil. It is not clear yet if he intends to deport them *"en masse,"* with or without their parents, or round them up in concentration (sorry, holding) camps.

Also, as a return to the heydays of McCarthyism, Trump promises to use an old law to bar *"Marxists"* from entering the U.S. Although this would piss off China, this restriction would certainly not please his buddy Putin. But again, in 2016, he tried to ban most Muslims from entering the U.S..

In a typical Trump move of doing exactly what he accuses others of doing, he will continue to implement what he started during his first term: The weaponization of the Department of Justice.

One of the first things Trump intends to do after taking office will be to appoint a Special Prosecutor to go after all the *"Vermin"* that did him wrong.

"We will root out the communists, Marxists, fascists, and the radical left thugs (Democrats) that live like vermin within the confines of our country,"

"That means that if I win and somebody wants to run against me, I call my attorney general, and I say, 'Listen, indict him!' " *....."[If the attorney general says], 'Well, he hasn't done anything wrong,' [I'll say], 'I don't know, indict him on income-tax evasion. You'll figure it out.' "*

It remains to see if his opponents will end up in Guantanamo Bay or face the firing squad. There is, however, an area where he does not leave any ambiguity: drug dealers and human traffickers should be executed. This is a point of view that many in the U.S. would agree with since 24 countries are already practicing it. This surely would be an alternative to Trump's musing of firing missiles and bombing drug labs in Mexico. But who knows, maybe he could do both.

It also appears that Javier Milei, the far-right new Argentina president has borrowed a page of Trump's re-election program by scraping all governmental departments he did not like. Goodbye ministries of education, public works, transport, women, health, and culture, just to name a few. Trump must be proud to have inspired such radical moves as he himself intends to continue the previous gutting of the Federal Administration by firing at least 50,000 civil servants once he takes office.

There is another area where Trump is truly in accord with himself. In order to continue to propagate his constant flow of misinformation (euphemism for lies), he would order the DOJ to investigate and prosecute any entity engaged in fighting fake news and misinformation. You read right. Trying to counter attempts by foreign or domestic entities to disseminate lies and fake news, even to influence an election, will become a crime. Elon Musk, as a libertarian, must be ecstatic.

Under the pretext of censorship, the Trump party has engaged in political pressure to dismantle groups or individuals reporting false voting information or fraud in the 2020 election. This seems paradoxical for a party that is building its whole 2024 presidential campaign on alleged voting frauds in the previous election. Of course, the Biden administration's attempt to set up a *"Ministry of Truth"* did not help. That sounded too much like something the Nazis did or something the Republicans would rather do themselves. To make sure that the Biden Administration got the message that the Trump Party would not tolerate any attempt from the Federal government to regulate the spread of misinformation, the Republican attorneys general of Missouri and Louisiana filed a lawsuit accusing the Biden Administration of colluding with social media companies to censor conservative speech. In case the lawsuit is not enough, the GOP Rep. Jim Jordan of Ohio is conducting his own probe in Congress into alleged collusion between the Biden administration and tech companies to unconstitutionally shut down political speech.

The net effect is that contrary to 2020 for the next presidential election, social media companies will be more reluctant to label as "*false*" or "*misleading claim*" any misinformation or lies posted by Donald Trump or foreign entities seeking to influence the election. And as we all know, once the lie goes viral, it is too late to put the Genie back into the bottle.

But most importantly, Donald Trump has made it very clear that once re-elected, he will have full control over the three branches of government and end the charade of the so-called balance of power. This prospect has been a long-time dream of the Republican Party that Trump is about to deliver. And if anyone has to guess about which way the republic is heading, one only has to remember the dysfunction of the Republicans in Congress to realize that the Party has no interest whatsoever in governing and that its only ambition is to exercise power.

Based on Donald Trump's record

"The most corrupt election in U.S. history!"

So said Donald Trump about the 2020 Presidential election. But what he was certainly thinking was:

"The next election will be the most corrupt election in U.S. history. I will make sure of that, believe you me!" From Donald Trump's little voice in his head.

Donald Trump has been explicitly clear: our institutions and democracy are not his things.

"President for life ... maybe we'll have to give that a shot someday."

"Maybe at some point, we'll have to take those rules on because things will have to be different for the good of the nation."

Donald Trump referred to the system of checks and balances between the legislative and executive branches as an *"archaic"* system, as well as the 22nd Amendment to the Constitution, which prohibits a president from running more than two terms.

For the 2022 Midterm Elections, the Trump Party might have gained a majority in both the Senate and Congress. But even if that prediction did not materialize, that does not change anything for the 2024 Presidential elections, and that is for a simple reason: the democratic voting process is utterly rigged in favor of the Trumpsters. Next time, it is almost certain that Donald Trump will not ever utter the word *"rigged"* because, having learned the lessons of the dry run 2020 attempted coup, he is the one who is about to *"Steal"* the election with impunity.

- In 2020, Trump seriously considered suspending the Constitution, decreeing Martial Law, silencing the press, seizing voting machines, and holding a new election under military supervision. For 2024, Trump does not have this power anymore. Still, nothing can stop him from appealing to his paramilitary militia's supporters to create enough chaos to force the government to do just that.

- In 2020, Trump had contingency plans to bypass election results and appoint loyal electors to do the vote counting and decide who wins. This time, everything is in place to ensure that such a thing happens in all States where the Trump Party has a majority.

- In 2020, Trump's appeal to the Supreme Court to invalidate votes and declare who won the presidential election went nowhere. This time around, based on the circumstances, such a possibility could very well happen, like in 2020 when the Court stopped the voting count in Florida to favor Bush against Al Gore..

- In 2020, when Trump asked a state legislator to find him 14,000 votes, in 2024, the answer will likely be: how many do you want, Sir?

- In 2020, in states won by Biden, attempts were made at the Electoral College to have "*alternate electors*" ignore voting results and appoint electors who would vote for Trump, which is illegal. Since when has anything illegal stopped Trump supporters from doing his bidding?

- Since 2020, Republican-controlled legislatures had ample time to pass vote-suppressing legislation to keep minority voters from exercising their democratic duty. In response, the Biden Administration ignored it by telling its supporters just to vote. How stupid is that when you cannot vote?

- In 2020, in a typical banana republic style, pressures were made on the Defense Department to seize ballots to prevent the election results from favoring the Democrats. If Trump's supporters were ready to go to such extremes, what could stop them from doing just that themselves?

- What if the scheme to have the voting results invalidated in Congress succeeds? It almost worked the last time.

- In 2020, for months after the election, angry Trump supporters threatened election officials, elections staff, and their family members with harassment and death threats. Next time, if you are not a Trump supporter, who will dare to participate in a democratic process and prevent them from stuffing ballots in favor of their candidate while suppressing others?

- For 2024, Republican Legislatures are well-packed with officials willing, able, and ready to invalidate any votes they don't like and decide who won in the State. The Trump Party made no bone about it and is quite comfortable to fuck democracy in the process.

It should now be evident that up to this point, Donald Trump has attempted all the tricks in the "*How to Subvert Democracy for "A Dear Leader" Wannabe*" playbook to stay in power and demonstrated at the same time his willingness to make minced meat of the democratic process and the rule of law. All is now ready for an American Armageddon.

"*We know that no one seizes power with the intention of relinquishing it,*" G. Orwell.

Based on what is lurking in the shadow

"It is the President's agenda that should matter to the departments and agencies, not their own." Russ Vought[67]

The last time Trump ran for Office, his political program could be summarized as *"Make America Great Again."* A single catchy slogan that encompassed *"Build the wall,"* *"Drain the Swamp,"* and *"Lock Her Up".* Not much of a program. This time over, Trump's re-election campaign is even more limited to a single topic: *"I am the subject of a witch hunt, and I have not done anything wrong."* Portraying himself as a victim works wonders for him since God knows how we Americans love underdogs.

But all this is irrelevant since dozens of Conservative groups have developed a plan for Trump's re-election:

When an individual or a political party intends to seize power and keep it, no one should be surprised when whatever they say will happen happens. For instance, in *"Project for the New American Century,"* the neocons of George W. Bush definitely identified the need for a *"New Pearl Harbor"* to justify the *"War on Terror"* and make America Great again after the Vietnam debacle. What followed was 9/11 and the Patriot Act that gave the State the legitimacy to spy on its citizens. By the same token, if in 1939, someone in the government of France and Great Britain had taken the time to read Mein Kampf, both countries would have been better prepared for what was coming, including the Holocaust.

---

[67] Russ Vought, budget director in the Trump administration, and a driving force behind House Republicans' hostage strategy.

Unfortunately, those road maps are almost always ignored or not taken seriously until it is too late to do anything about it.

It is a common saying that states that the only thing we learn from history is that we learn nothing from it. Well, the Trump Party, for its part, has learned something from Trump's last bout with power. If in 2016, it took months for the Trump Administration to nominate their people at the head of most Federal Agencies, this time, the Republicans are more prepared, more structured, and know exactly what to do during the first 100 days of Trump's Second Coming. And it does not look pretty, at least for those who value their civil rights and America's democracy. Its mission:

To hit the ground running to allow Donald Trump to exercise the full power of his Office as of 12:00 noon, January 20, 2025.

"The president Day One will be a wrecking ball for the administrative state." Russ Vought.

The political program is tasked with planning the implementation of a rapid and effective transition of Donald Trump's conservative agenda. In effect, this is a continuation of Trump's previous attempt to control everything by gutting all the Federal Agencies that he did not like. So what to expect?

In a broad sense, the plan is to dismantle the U.S. Government by controlling all three branches of government as directed by the Constitution, including the Legislative and Judicial, to give all the powers to the Executive Branch of government. In over words to Trump. This plan is the clearest indication that the Trump Party is more interested in exercising power than in governing.

As a supplement to *"How to Subvert a Democracy for "A Dear Leader" Wannabe,"* the nearly 1,000-page *"Project 2025"* handbook[68] outlines in detail how to do away with what the Trump Party derides as the *"deep state"* bureaucracy by firing as many as 50,000 federal employees[69] and replace career Civil Servants by political appointees, just like in Russia and other undemocratic states. In fact, it is no secret that the sponsors of the plan openly admit that their role model for Trump is Viktor Orbán, the authoritarian Hungarian president since 1993 and an embarrassment for the European Union for his fascist tendencies and proof of how people have a shot memory. Indeed, most people in Hungary are still alive to remember when Russian tanks rolled into Budapest in 1956 to crush a popular revolt against Soviet occupation that cost the lives of up to 3,000 Hungarians.

Obviously, who needs federal workers when everything can be decided by one man who knows everything? This plan is perfectly in sync with the Conservatives who have traditionally sought to limit the federal government by cutting federal taxes and slashing federal spending. It remains to be seen if all the money saved by firing all those workers will end up lining up Trump's pockets since he will be doing all the work.

While Project 2025 is an extensive policy roadmap containing many worthwhile policies on how to reform the Government, it nevertheless contains many others that every American should worry about. Since it would be too cumbersome to outline all the

---

68

https://thf_media.s3.amazonaws.com/project2025/2025_MandateFo rLeadership_FULL.pdf

[69] Much of that could be accomplished by re-instating *"Schedule F,"* a Trump-era executive order rescinded by President Biden.

specifics of "Project 25-*Mandate for Leadership: The Conservative Promise*," some of its theocratic elements outlined here deserve to ponder.

- "*I have an Article 2, where I have the right to do whatever I want as president.*"
- Atler the balance of power by giving the Executive Branch more power over the Legislative and Judicial Branches and every part of the Federal government.
- Gut all agencies that enacted regulations aimed at keeping the air and water clean and food, drugs, and consumer products safe.
- Make faith the primary direction of government. In effect, blurring the separation of religion and state and put the Bible ahead of the Constitution.
- Ending the FBI's efforts to combat the spread of misinformation.
- Dismantle all previous climate change policies.
- Breaking up the Department of Education to stop School Boards from brainwashing kids.
- A "*top-to-bottom overhaul*" of the Department of Justice, particularly curbing its independence.
- Going full climate-skeptic by shredding regulations to curb greenhouse gas pollution, dismantling almost every clean energy program boosting the production of fossil fuels[70], and drilling inside the pristine Arctic wilderness.
- Reverse a 2009 scientific finding at the Environmental Protection Agency that says carbon dioxide emissions are a danger to public health.
- Reinstate the practice of "*impounding funds*," by refusing to spend money Congress has appropriated for programs a president doesn't like.

---

[70] About 70 percent of Republicans said global warming was either a minor threat or no threat at all.

- Abolishing equity and inclusion initiatives.
- Fire nonpartisan professionals and experts with protections against being fired for political reasons.
- Bolstering the number of political appointees in Homeland Security.
- Replacement of the Entire Homeland Security Advisory Committee.
- Installing top allies in acting administrative roles, as was done during the Trump administration to bypass the Senate confirmation process.
- Diminish the role of Congress. Eliminate Congress' power over Federal Agencies to give it to the President.
- Put regulations in place to ensure that everybody knows that the President is in charge and that everyone has to do what he says, dismantle all rogue agencies, and put an end to the notion of independent federal agencies or federal employees who don't answer to the president. This includes, in theory, the independence of the Federal Reserve.
- Identify the pockets of independence within the government and remove them.
- Get out of multinational agreements that the U.S. does not directly control. Paris climate Change Agreement. Again? And potentially, NATO. Etc. etc.

Project 2025 of the Heritage Foundation is far from being alone in planning the Trump Party's return to power. Another conservative think tank, "*The Conservative Center for Renewing America*," has similar plans.

- Limit FBI efforts to combat the spread of misinformation.
- Inhibit Department of Justice and FBI investigations into far-right extremism.
- Unleash the Bureau against the right's political enemies.

- Investigate the DOJ and FBI for a supposed anti-conservative bias.
- Set up a panel under the House Judiciary Committee for the Weaponization of the Federal Government.
- Increase the FBI's ability to "thwart" efforts at criminal justice reform.
- Cut funding to the Civil Rights Division and Environment and Natural Resources Division.
- Eliminate the 'equity' obsessed Community Relations Service.
- Terminate the Office of Environmental Justice.
- Give the president the power to dispatch the FBI against localities deemed as hostile.
- Elimination of a State Department office tasked with "eliminating corruption.
- Eliminating funding for the hiring of 87,000 new IRS agents tasked to go after people who dodge taxes.

Based on a consensus of people in the know

If many of Trump's supporters see Donald Trump as the Messiah, many others consider him as the devil incarnated. In its annual "*World Ahead Guide*," published by the Economist, a wide range of business, economic, and political professionals throughout the world give their expert opinion in predicting what lies ahead for the world in 2024. And their prediction is scary.

The Economist's *'World Ahead'* Guide Called Donald Trump the "Biggest Global Threat" in 2024

For those tasked with the job of hoping for the best but preparing for the worst, **a fifty-fifty chance for a Trump Second Coming is just too much of an odd for not believing in the Apocalypse**. Because what had until recently been a hypothetical possibility has brought most political and economic stakeholders on the planet to the brink of apoplexy now that this probability is beginning to sink in.

Regardless of how you personally feel about the return of Donald Trump as the head of the most powerful and influential country in the world, those who make it their business to anticipate the consequences of such a prospect are beside themselves.

Welcome to the return of political retribution, economic protectionism, and chaos in predicting where and for what America stands for. Globalization works on predictability and hates chaos, especially at a time when proponents of a New World Order are challenging America's economic, political hegemony and democratic role model.

If, historically, the American economy has proven itself to be more resilient than most, there is no guarantee that it will experience a soft landing from the curse of inflation. And despite all his rhetoric, it is more than likely that Donald Trump will not be able to wave the magic wand to make it disappear.

Of all the challenges faced by the United States, in the eyes of the world, the sorry display of its dysfunctional democracy is the one that most preoccupy corporation boardrooms and foreign chancelleries across the globe. In their eyes, the advent of Trump Version 2.0 will simply transform global markets into a transactional one where each country will play the "*Make.........*" fill-in-the-blanks "*Great Again.*" In the meantime, here are some of the areas where a return of Donald Trump will have the most impact around the world.

THE RE-EVALUATION OF NATO

"You need to understand that if Europe is under attack, we will never come to help you and to support you. By the way, NATO is dead, and we will leave, we will quit NATO." D. Trump.

Already in 2019, thanks to Trump's misgivings regarding the alliance, France's Macron called NATO *"Brain Dead."*. Trump's departure from the world scene and Ukraine's Russian invasion changed all that. Today, NATO is stronger than ever, and it has even added two new members, Sweden and Finland. But Trump's return will put the alliance on shaky grounds again.

Donald Trump has boasted many times that he would *"End the war in Ukraine in one day"* and that it would be *"very easy."* Setting apart his overconfidence in the *"Art of the Deal"* illustrated by his total failure to deal with China, Russia, North Korea, and Iran, it is a stretch to assume that he would be more successful in bringing both Ukraine and Russia to a negotiating table. The more likely scenario is that Trump would call his mentor Putin to let him know that the United States will no longer support Ukraine in its fight for independence.

As for NATO, since the main raison d'être of the Alliance is to act as a deterrent against Russian territorial extension, Trump would most likely oblige Putin by telling him not to take Article 5[71] of the Alliance too seriously.

This action would, however, have three major unintended consequences:

1. This would validate Macron's long-term argument that the European Union should be more than an economic and political union and should start developing its own

---

[71] Article 5: An attack on one is an attack on all the members

defense industry instead of buying American-made weapons.
2. America reneging on its commitment would act as a green light for China to invade Taiwan.
3. If this happens, America will see all the countries with which the U.S. has a military alliance collapse.

And if the U.S. ultimately decides to support Taiwan, it will ask its allies to line up against China, enforce an economic embargo, and support them militarily. To which the E.U. and the rest of the U.S. allies will probably tell them to go and suck an egg.

INTERNATIONAL TRADE

Donald Trump has already signaled his intention to renegotiate NAFTA. Yes, the same trade agreement between Canada and Mexico that he re-negotiated with fanfare during his presidency. So, so much for the art of the deal that Trump is so proud of. The dispute centered on the interpretation of the percentage of foreign parts that can be made in cars sold in the U.S. Since an international panel has already ruled in favor of Canada and Mexico, it remains to be seen if Trump will decide to invade both countries or build a wall on the U.S. northern and southern borders.

Setting aside that the Biden Administration has continued Trump's policy of China's economic confinement, it is very likely that Trump will double down on the tariff wars he started with China during his administration. Engaging in an economic war with China is very important to Trump since he knows that he will always need somebody to blame in case things don't go his way.

On the global trade scene, Trump's protectionist instincts may tempt him to go ballistic. Having made *"America First"* his trademark, Trump sees globalization as a series of transactional deals with the "*I win, you lose*" mentality. With the re-alignment of planets where each country seeks to serve its own interest, America is no longer swimming in an ocean where the bigger fish eat the smaller ones, but in a pond where all the fish are sharks. Translation: "*America First*" may translate to "*America Alone.*"

CLIMATE CHANGE

Since Donald Trump, along with many of his supporters, believes that climate change is a hoax, he will probably take the U.S. out of the Paris Accord on Climate, again.

This action could have disastrous consequences not only for the planet but also for American competitiveness, as those industries are already engaged in the transition to be more energy efficient.

Trump said that human-caused global warming is fake, and that if elected, he would be a " *dictator for one day*" in part so he could "*drill, drill, drill.*"

As a consequence, Trump's policy think tank Project 2025, led by the Heritage Foundation, is planning to turnkey government agencies, such as the Environmental Protection Agency, toward increasing fossil fuel production rather than public health protections. This will fly in the face of seventy-three percent of U.S. adults who want the government to do more to address climate change. Most want the government to cut emissions in half by 2030, including 50 percent of Republicans and 95 percent of Democrats (Jan 2024 CNN poll).

"It's freezing and snowing in New York – we need global warming!" D. Trump.

In a typical display of ignorance that even a goose can tell the difference, Trump is confusing weather forecasting with global warming. That explains why his administration gutted all regulations and government initiatives aimed at curbing our carbon dioxide emissions and footprint for the sake of the next generation. And that was too bad because our country could make a big difference in the fight against polluting the planet.

With 6 million tons of CO_2 per year, the United States only comes second to China (14 million tons) as the planet most polluting country.

Fortunately, the Biden's administration passed the Inflation Reduction Act, an ambitious legislation that proposes to invest approximately $300 billion in Deficit Reduction and $369 billion in Energy Security and Climate Change programs over the next ten years. In addition, the act calls for comprehensive reform legislation and tax credits for renewable initiatives to accelerate the transition toward a decarbonized economy. The only caveat is that all this is at risk of getting flushed down the proverbial toilet if Trump has anything to say about it.

If this happens, nobody can predict the consequences of our inaction for the planet, but the **scientific consensus is certain: the consequences will be fast, extreme, and irreversible**.

So, if we hope that the transition to a climate apocalypse will be gradual, steady, and linear, nobody can predict when the planet will reach a tipping point that will trigger a tripwire that we can no longer control.

The French love phrase *"I love you more than yesterday, but less than tomorrow"* is a perfect analogy to global warming since every year is warmer than the one before while being the coolest than it will ever be in the future. We can deny reality, but reality does not care because one day, nobody will be left to deny its existence

TELLTALE SIGNS THAT DONALD TRUMP WILL TRY TO RUN A FASCIST DICTATORSHIP IN A SECOND TERM

If you still have not made up your mind about whom to vote for in the next presidential election, just pick the one who lives in your reality.

"He's been weaponizing government against his political opponents like a Third World political tyrant. Biden and his radical left allies like to pose as standing up as allies of democracy, Joe Biden is not the defender of American democracy; Joe Biden is the destroyer of American democracy." [72]

If that sounds true to you, your choice is clear. In your reality, Hitler blamed Einstein for being an anti-Semite, Putin invaded Ukraine to prevent it from invading Russia, Muslims are in the process of taking over India, and the Uyghurs are committing genocide toward the Chinese people to protect their identity.

If that is the case, your conviction is probably reinforced when Donald Trump declares:

"Do you throw the Presidential Election Results of 2020 OUT and declare the RIGHTFUL WINNER, or do you have a NEW ELECTION? A Massive Fraud of this type and magnitude allows for the termination of all rules, regulations, and articles, even those found in the Constitution."

---

[72] *Trump addressing a crowd in Cedar Rapids, Iowa in December 2023.*

Fourteen signs that should even scare the Bejesus out of Evangelical Christians[73]

Sign # 1: The doubling down on the big lie

*"So, with the revelation of MASSIVE & WIDESPREAD FRAUD & DECEPTION in working closely with Big Tech Companies, the DNC, & the Democrat Party, do you throw the Presidential Election Results of 2020 OUT and declare the RIGHTFUL WINNER, or do you have a NEW ELECTION? **A Massive Fraud of this type and magnitude allows for the termination of all rules, regulations, and articles, even those found in the Constitution.** Our great Founders did not want and would not condone False and fraudulent elections!"*

Posted by Trump on Truth Social on Dec. 3, 2022.

If progressive media had a field day describing Trump's tweet as proof of his anti-democratic tendencies, conservative media were quick on the defensive that this is not what Trump meant. If Trump indeed rebuked for a call to suspend the Constitution, this was not the first time that such an extreme idea had crossed his mind.

Back in December 2020, General Flint retweeted a tweet from Tom Zawistowski, the president of a right-wing Ohio activist group calling on U.S. President Donald Trump to "*suspend the Constitution,*" declare martial law, and have the military hold a new election. The fact that Trump did not act on that advice at the time only means that he regrets not doing it and is bringing the idea back if he loses the next presidential election. Thus, his doubling down on his non-existent 2020 *MASSIVE and*

---

[73] Assuming that they are American first before being Christians

WIDESPREAD FRAUD and DECEPTION claim to prepare us for a repeat in 2024 when "*steps will have to be immediately taken to RIGHT THE WRONG of election fraud.*"

Interpreted in that context, Trump still pretends to believe that any candidate who lost an election can, by simply invoking fraud, suspend the Constitution to be re-instated as the RIGHTFUL WINNER or HAVE A NEW ELECTION. However, that is simply not true since only an act of Congress can temporarily suspend the Constitution in very rare instances, such as cases of rebellion or invasion. Unless Trump is counting on his natural ability to create chaos with a call to an armed uprising, even if he declares himself president, he cannot unilaterally suspend the Constitution.

Sign # 2: Love for dictators

"Sure, he is a tyrant and a low-life human being, but he likes me, so I love him." D. Trump referring to Kim Jong Un, the North Korea Dear Leader.

Trump's love for dictators. It should not be a surprise to anyone if among the documents taken by Trump to his residence at Mar-a-Lago was North Korea dictator Kim Jong-un's "*love letter.*" As a Putin wannabe, Trump must dream of being elected for life and envy his ability to murder journalists and opposition members with Impunity. Sure, Trump will deny such ambitions, but his praise for dictators proves otherwise, such as when he could not help but compliment them.

- Trump complimented Rodrigo Duterte, President of the Philippines, for "*a job well done,*" on his war on drugs after Amnesty International reported "*more than 2,500 deaths at the hands of police, fabricated reports, falsified* or planted evidence, thefts of property from the accused, and police opening fire on unarmed accused individuals."

- Abdel Fattah el-Sisi of Egypt. *"He has done a fantastic job in a very difficult situation, and I just want to let everybody know, in case there was any doubt, that we are very much behind President el-Sisi.".* Main accomplishment: hijacked a popular pro-democracy revolt against a dictatorship in a military coup to replace a dictatorship with another.

- Recep Tayyip Erdogan of Turkey *"Very high marks."* Probably in reference to the way he repressed a 2013 anti-government protest by killing and jailing tens of thousands of dissidents.

- Mohammed bin Salman of Saudi Arabia: *"a person who can keep things under check and a strong person with very good control.". as a response* to the death of Jamal Khashoggi, cut in pieces while visiting a consulate of Saudi Arabia.

- Xi Jinping of China: *"It's great for him to be President for life,"* Said Trump with envy while fantasizing about his own prospects.

Sign # 3: Willingness to resort to force to achieve his goals

- The January 6, 2021, Capitol riot when Trump's supporters answered the call to *"fight like hell,"* *"Be there, will be wild,"* and *"lock and load"* orders.

- Trump wants to bring back firing squads, hangings, and *"possibly even the guillotine,"* should he return to the

White House. He has also apparently "discussed group executions,"[74] such as "*creating a flashy, government-backed video-ad campaign that would accompany a federal revival of these execution methods.*" The videos reportedly include "*footage from these new executions, if not the exact moments of death.*"

- Trump explicitly called on right-wing extremists and white supremacist groups to support and protect him. "*Stand back and stand by.*"
- Trump's reported desire to have the military shoot racial justice protesters.
- Trump's endorsement of assaulting reporters.

- In a typical Chinese style, Trump also proposed that the government should execute drug dealers by shooting them and then "*send the bullet to the family*" and make them "*pay for the cost of the bullet.*"

Sign # 4: Mafia-style mentality and demeanors

- Trump is obsessed with loyalty and respect, although he does not think twice about throwing former allies under the bus.

- Trump constantly makes veil threats and innuendos mafia style to intimidate those who oppose him, including the threat of a popular insurrection if he ever gets criminally indicted in one of his many legal exposures, which, of course, would prevent him from seeking re-election. "*I think if it happened, I think you'd have*

---

[74] From former attorney general Bill Barr in an interview to the *Rolling Stone Magazine*.

problems in this country the likes of which perhaps we've never seen before. I don't think the people of the United States would stand for it."

- Trump has no compunction about inciting or praising violence so long as he gives himself some legal deniability. This is typical of mafia bosses employing Mafia *"soldiers"* to do their dirty work, like Al Capone, who was never convicted for all the crimes he had ordered but was sent to the slammer on tax evasion charges.

Sign # 6: Near total control of the TADPOLE-GOP

- The number of TADPOLE-GOP lambs not grazing on Trump's bullshit can be counted on one hand.

- Potential challengers to Trump's nomination to the Trump Party had a big problem: how to be like Trump without being like him?

- Following Trump's cue, many TADPOLE-GOP members have wholly adhered to Far-right supremacist theories or QAnon conspiracy rhetoric, making them more extremist, uncompromising, dangerous, and receptive to the use of undemocratic means to achieve their goals.

Sign # 7: Tried to suppress free speech

- On journalists: *"These people should be executed. They are scumbags.". "They are both a disgrace to our Country, the Enemy of the People, but I just can't seem to figure out which is worse?"*

Sign # 8: Putin Wannabe

- In his moment of candor, Trump could be very transparent. Wouldn't it be great if he could be elected for life like his mentor, who still can send dissidents to rot in Siberia? "*The news is that at the end of 6 years after America has been made GREAT again and I leave the beautiful White House (do you think the people would demand that I stay longer? KEEP AMERICA GREAT).*"

- "*Under the normal rules, I'll be out in 2024, so we may have to go for an extra term,*" and, "*President for life ... maybe we'll have to give that a shot someday.*". Now you have it, right from the horse's mouth.

- If there is one similitude between Trump and Putin, it is that both are experts in recasting their roles from being the perpetrator to being the victim. Sign that they are both sociopaths.

Sign # 9: Clear disdain for democratic institutions and the rule of law

- One of the reasons for Trump's affinity and admiration for dictators is their ability to dispense with democratic principles and the rule of law. While in Office, Trump had a tendency to consider Federal Agencies as his own, dedicated to his service, and gutting those he did not like, like anything close to consumer protection, climate change, or education.

Sign # 10: Wanting to control the judiciary system

- One of the first things authoritarian leaders do is to control the justice system and the country's highest Court, in our case, The Supreme Court. Trump has done an outstanding job in that domain and should be proud of himself. No doubt, the Supreme Court could become handy in a contested election to extend the limit of time a president can stay in power or, pass laws that support his political agenda, or nullify the laws he does not like. *"I have the absolute right to do what I want to do with the Justice Department."*

- And so he did. Trump had no qualms in using the Justice Department as his own Special Op to go after political opponents of those critical to his policies.
  " I have an Article II, where I have the right to do whatever I want."
  And the one that takes the cake, "**I have the absolute right to PARDON myself.**"

- Short of being openly able to send in exile members of his administration he judged being a threat, like a king, he still could dismiss an FBI director and a deputy FBI director, as well as five inspectors general and U.S. attorneys who had the guts to investigate his abuse of power or alleged crimes of his cronies.

- And when someone got too close to investigating one of his alleged malversations, Trump had no problems using the Justice Department to begin a criminal probe into the origins of the inquiry *"investigate the investigators."*

- And when someone indeed managed to make one of his misdeeds public, Trump had a radical explanation: it is treason. "*I want to know who's the person who gave the whistleblower the information. Because that's close to a spy. You know what we used to do in the old days when we were smart? Right? The spies and treason, we used to handle it a little differently than we do now.*"

Sign # 11: Wanting to control information media

- Trump would love to be able to suppress any free press and propagate his gospel through state control media, Chinese and Russian style. Sure, as an alternative, privately owned propaganda machines such as Fox News are useful, but they are unreliable and could turn against you.

Sign # 12: Trump has a messianic delusion

- Indeed, Trump was sent by God to do great things. "*I am the chosen one,*" which probably explains why one of Trump's evangelical supporters was so moved that she began speaking in tongues when she saw him kissing the Bible at a photo op in front of Lafayette Square's St. John's Episcopal Church.

Sign # 13: Trump has all the psychological characteristics associated with dictators

- There is no point in revisiting those particular Trump character traits that have been extensively covered in other chapters of this book. Suffice it to say that without them, Trump would not be Trump.

Sign # 14: Trump fascist rhetoric.

- Finally, if you still have any doubts about how Trump intends to govern if reelected, the plan is clearly outlined in "***Project 2025"* handbook**" already discussed on page 360 of this book.

Now that Donald Trump is no longer an unknown incumbent to the supreme Office post of the land, and considering that the present political divide is driving us right into a wall, it is time to answer the main question this book was alluding to:

Are American voters condemned to forever have only one democratic choice between a Republican and a Democrat party and having to choose between the Plague and Cholera, or

Could a brand-new political party save us from collective self-destruction?

A BRAND-NEW THIRD PARTY

CAN A BRAND-NEW POLITICAL PARTY
STOP A SLOW-MOVING COUP?

We all have seen one of those mile-long slow-moving freight trains that drive you crazy because you are sitting at a railway crossing, and the train takes forever to move along, especially when you are in a hurry. So, what do you do when you have the misfortune of getting your car stalled on train tracks in the middle of a railway crossing, and you can hear a freight train coming your way in the distance?

1. You freeze like a deer caught in a car's headlights?
2. You yell for help?
3. You get out and try to push your car off the tracks?
4. Call an emergency number, hoping the train can be stopped before it reaches you.
5. You hope the train engineer will see you in time to stop the train?
6. Get out of the car and run out of the way as far away as possible.

In this analogy to a slow-moving political coup to subvert democracy, what would you do?

1. You think that the outcome is unavoidable and do nothing?
2. You become a militant and try to warn everybody of the incoming threat?
3. You place all your hopes in the possibility that the opposing party will change its mind about attempting a coup and accept the voting results.

4. You hope that your party will garner an overwhelming majority to ward off the potential threat?
5. You quit your job, garner all your belongings, and move to Canada?

You can see that none of the above scenarios will prevent the train from coming or stop an attempted coup from happening.

In the case of being stuck at a railway crossing, the best way to avoid a tragedy is to prevent your vehicle from getting stuck on the tracks in the first place. Like making sure there is enough room to clear the tracks before you move forward so you don't have to stop your vehicle in the middle of the tracks.

STOPPING A SLOW-MOVING COUP IS LIKE STOPPING A SLOW-MOVING FREIGHT TRAIN. CHANCES FOR SUCCESS ARE SLIM BUT NOT IMPOSSIBLE.

The best way to avoid getting hit by a slow-moving freight train at a railway crossing is to prevent the possibility of getting stuck on the tracks in the first place. In America, the political equivalent of getting hit by a slow-moving train is baked into our electoral system. It is called **the two-party deadlock system.**

In one hundred percent of cases, a political coup happens because of the inability of the political party in power to govern. This can happen with or without a democratic election. In the latter case, all a party has to do is engage in voting fraud or allege fraud from the other party and contest the voting results.

On the subject of voting fraud, what should we think of the party that rails against voter fraud and rants about "*stolen elections*" to see high-profile instances of voter fraud and alleged fraud committed by high-profile TADPOLE-GOP Republicans and ordinary Trump supporters?

- The local TADPOLE-GOP official in Ohio who forged the signature of his recently deceased father on an absentee ballot?
- What to say about Trump supporters like the one in Nevada who claimed that someone voted in his dead wife's name only to later plead guilty to having done it himself?
- Or the case of another Trump supporter from Iowa convicted of voting twice and said that she did so because she worried, as Trump warned, the election would be rigged.

All of this would be funny if it were not downright pathetic.

But do not worry about future voting fraud since, for the next presidential election of 2024, the Trump Party has made it its priority to block any type of legislation that would permit the Democratic Party to implement its political and social agenda and effectively govern the country. The Trump Party has also learned from its previous failed attempt to subvert democracy and, this time, has stacked all the odds in its favor to achieve its ultimate goal: total power.

That is not what the Founding Fathers envisioned when drafting our Constitution. By establishing a rule of governance with a separation of power between the Executive, the Legislative, and the Judicial Branches of government, they were confident that those provisions would serve as an effective guardrail to any attempt at despotism. What our Founding Fathers did not predict is that our two-party political system could possibly put all the power in the hands of a single party or a single person, should one of the two parties refuse to play the alternation of power inherent to any democratic system.

It is a hard fact to acknowledge, but our electoral system is archaic, convoluted, and undemocratic. At the very least, most Americans would recognize that our political system is gangrened by partisan animosity, gridlock, and gamesmanship. To be sure, the framers of our Constitution were leery of a two-party system when George Washington, in this final presidential address, warned of the danger of *"the alternate domination of one faction over another."*

"A division of the republic into two great parties . . . is to be dreaded as the great political evil." John Adams

But here we are

OVERCOMING ROADBLOCKS

An uphill battle

Barriers to third parties appearing on ballots are ingrained in our electoral laws, which have been engineered by those managing the current system. Of course, new laws and electoral reforms addressing voting disparities and inequalities could be enacted. Still, there are no incentives for the major parties to reshuffle the cards they have already stacked. Worse, Republicans have strengthened old laws and enacted new ones to suppress votes and staked their state with the very legislators who decide who votes, how the ballots are counted, and who wins.

Structural barriers

For starters, a two-party system is *"baked in"* into our country's existing legislative rules and election laws. Only in America can a third-party movement amass a significant percentage of the overall national vote without securing a single seat in either house of Congress.

But more importantly, the two major parties don't want competitors, and they've designed a system that makes the advent of a third party difficult, if not impossible, against overwhelming odds to impact a presidential election.

The winner-take-all characteristic of the American voting system

By widely accepted democratic standards, our voting process is antiquated and archaic. Winner-take-all systems are virtually unknown in other developed countries. It is an American anachronism that lies at the root of our failing democracy and is the source of many of our political problems. Still, it remains the rule under the American voting system, allowing a slim majority of voters to possibly control 100% of seats, leaving everyone else effectively without representation. **The net effect is that it translates millions of votes to zero.**

There is barely any other country in the world where a candidate can win the popular votes and still lose the election. Both Republicans and Democrats agree: the "*winner-take-all*" voting scheme is anti-democratic. Furthermore, according to most law experts, the practice could even be unconstitutional under modern voting jurisprudence. However, it is unlikely that either major political party will do anything to change the status quo since every House and Senate member is elected in an individual winner-take-all race, and a third party, even one with substantial support, can still be shut out of power.

Electoral College

Contrary to popular belief, American voters do not elect presidents; the Electoral College does. Because presidential votes are tallied on a state-by-state basis, even if a candidate receives a substantial number of votes nationally, as long as he does not win a majority in a state, he will receive no vote in the Electoral College. This is why a candidate can still lose the presidential election even when winning the popular vote. Since presidential ballots are tallied on a state-by-state basis, the only way for a third party to win a presidential election is to win at a state level.

Until the Electoral College reforms itself or is scrapped altogether, millions of voters in dozens of states will continue to know that their votes make no practical difference in the election. Using an Electoral College is why the United States is still a second-rated democracy.

The Weight of History

From experience, third parties in America have always ended the same way: **spoilers but not winners. Their only accomplishment has always been to siphon off votes from one of the two major parties without achieving any real influence in either the House or Senate. But this time could be different; remember the French**[75].

Financing

While there are very few limits on fundraising and campaign contributions favoring big parties, donors and lobbyists have little incentive to financially support new political kids on the block with unpredictable outcomes.

Getting voting ballots

Republican and Democrat-controlled legislatures have put in place onerous and time-consuming petitioning requirements to hinder other upstarts, like third parties, from being put on the ballots.

---

[75]in 2017, Emanuel Macron created a brand New Party that in a matter of months obliterated the traditional Parties of the Left and the Right and was elected President. Can we do less than the French?

A TIMID ATTEMPT TO ESCAPE THE MUSICAL CHAIRS GAME OF A TWO-PARTY POLITICAL SYSTEM

American interest in a third-party

Save the naysayers who negate or minimize the widespread interest in a third party, it is true that given the consequences of the next presidential election; it is now or never.

Political polarization

When the major parties are highly polarized, larger groups of voters end up not being represented by either one or the intense contention between them also increases political dissatisfaction.

According to recent Gallup polls, 62%, nearly two-thirds of Americans, say that they are more than fed up with the toxicity of politics in general and their political party affiliation in particular and would favor the end of the two-party gridlock that paralyzes the government from governing effectively. The only caveat is that they doubt that there is a realistic way to see it happening, given the roadblocks that the two major parties would put up to prevent such a possibility.

The same polls reveal that 33% of Americans believe the two major political parties are doing an adequate job representing governing the country, one of the lowest ever.

Contrary to what the TADPOLE-GOP proclaims and the apparent lasting popularity of Donald Trump, Americans' opinion of the TADPOLE has reached a new low of 37%, while 48% have a favorable view of the Democrats. More interestingly, it appears that 50% of Americans identify themselves as politically independent, the highest ever measured by Gallop. This fact could turn out to be good news for the proponents of a third party because counting on dissatisfied Democrats and disgruntled Republicans would not be enough to provide the mass appeal to force legislators to permit a third party to emerge.

If it sounds logical to expect independents to favor third parties, more surprising is that at 63%, Republicans are almost as open as independents to allowing third parties to run in a presidential election.

Democrats' internal divisions between its moderate and liberal wings appear equally divided on the opportunity to see third parties emerging. Perhaps because they still have not fully decided if such a competition would be detrimental or beneficial to them.

Regardless of their political color, it appears that most Americans would favor breaking the deadlock of our two-party political system in favor of a multi-party system. As auspicious as a third party seems to be, nothing will happen without us, the people.

WHAT IS NEEDED

It has been advanced that American voters are not so stupid to re-elect a demagogue. You wish.

What any third party undoubtedly needs is a brand and a constituency that is powerful enough to transcend the tribalism of both the left and the right in order not simply to be a spoiler of votes but to win a majority of votes to govern.

One thing is certain: it is doubtful that a new party will emerge out of a few disgruntled Republican conservatives seeking to rededicate a new political party more in tune with its founding principles and ideals. By the same token, forming a new party cannot wait until disaffected minority, centrist, or moderate voters get organized around a specific issue or set of demands. We should also not count on the initiative of another billionaire in search of making his mark in politics as the most powerful man in the world. If we truly want to save our democracy from going down the toilet, it is only up to us, the people.

A vision, not a division

Ok, for a brand new party, but to do what? How can a new party cure the problems that ail us and save our democracy? What political programs, policies, democratic, economic, and social reforms would unify various political aspirations under a common denominator that would move the masses? The answer: who cares? Because here is the sad truth: People's votes are not rational but emotional. They pay little attention to campaign promises, moral values, or specifics on how their life will improve. People do not want to hear the truth anyway, and being frank and honest is the best way not to get elected. So, what could the vision of a new political party be?

A FAINT GLEAM OF HOPE

The new kids on the block

With the perspective of a Trump-Biden rematch, potential voters are becoming increasingly leery of a "*Stop the Steal*" redux.

To date, three political groups have emerged to make enough waves to worry the two traditional political parties:

NO LABEL touts itself as a centrist political group with the ambition to offer an alternative option to voters while denying the Democrats' accusation that it would only end up as a spoiler to serve the interests of Donald Trump. Third-party history indeed retains the memory of the Green Party, the Libertarian Party, or Ross Perot, who narrowly contributed to the defeat of George H.W. Bush against Bill Clinton in 1992.

THIRD WAY is not a political party but a center-left Washington D.C. think-tank. To quote their agenda: "*We are fighting for **opportunity**, so everyone has the chance to earn a good life; progress on social issues, so all have the **freedom** to live the lives they choose; and **security**, so we are protected from 21st-century global threats.*" Their program is the only one not focussing on not re-electing Trump.

Then there is the **LINCOLN PROJECT** with the distinction of being a TADPOLE-GOP group that ironically aligns itself with the "*Never Trumpers.*" Its prime goal purports "*to hold accountable those who would violate their oaths to the Constitution and would put others before Americans.*" In other words, almost the entire TADPOLE-GOP, and realistically, an untenable goal.

Finally, there is the case of **ROBERT F. KENNEDY Jr.**, who is running as an independent.

The Democrats say that he is a conservative, while Donald Trump says that he is a liberal. If that is the case, his effect as a spoiler is fifty/fifty = zero.

Whatever RFK Jr.'s presidential program professed to be, his assumed main objective is to run on a *"Never Biden"* mantra professing that Joe Biden is a greater threat to democracy than Trump. Sure, the majority of the Kennedy Clan is distancing itself from what it considers as a lunatic character running on the Kennedy's prestigious name, except that his views find an echo among certain Republican and Democrat voters.

However, RFK Jr.'s advocacy for strange conspiracy theories would logically attract more voters supporting worldviews closer to those of Trump's and QAnon followers. So, aside from counting on his prestigious name, what does RFK Jr. have to offer as an alternative to the two-party system trap, and what are his beliefs?

First, his beliefs:

- **The CIA was involved in the assassination of former President John F. Kennedy**: This is not an outlandish claim. Many Americans believe that the Warren Commission convened to study the killing was nothing more than a whitewashing attempt to conceal the fact that Lee Harvey Oswald was a patsy, just like he claimed to be.
- **The COVID-19 virus was genetically engineered:** No one knows for sure that it was manufactured as a biological weapon, but its intentional release is doubtful. Who would intentionally release a deadly virus without having a vaccine?
- **The 2004 presidential election was stolen**; RFK Jr. is convinced that voter fraud in the 2004 presidential

election allowed former Republican President George W. Bush to steal the victory from Democrat John Kerry. The Supreme Court actually made the decision of who won the election. One of its worst rulings.

RFK Jr's policies

The following is just a summary of RFK Jr.'s policy taken directly from his website[76] , which is reproduced here without comments.

- **Economy**: People who work hard should be able to afford a decent life.
- Housing - Homeownership: The dream of home ownership is slipping away for many Americans.
- **Environment**: Clean it Up - We're going to unite Americans around safe and healthy food, pure water, clean air, and living rivers, forests, grasslands, and wetlands.
- **Honest Government** For the People: We are going to remake public institutions to serve the public.
- **Reconciliation** - Heal the Divide: Robert F. Kennedy, Jr. will lead the country toward an ethos of respectful dialog and reconciliation across divisions.
- **Peace** - Bring it Home: Robert F. Kennedy, Jr. will end the foreign wars, bring home the troops, and devote the freed-up resources to revitalize America.
- **Border** - A Humanitarian Crisis: Robert F. Kennedy, Jr. sees the situation at the border primarily as a humanitarian crisis.
- **Civil Liberties** - Restore our Rights: RFK, Jr. will end censorship and surveillance, reduce incarceration, and respect the rights and dignity of all citizens.

---

[76] https://www.kennedy24.com/policies

- **Racial Healing** - Civil Rights: Robert F. Kennedy, Jr. believes that the current situation is the result of the unhealed legacy of racism in this country.
- **Native Americans** - Deep Commitment: Robert F Kennedy Jr. inherited from his father a deep commitment to improving the lives of Native Americans.
- **Revitalization** - Turn it around: The time has come to reverse America's economic decline.
- **Veterans**: Mr. Kennedy embraces the sacrifice made by veterans to the country, your sense of honor, and your desire to serve.
- **Higher Education**: Today, the higher education system is trapped in a vicious circle where rising tuition forces students to struggle.
- **Americorps** - Expand Americorps: Robert F. Kennedy Jr. is going to transform the existing Americorps program to offer a new option to young people who want to gain skills.
- **Labor**: Strong Support of Labor Rights.

In short, nothing that any normally breathing American would not agree with.

So, what do those potential vote spoilers have in common? They are fiercely opposed by both traditional political parties and, more so by the Democrats, who could see the appeal that such an alternative vote would have on independents. So, realistically, the chances for any third party to re-draw the political map look bleak and are a long shot. But more than anything, what a new political party needs is a providential savior.

The 2024 U.S. presidential election presents a unique opportunity for a Third Party to break the undemocratic American Two-Party political system. If not now, it will never happen, and America will remain forever a flawed democracy.

A PROVIDENTIAL MAN (or woman)
OF DESTINY

More than ideas, a charismatic leader moves people into action. Although common to all dictators, words are not enough. Hitler, Mussolini, Fidel Castro, or Hugo Chavez could talk for hours, haranguing crowds. Others with limited vocabulary, like Donald Trump, can accomplish the same thing as long as he keeps repeating the same words. But were they men of destiny? Most dictators do not start that way. They appear on the national scene at a critical time for their country and often begin as liberators or the providential man who will restore moral values, economic prosperity, or national pride. Trump's "*Make America Great Again*" is precisely on that trajectory, except that his disregard for the law, the institutions, the Constitution, and his dictator's tendencies were apparent from the start. Regardless of Donald Trump's record, the main question remains: **Is Donald Trump America's providence man?**

The providence man concept is the belief that God has temporarily lent some of his spiritual power to a man to do extraordinary things to save humanity from some unspeakable perils. For many, Donald Trump is the man sent by God to destroy a secret cabal of blood-drinking, child-sex-trafficking members of the liberal elite. For others, Trump has been sent by God to restore white evangelical power in America in a fight of good against evil and rights against wrongs kind of war. Others are less vocal but no less influential, like the Jewish community, which sees Trump as the providence man sent by God to support Israel in the coming apocalypse.

America has never had a shortage of "*providence men*" in times of need. From George Washington during the War of Independence, Abraham Lincoln during the Civil War, and Franklin D. Roosevelt during the Great Depression, it appears God has always shown his mercy for America. However, it seems that this time, his leniency is wearing thin.

Today, if Donald Trump succeeds in his plan to subvert democracy and America becomes a banana republic, all those who see him as the "*Second Messiah*" will interpret that outcome as God's will.

Conversely, it is also possible that God sees Donald Trump as the "*Devil Incarnated*" or as the "*Anti-Christ*" and sent him to test America to see if it deserves to be saved.

The gulf that separates Republicans and Democrats is greater than the Gulf of Aqaba separating the Sinai from the Arabian Peninsula in the Red Sea. Even Moses would find it daunting to try to find a path bridging the two sides of their political divide. Nothing short of divine intervention would accomplish such a miracle, like a providential man who would create a new political party.

Please, God, send us a George Washington, a Roosevelt, a Churchill, a De Gaulle, a Joan of Arc, anybody, to save us from ourselves.

A FEW GOOD MEN

In the final analysis, what if America's fall was simply due to an increasing shortage of good men? Men who do not confuse their wishes for reality, men who do not equate compassion with a lack of masculinity, and men capable of admitting when they are wrong. In short, men that women would like to see as the father of their children as a model of the moral values you expect from a human being.

Worrying about the state of men's masculinity is an American tradition that dates back to the 1800s. So, talking about the crisis of American manhood is not new. American manhood has always been in crisis. What is new this time is that the latter "*crisis*" might be, if not the cause, at least the contributor to the societal decay that could lead to the end of America the way we know it. To just say that we live in a macho society where confrontation, "*Stand-your-Ground*," shoot first, and talk later is just our heritage of the American West would be a negation of an alarming social trend: men, especially younger ones, are increasingly confused, struggling both physically and mentally and becoming lost. If it is true that our young boys are our country's future, we are in deep trouble.

Few in America would agree with the French poet Louis Aragon's maxim, "*The woman is the future of man*." But if the statistics hold true, men are losing ground in all attributes that would make a man attractive as a husband to a woman. And for those already married, women are ditching their significant other at an alarming rate. Continuing on this trend, the only relationship that many men may hope to achieve would be with an App or a blown-up inflatable life-size doll.

In the meantime, young women continue to out-learn and out-earn young men as women capture 60% of all higher education degrees and have increased their lifetime earnings by 33 percent while those of men have decreased by 10 % since 1983.

In their defense, the men said that women work harder, are more motivated, and plan ahead better. It is then no wonder that because of their lack of motivation, faith in themselves and the future, men account for close to three out of every four "*deaths of despair*," such as suicide and drug overdoses.

On the social side, young men are not fairing any better. A recent survey reveals that about 15 percent of men do not have a close friend. It is true that if you discount the fake friends you garner on the internet and spend most of your time between watching porn and playing video games, your best options for finding friends are joining a group of people that share your worldviews on the Manosphere[77], joining a gang, QAnon, rent a friend like they do in Japan or joint a far-right political movement, the kind that sees Donald Trump as the only political person that embodies all the macho allures of a strong man. And here lies the potential danger for our democracy: the shortage of "*good men*" that redefines the notion of what we used to call a "*real man.*"

---

[77] Manophere , encompasses a range of misogynistic communities that vary from anti-feminism to more explicit, violent rhetoric towards women.

COULD THE REAL GOOD MEN PLEASE STAND UP AND BE COUNTED?

In 2021, save a few good men, mainly Republicans, America came to a hairbreadth away from becoming a banana republic. Without those very few who stood by their conscience and oath to protect our Constitution, any of the many nefarious attempts to subvert our democracy could have succeeded.

Those were the real patriots of the day, not the morally bankrupt elected officials or so call patriots who dressed in the Star-Banner flag were pissing on our Constitution.

Now that most of the same men have joined the dark side, it is almost guaranteed that the next time *"the few good men"* left won't matter.

But first, what is a good man?

The only time we hear of someone having been a good man is during his eulogy. But what does it mean? In most cases, it means that he did everything expected of him with his family, friends, job, country, and society in general. But how many times have you heard it when referring to a politician? Good men in politics are few and far between.

To paraphrase Jesus' words

"It is easier for a camel to go through the eye of a needle than for a politician to be a good man."

Not easy, indeed, but not impossible, even for a Republican. In fact, most good men in politics were Republicans. They were the ones who, after the 2020 presidential election and at great risk to themselves, placed their professional integrity ahead of politics. Men who took responsibility for their actions chose truths over expedients, their country above personal ambition, and above all, kept their moral compass in a storm of lies and deception.

Those were the men and women who stood steadfast in telling the truth in their testimony of Donald Trump's impeachment investigations.

Those were the judges who showed integrity in applying the laws in judging the merits of the many legal recourses to have the presidential votes invalidated.

Those men of the fine blue line defended the Capitol and saved Mike Pence's hide from the noose.

Those were the elected Republican officials who, under threats, refused to surrender to political pressures to do unethical or immoral bidding for their party.

Those men refused to do Trump's illegal and criminal biddings.

All were indeed good persons.

Unfortunately, that does not include all those people who did or said something that was expected of them too little too late, like William Barr, who resigned from his post when the rats were abandoning the ship.

But make no mistakes. Most of those "*good men*" who put their finger in the last levee that protected our democracy are now gone.

Next time Trump asks a state legislator to find him votes, the answer will likely be: how many do you want, Sir?

Next time Trump thinks of using the National Guards to size voting machines in states he did not win, he might certainly ask the right-wing militia to do so.

Next time, Trump won't even have to ask State legislators not to certify votes in States he lost; they will do it on their own.

Next time Trump asks any Republican official to commit illegal actions that serve his purpose, he will do his "*patriotic duty*" to comply.

But here is the kicker:

What will Donald Trump do on January 21, 2025, on Inauguration Day, if Trump loses the election again and presents himself at the U.S. Capitol to be sworn in?

The next time, will there be enough good men left to stand up for democracy?

We already know the answer:

The answer is no!

It is absolutely within the realm of possibility that Donald J. Trump be re-elected President of the United States without him having recourse to cheating. In that case, the Universe has spoken: America's exceptionalism deserves to go down the toilet.

GOD'S PROVIDENCE

*If there has ever been a time when God's
Providence is needed in the affairs
of America, it is now*

Since the initial founders of America, the prevalent view of the exceptionality of our country has been based on the belief in the supernatural intervention of God in our affairs. *"In God we trust"* can mean different things to many people, but the underlying meaning of our belief is in the unshakable confidence that God will always be there to save us from ourselves in moments of need.

To be sure, America has had no shortage of *"Providential Man"* to save its bacon when it needed it the most. George Washington, Abraham Lincoln, and Delano Roosevelt, just to name a few among many more.

But considering that America is today facing an existential crisis of apocalyptic proportion, it is all natural to seek succor and solace in a messianic hope of divine intervention. If, for the Republicans, God has already answered their ultimate messianic hope in the person of Donald Trump, the rest of the country is still waiting for the ultimate savior that would save America from Trump. And here's the rub: because while we wait for an eventual messiah to show up, we may just sit on our hands and do nothing in the expectation that when the Messiah comes, all our problems will miraculously disappear without major upheavals.

But what if no messiah is coming to save us?

All the recent polls concur: three-quarters of Americans want political reforms. Short of actively listening to popular demand, America is committing a collective societal suicide with only one outcome......

..........AMERICAN DEMOCRACY APOCALYPSE

2024

DEMOCRACY APOCALYPSE

THE END OF AMERICAN EXCEPTIONALISM

We used to be so proud of our democracy. After all, America is the light of the world, the land of the free, and the home of the brave. That was then, at least until the advent of a demagogue that would reshape the American psyche, self-image, and confidence in our institutions at home and abroad. Thus, the question: Are we still exceptional?

Partly because of globalization and the failure of democracies to meet their people's aspirations, the world is now in competition between two diametrically opposed political systems. One is where people still have a voice in the manner in which they live, and the other is where their daily lives are constantly monitored and directed by the omnipresence of the state.

For the time being, America is still the land of the free, but people are becoming more aware that the country is quickly sliding on the slippery slope of intolerance, greed, and tribalism. To that extent, either from apathy or by design, America is on its way to joining a global trend of countries where the people accommodate themselves in tolerating autocratic leaders. Make no bones about it. The free world is shrinking fast. Indeed, the prospect of the free world becoming a euphemism for "*The Old World*" is dire. According to Freedom House[78]

---

[78] A Washington-based pro-democracy think tank and watchdog. https://freedomhouse.org

- Three-quarters of the people on earth live in countries where freedom is declining.
- Fifty-four countries are now labeled *"Not Free,"* or about 38 percent of the world's population.
- Of 39 countries and territories that experienced pro-democracy protests in 2019, 23 saw their scores decline the following year.
- India, the world's largest democracy, went from "*Free*" to "*Partly Free.*"
- Though still classified as *"Free"* and as a "*flawed democracy,*" the United States fell to 26 on the Global Democracy Index..
- Out of 167 countries, only 21 are fully democratic, 59 are authoritarian, and the rest are in transit or in a grey zone, meaning nations with regular electoral fraud, contested election results, and voting restrictions.

Considering the global general trend towards illiberalism, the obvious relevant question is which path America will follow, and in doing so, shall we learn from our own history?

> *"We learn from history*
> *that we do not learn from history."*
> Georg Wilhelm Friedrich Hegel

It is an often repeated quote, and it is why history is bound to repeat itself.

In 1824, exactly 200 years ago, an unprecedented event happened in American politics:

In that year's presidential election, Andrew Jackson won the most popular electoral votes from the Electoral College but failed to receive a majority. As a result, the House of Representatives assumed the responsibility of designing a winner and elected John Quincy Adams as president.

The major consequence of this outcome was the birth of the two-party system responsible for today's political imbroglio of American politics.

Like a wink from history, Jackson got his revenge in 1828 when he defeated Adams to capture the presidency. Fast forward to 2024. Will history repeat itself?

1824 REDUX

In 2024, America had only one chance, albeit a feeble one, that the *"Shining City on the Hill"* would not become a banana republic or a dictocracy.

Granted, for this possibility not to happen, our country had to find a charismatic leader who can unify all the Americans who are still living in this reality, not an alternate one. True, we already have one charismatic leader, *"Dear Leader,"* AKA Donald Trump, dictator in waiting, and Putin wannabe. But is he the one who will save our democracy or the one to F#%& it up?

All the measures designed by the Trump Party to guarantee the next presidential elections are now in place, and the Republicans are now ready to cash in.

In Red States, hundreds of voting-suppressing laws have been enacted to make it as difficult as possible for minorities to vote.

"Watchers" have been put in place to intimidate and threaten officials in charge of counting votes in case the results turn out not to be those expected.

As a failsafe measure, many Republican states have put in place laws to allow legislators to completely reject the voting results they do not like and to decide who wins the popular votes.

Finally, by packing the Supreme Court with Trump-minded judges, everything is in place to have the Court declare Trump the winner. Cherry on the cake, the Supreme Court is ready to remove the Constitutional two-term presidential limit placed on re-election, opening the door for a president for life Putin's style.

So, to quote Voltaire: *"Everything is for the best in the best of all possible worlds."* For Trumpsters, that is to say.

WHAT HAPPENS NEXT?

You do not have to be a bird of ill omen, a tea leaves reader, nor be gifted with any special divination powers to predict how the 2024 U.S. presidential election will turn out. However, somewhere, someone will discover in the cryptic prophesies of Nostradamus that *"the fall of the shining city upon the hill"* was there for all to see.

Unfortunately, the 2024 U.S. presidential elections can only go in one of two ways with the same ineluctable result.

Scenario 1: The Trump Party wins

Because of the 6/01/21 failure of the insurrection riot at the Capitol to invalidate the voting results and The Trump Party's total routing of all the legal challenges meant to prove voting fraud, there is absolutely no way that the Trump cult members will allow a repeat of *"Stop the steal."* The fact that no one in The Trump Party noticed the irony that the *"Stop the Steal"* slogan indeed applied to themselves shows how far they have fallen down the rabbit hole. It was a bit like the Nazis marching in the streets with *"Stop the Jews from killing us"* banners, but since the Democrats did not even point out the irony, why stop?

This time around, the Trumpsters have left nothing to chance, and any attempts by the Democrats to counter a trumped-up election will be met by fierce Trumpsters *"resistance is futile"* Borg style.

Contrary to Trump supporters, the Democrats have neither the appetite nor the inclination for an armed insurrection, which leaves them with only one option. The nuclear one: SECESSION.

On the practical side, it isn't easy to comprehend how such a thing could happen in reality. True, the nation is ineluctably fractured into almost equal irreconcilable camps. One lives in an alternate reality sustained by lies, hate, and conspiracy theories, and the others, mainly Democrats, are affected by the Rodney King's *"Why can't we all just get along?"* syndrome.[79]

Given this perspective, it will be up to Trump's supporters to take arms to prevent such an *"unpatriotic"* thing from happening. With *"Captain Chaos"* in charge, things will go from very bad to extremely bad very quickly.

Scenario 2: The Trump Party loses

This is not even a plausible scenario. If such an improbable thing were to happen, it would be 1824 over again. Trumpsters will ask the House of Representatives that they control to designate the president. In this case, we are back to scenario 1.

In this scenario, this is the election of 2020 redux, with the same claims of voting fraud and non-acceptance by the defeated Trump Party to accept the democratic process, with one big difference. This time, it is a civil war that leads to only one logical conclusion: the NUCLEAR OPTION, meaning secession.

In both cases,

America is F@%#&ed!

Perhaps this is a good time to use Trump's directive against him.

"We fight like hell, and if you don't fight like hell, you're not gonna have a country anymore." Donald Trump.

---

[79] Rodney King, the man whose vicious beating by members of the Los Angeles police department in 1991 was caught on a video that started a riot after the officers involved were acquitted.

Before you deposit your vote in the ballot box, your choice is not about the economy, stupid! Nor the unchecked immigration, the moral values of the man to hold the highest office of the land or even the future of our democracy. You are voting for the soul of America.

THE NUCLEAR OPTION

Can America secede?

Shit never happens at random. It is just a failure of the imagination to forecast the future and accept the possibility that the worst may happen.

Here is a question that many people inside and outside the U.S. have been asking:

If Donald Trump is such an existential threat to American democracy, why can't one of the many American patriots take him out?

The short answer could be resumed in two reasons:

The first one is that today's patriots are the ones trying to trample on democracy while draping themselves in the Old Glory flag.

The second reason is that although America has a long history of assassinating political figures[80], the majority of them had been for petty personal reasons that had nothing to do with achieving a specific political goal. Furthermore, **when it comes to assassinating its leaders, judging from the past examples of Abraham Lincoln, Martin Luther King, John, and Robert Kennedy, Americans only take down the good ones.** So, for Donald Trump, the answer is no, not a chance.

But let us not kid ourselves. The 2024 presidential election has all the hallmarks of an existential event for the Republic. As Donald Trump has proclaimed many times before, it is almost certain that the 2024 election will be rigged, and he knows what

---

[80] At least 54 since America became a republic

he is talking about because this time, he will succeed. So, we better prepare for contested voting results, civil unrest, and possible civil war leading to the secession of several states from the Union. But is this outcome even possible?

Legally no! **The Constitution has no provisions for a State to leave the Union.**[81]

"*There is a lawful way to secede – it's called emigration. They can move to Canada,*" Akhil Reed Amar.[82]

But like the 1861 American Civil War surely demonstrates, "*legally*" means diddly-squat!

Already back in 2020, a survey revealed[83] that 41% of Biden's supporters and 52% of Trump's voters thought that "*it's time to split the country, favoring blue/red states seceding from the union.*". More ominous was a 2020 Hofstra University poll that found that nearly 40 percent of likely voters would support state secession if their candidate loses. And here we are, a secession of Blue and red states from the Union is rapidly moving from a hypothesis to a real possibility.

But secession could be made possible. All we have to do is to amend the Constitution to allow the people to vote for the right to leave the Union. It is that or a civil war.

But if allowed, what would secession realistically look like? Would we see a mass migration of the Red States toward the Blue States and vice versa?

---

[81] The United States Supreme Court established a new constitutional principle in *Texas v. White*, holding that states cannot unilaterally secede.
[82] Professor of Law and Political Science at Yale University.
[83] 2021 University of Virginia poll.

If it is hard to predict the future, we can already observe the present to detect an ominous trend of things to come. Americans are already segregating at an alarming pace by political preference, accentuating the country's political divide and polarization. Conservatives are moving to Red States while Liberals to Blue ones.

In a move dubbed the *"Big Sort,"* Conservative Americans are moving to States where one party has a supermajority that controls the entire Legislature, as it is already the case in 28 States. In all other States except two, one party already controls the Legislature as a whole. So Liberals also have a place to go where they could be sure that local Government policies reflect their values.

If we follow the logic of the political divide, it appears that Republicans are more secessionist in the South, whereas, in the North East and the West Coast, Democrats would feel the same. But where would the independents go? The Midwest?

There is, however, a simpler solution. The United States is a federation of 50 states, which, in effect, are governed like independent countries. Each state already has its own government, constitution, legislature, economic powers, and different rules on how to elect the president, all independent of the Federal government. In the scenario of catastrophe where the nuclear option becomes the only way out of a civil war, all states are not created equal and would fare differently as truly independent states. For example, based on their GDP,

- California would compare to Canada.
- Texas to Mexico.
- New York to South Korea.
- Illinois to Saudi Arabia, etc..

Many other states could very likely make it on their own, while others with a lesser population will have to work out some sort of union with other states to survive. What remains would not be as easy to settle. For instance, who will own the mighty U.S. military? With the majority of military bases in the South, the Plains states, and Rocky Mountain areas, wouldn't that leave the other States under the threat of an invasion? Sure, each state already has its own military and air force, but what about the Navy?

Of course, secession will have substantial unintended consequences on the global stage. America will no longer be able to count on its military might to keep military alliances credible. It will indeed cause the end of NATO's credibility as a deterrent to Russia's and China's territorial ambitions.

On the economic side, **China would de facto become the first economic world power**, well ahead of its most optimistic previsions, and Trump's motto, "*Make America Great Again,*" would become a standing joke across the world and be replaced by "*Make Florida Great Again*" and "*Make Texas great again.*"

Also, who will own the humongous U.S. debts? Of course, the easiest would be to default on the debt and go bankrupt. Who is China going to sue if there is no more United States?

There is also an alternative solution based on the television series/novel "*The Handmaid's Tail,*" where a radical Christian movement called the Sons of Jacob forms a new state called Gilead. In the Novel, the Sons of Jacob instigated a *coup d'état* against the United States government in one attack against all three branches of government. In this scenario, where reality copies fiction, about half of present America could have the state they literally want: authoritarian, Evangelical Christian, anti-abortion, anti-WOKE, anti-LGBTQ+, and whiter than white:

a paradise on earth. Let's just hope that in this scenario, like in the novel, Gilead's neighboring country in the north, Canada, remains free.

However, if this doomsday scenario ever materializes, each citizen of the new state will be able to reminisce about the good old days by listening to a Bruce Springsteen version of Woody Guthrie's informal National anthem,

"This land is my land, and this land is your land........
.......This land was made for you and me."
And replace it by

This land is my land, and this land is not your land........

..........This land was made only for me.......

Perhaps it would be a good thing if Trump becomes president again because we have not reached rock bottom yet. It will only be after America experiences the fascist government of Trump that America will be ready, like the phoenix, to be reborn from its ashes.

THE MOST FRUSTRATING FEELING
IN THE WORLD

Here is a question with no answer:

If someone's nose is in cow dung, how do you convince that person of the contrary if he continues to insist that it is chocolate pudding? Because if there is anything more futile than trying to convince an imbecile, it is trying to convince a person of bad faith. You will always lose, for he has more experience defending something with no arguments than you do.

This must have been the sentiment felt by most Democrats after the January 6 Commission hearing exposing all the malversations perpetrated to subvert our democracy was exposed for the world to see. Because far from opening the eyes of people with a minimum of honesty and good faith, it had the opposing effect of strengthening the conviction of those already convinced of the big lie while shifting to the dark side those sitting on the fence.

Of course, it did not help that the Democrats took two years to seriously start to investigate the origin and the actors of the January 6/21 Capitol riot perceived mainly by the Republicans as politically motivated.

Indeed, in the course of its investigation, the House Committee unearthed some damming pieces of evidence detailing intent, conspiracy, and actions supporting criminal charges against the perpetrators, including:

- **Obstruction of an official proceeding:** This law makes it a crime to "*corruptly*" seek to obstruct, influence, or impede "any official proceeding" or to attempt to do so.

- **Conspiracy to defraud the United States:** The committee says that Trump did not work alone in committing the above offense.
- **Conspiracy to make a false statement:** The committee alleges that Trump conspired with others to submit alternate slates of fake electors to Congress and the National Archives, which in some cases involved falsely asserting in a legal document that they had been duly elected.
- *"Incite," "assist,"* or *"aid and comfort,"* an insurrection.

But the most damming evidence from the investigation is the extent to which Trump's inner circle of staff and advisors told him repeatedly that his claims about Dominion voting machines and rigged elections were unfounded.

The takeaway

It appears that for an insurrection against the state that would typically land any private citizen a life sentence behind bars, none of Trump's enablers and the mastermind in chief of the conspiracy himself will suffer any consequences. If that simple fact does not illustrate the abysmal level of our judicial and political system, nothing will. By this action, or lack thereof, our great country has officially joined the rank of banana republics.

THE MINORITY RULE

or

The power of one

All rulers of autocratic countries will tell you the advantages of being the supreme leader. After all, look at what kings and emperors have been able to accomplish. They had a long-term vision of their country and their own legacy to envision the future. This, in part, explains why, with their short-term vision riveted toward the next election, today's politicians are not expected to do anything that would endanger their political future. China, for instance, is the prime example of a country that wants to prove the superiority of a supreme leader over democracies, where you have to ask everyone's opinion before doing anything. Even countries that have experimented a bout with democracy are longing for the return of some sort of strongman rule. But what can we say about countries with long and strong democracies, such as India and the United States? So far, India is leading the way to becoming an autocracy, but it appears that America is not too far behind.

Donald Trump, for one, truthful to his enormous ego or boundless optimism, since 2022, has already called himself the 45th and 47th president, indicating that he has no doubts about all the preparation put in place to steal the election, this time for good.

In reviewing the January 6 Committee findings, there can no longer be any ambiguity on the intent of Trump and the TADPOLE-GOP to trample the rule of law, our institutions, and our democracy. It has been estimated that 79% of Republican voters still support Trump. But what does that mean? According to ongoing polls, the number of MAGA Republicans[84] has been relatively consistent. They represent about 14% of American adults of voting age compared with 11% of Republican-independent. However, the percentage of voting adults supporting the January 6/20 riot on the Capitol falls to 6% compared to 25% for Republicans. Based on those statistics, it is comforting to find out that, taken together, the percentage of "*fools*" does not exceed ten percent of the population. A minority which, in theory, should, with a caveat, reassure us of the future of our democracy. Except if you ignore the minority rule.

If there is one widespread misconception regarding who governs a country, it is the fiction that the majority rules. With few exceptions, it is the minority, being ethnic or political, that governs a country, including democracies where elected government rarely exceeds more than a quarter of the votes cast. This can be explained by the fact that even in democracies, only a small proportion of the population bothers to vote. Either by apathy, disillusion with the political process, or the lack of personal appeal of the candidates. For whatever reason, it appears that the will of the majority has little value and is repeatedly ignored, so why bother?

On the other hand, minorities are more politically active, more dedicated, more organized, and more ruthless in achieving their goals, and America is no exception. If the majority of Americans are in favor of universal health care, abortion rights, gun control, equal voting rights, police accountability, and against Republicans' anti-democratic stance, Donald Trump's rhetoric, and blatant lies, shouldn't they make sure that next time they

---

[84] MAGA republicans believe that Trump was the legitimate winner of the 2020 presidential election.

vote, their ballot does not go to the minority that does not represent them?

Americans have already recently witnessed the dysfunction of their government and the ability of one single person to hijack the entire political process of governing. In this sad state of affairs, both political parties are on equal footing. For the Democrats, key legislations were derailed by senators, Joe Manchin and Christine Cinema, every time a proposed legislation ran contrary to their personal interests. As for the Republicans, how can we forget the day the Speaker of the House of Representatives, Kevin McCarthy, was thrown out on the initiative of one single person, Florida Rep. Matt Gaetz? This last episode of democracy dysfunction should become a textbook case of political power ambition gone bad. While completely predictable, one could question the lengths McCarty was prepared to go to gain political power by accepting to be permanently blackmailed and have his head chopped off by one single vote. This is not the way democracy is supposed to work.

Among democracies, America is now becoming a model of minority rule in politics. The American voting system has, without any doubt, demonstrated how lopsided our voting system is at both the presidential and Congressional levels. But in the United States, the Minority Rule goes far beyond voting results. Considering all the progressive values that the majority of Americans want, the majority that the conservatives hold in the Supreme Court guarantees that the wishes of the majority of Americans will not materialize anytime soon. Indeed, in effect, the Supreme Court has now become the poster child of minority rule in America. Worse is the fact that by overturning Roe v. Wade and years of jurisprudence, the Supreme Court has demonstrated that by the stroke of a pen, a conservative minority can wipe out fifty years of hard-won progressive social gains.

There is another voter representation imbalance that will ensure the continuity of minority rule until we dispose of the Electoral College altogether. The situation where when counting presidential votes, Wyoming, with a population of 578,000 people, counts as much as California, with 34.5 million, is untenable. On the scale of minority rule, the United States is the only democratic country in the world where a presidential candidate can win the popular vote and still lose the election.

American voters should understand one thing: they do not elect presidents; the Electoral College does, and even Trump understands that. That is why he orchestrated a fake elector's fraud to overturn the election.

PART IV

THE CROSSROADS OF DESTINY

Grandpa, where were you during the war?
Daddy, for whom did you vote
before the fall of America?

It happens perhaps only once in a lifetime or at particular times in history when a nation is on the brink of seismic changes that would precipitate it towards the abyss or a completely new path toward redemption.

2024 is that extraordinary moment in time when America will lose or redeem its soul. If this is not the first time that America has faced an existential threat of this magnitude, this could very well be the last time a fair and free election is held in America.

AN ATTEMPT AT RATIONALITY

What do religious faith and conspiracy theories have in common? They are both based on the belief of unproven allegations. No wonder fundamentalist Christians, QAnon, and Trump believers in B.S. are often the same people.

A PLAUSIBLE EXPLANATION FOR WHY PEOPLE BELIEVE TRUMP'S LIES ABOUT THE ELECTION

Since Joe Biden won the election, numerous polls throughout the country have been relatively consistent. Some 35 percent of Americans, including 68 percent of Republicans, believe in the Big Lie. Since it would be very depressing to assume that they are all stupid, something else must be at play in their rational mind.

Trying to explain why so many people believe in Trump's lies is virtually impossible for a very simple reason: they themselves do not know why. Aside from the media echo chamber effect and the sentiment of belonging to a tribe, most people would struggle to explain precisely how and why they believe something nefarious occurred. And for a good reason: proofs, there are not any, as evidenced by the famous,

"Just give me five dead voters."

a desperate plea by Sen. Lindsey Graham pleading with Donald Trump's lawyers to give him a shred of evidence that there was election fraud.

This is why, if pushed to their last entrenchments, they would finally admit that the voting results did not seem right, that there was something fishy about it, that even though they cannot put their finger on it, they know that Trump could not have lost and that for sure it did not feel right. In other words, it is all a matter of feelings.

"I don't know it for a fact....I just know it's true " Real Time with Bill Maher.

Since feelings have never been accepted as evidence in a court of law, perhaps we should investigate the reasons leading to those feelings. Here are some probable causes:

- Trump's voters have been primed for voting fraud for a long time, since 2016 exactly. When you are repeatedly told that something will happen, the brain not only expects it but does not accept any possibility that it has not already occurred.

- Others did not get the memo that in a presidential election, it is common for the voting temporary results to flip overnight as mail-in-ballots start to be counted. Indeed, it must be disorienting to go to bed thinking that your candidate has won to wake up the next day, realizing that he has lost. This is called the *"Red Mirage"* and the *"Blue Shift."* Nothing nefarious about it; it happens frequently. For some people, such a shift in reality is inexplicable and unbearable to accept.

- But probably the main reason for the *"feeling"* to persist is the persistent bombardment of echoes validating your beliefs. When The Big Lie has been embedded in your daily life for such a long time, you inhale it as your natural breathing, even if it is polluted air. In the end, your brain becomes mush and hermetic to any new information that could put into question your reality. In essence, this psychological state is similar to the one experienced by some people going through police interrogations. After being presented with false proofs and allegations and repeatedly told that somebody has committed a crime, nearly 30 percent of suspects finally admit to a crime they did not commit.

Unfortunately, all those probable reasons mean diddly-squat to "*believers-by-feelings,*" and any attempt to rationalize their beliefs becomes counter-productive since, to them, the more you attempt to deny that the election was rigged, the more they see it as evidence it was.

Trump's "*believers-by-feelings*" should now adapt Bill Maher's line to:

"*The election was rigged. I don't know it for a fact....I just know it's true.* "

In America, truth has been replaced by feelings; no evidence is necessary. So, if I feel that you are an idiot and a complete moron, that is the truth.

LAST-DITCH EFFORT
TO RESTORE SANITY

Here is the last stupid question of this book:

How sure are you that your beliefs are your own?

Whatever happened in the history of this country, this period we are living in is unique. It is unprecedented in the sense that,

It is a paradox that never in the history of the world has so much information been made available to so many ignorant people without any positive results.

We could argue that this information overload is making man stupider instead of wiser, but it would be barking at the wrong tree. Man has always been stupider than wiser, and if you don't believe it, ask Eve's descendants. They will attest that man has rarely capitalized on the very reason he was cast out from the Garden of Eden: his newfound ability to acquire knowledge and be able to tell good from wrong.

It appears that nothing has evolved since the days when mass was only said in Latin, and translating the Bible into a language that everybody could understand would send you directly to "*Inquisition Central*" before being burned at the stake. In those "*good old days*" (for the Catholic Church), only the priest was allowed to be the intermediary between you and your God. First, to interpret his will and then to tell you what to do and think.[85] Today, the only difference is that new priests don't have to rely

---

[85] It took almost 20 centuries, at the 1965 Vatican II Council for the Roman Catholic Church to authorize mass being told in any other language than Latin.

on the faithful to attend mass to preach the Gospel of new Messiahs like Donald Trump. They flock on their own to the echo chambers that reaffirm their beliefs and be told what to do and think.

> *When you yell "Fire" in an echo chamber,*
> *do you expect the echo to return "Water"?*

Having dispensed with the last stupid question of the book, it becomes fitting to conclude this book with a last question that is at the core of all our experiences and actions:

WHAT IS OUR PURPOSE IN LIFE?

INDEED WHAT IS OUR PURPOSE IN LIFE?

At the outset of this book, it was stated that this book was a non-philosophical book that talks about philosophical issues. It is, therefore, fitting that an attempt be made to answer that particularly challenging question with a philosophical answer.

The American Constitution proclaims that all men are endowed with certain unalienable rights, including the pursuit of happiness. But what is happiness, and is it the only purpose in life? If happiness could mean different things to different people, we could at least agree on one thing: happiness is people. We are social animals who need to interact with others to construct our experiences and reality.

True, Jean-Paul Sartre was not completely wrong when he said, "*Hell is other people.*" The internet and social media have proved his point. Social media has provided new ways of constructing realities that have left us decoupled from each other. Things we used to believe in, our identity, and our convictions have been replaced by fear, uncertainties, and anxiety, affecting our ability to reason and leaving us exposed to dangerous influences without proper defenses.

Through the weaponization of fear, we have become more susceptible to being manipulated by unscrupulous political leaders who reshape our realities by conditioning us to prepare for the worst. Should a charismatic leader claiming to be the only one able to bring back the certainty and security of the good old days come along, all doubts are off. This has now become an "*us against them*" where neither lies nor truths are relevant, undermining in advance any attempt at dialogue.

So, what is your purpose in life? What legacy are you going to leave to the world?

Maybe the answer lies in Walt Whitman's O Me! O Life Poem.

Of eyes that vainly crave the light, of the objects mean, of the struggle ever renew'd,
Of the poor results of all, of the plodding and sordid crowds I see around me,
Of the empty and useless years of the rest, with the rest me intertwined,
The question, O me! So sad, recurring—What good amid these, O me, O life?

Answer:
That you are here, that life exists and identity,
That the powerful play goes on, and you may contribute a verse.
What will your verse be?

INDEED, WHAT WILL YOUR VERSE BE IN THE FACT THAT YOU ARE HERE, ALIVE, WITH A CHANCE TO CONTRIBUTE IN SOME SMALL WAY TO THE SUM OF HUMAN ENDEAVOUR AND HAPPINESS?

Think about that the next time you go voting.

A SOBERING PERSPECTIVE

First, a sobering perspective. In the great alignment of planets, whatever happens to America in 2024 is inconsequential. This might be a difficult fact to accept for a country that considers itself the center of the known universe. Still, our fate or our demise as a nation will not even register as a whisper in the great galactic wind of planets, a ripple in the ocean of time, and a coma in the long history books of humanity that great past civilizations started to write ions ago.

According to mainstream historians, recorded history started roughly 5,000 years ago, beginning with the Sumerian cuneiform script. This arbitrary starting date based on ancient writings from a Sumerian civilization in Mesopotamia poses an irreconcilable paradox for historians who would like us to consider their field of study as a science. Let's be candid: **History is not a science. It is an interpretation of events that took place in the past based on records, being factual, hypothetical, or geological**. If history were a science, then historians would apply the scientific approach to their research and hypothesis and let the evidence take them wherever it leads them. But historians do nothing of that sort. They pick and choose whatever fits their theories and discard evidence that contradicts the general consensus. The rationale for using Sumerian cuneiforms as the basis to determine the start of recorded human history is exactly a case in point. How could the same historians assure us that Sumerian cuneiform texts prove that the history of human civilization started roughly 3,000 years B.C. when the same scripts give them a detailed list of their kings, with names, duration, and place of the city-state where they reigned, and their decedents, spanning a period of 241,200 years, before and after the flood which incidentally they also relate in the epic poem of Gilgamesh[86]. An event in which, by the way, the Bible had no problem plagiarizing almost word for word.

Another example of historians' denial of evidence is the dating of the Great Sphinx on the Giza plateau facing the Great Pyramid. Recent research has put in evidence that the erosion at the base of the Sphinx was not due to normal erosion caused by sand storms but by a constant beating of water that occurred at least 10,000 years ago. This assessment would make the Great Sphinx a pre-deluge construction dating as far as 12,000 years ago, at the time of the melting of the last glaciation. Needless to say, this interpretation is unanimously rejected by most archeologists in Egyptology who, in their great majority, are Muslims and who believe that according to their religion, the world was created 6,000 years ago. That explains why the Egyptian government has a long history of denying and rejecting any permit for diggings or searches that would put in evidence the existence of a civilization prior to their own. What is worse is when the evidence is too big to ignore, the Egyptian government simply destroys it. But don't count on the mainstream Egyptologists to raise an eyebrow. **They are still clinging to their fantasy that pyramids were tombs when not a single mummy has ever been found in any of them**.

Fortunately, Sumerian cuneiform script and the poem of Gilgamesh are not the only writings that attest to a longer human history than generally accepted.

---

[86] From which the Bible story of Noah and the big flood is extracted. If we are discounting the story of Gilgamesh, which also relates the story of the Garden of Eden and Adam and Eve, then we should logically also label the Bible as a fable.

In France, history books teach every child that their ancestors, the Gauls, feared only one thing: not Caesar's legions but that the sky would fall on their heads. Such a statement was ordinarily interpreted as a metaphor that they were fearless until it was found out that many cultures from all corners of the earth have the same apprehension rooted in myths and folklore that could be summarized like this:

A long time ago, the sun deviated from its regular path, and time stood still. Earthquakes tore the earth, and the sky fell until a great wave of water engulfed the Earth. Survivors were then taught by people from the stars how to grow crops, build things, astronomy, and all the sciences needed to restart civilization.

This common theme has persisted for ions despite humanity's general amnesia that only remembers one thing: the Flood.

We now know that during the last ice age, the ocean floor was about 400 feet lower than today's shorelines. We also know that about 12,000 years ago, the earth went through a series of upheavals, such as the tilting of the earth's axis that some astronomical events could have caused. It is, therefore, conceivable that any civilization, even one more advanced than ours, could have been completely wiped without a trace.[87]

The Takeaway

After receiving this bite-size of knowledge, your first reaction might be to say," *OK, thanks for the info. It's good to know, but what do you want me to do with that?*"

---

[87] This is not completely true, since it is not uncommon to find possible human artifact or Oopart (out-of-place artifact) like pots, tools, bells or jewelry made of gold or metal alloy embedded in coal veins dating to at least 300 million years during the Carboniferous Period.

The point is that whatever importance we give to ourselves, our personal experiences are only relative to the context we give them. Thus, by widening the field of vision of our actions, the real question that we Americans should be asking ourselves is: How is my action impacting me, my family, my children, my environment, my city, my country, and the world**? This is not a philosophical question because, in 2024, your vote and actions after that will indeed make relevant all those hypothetical questions**. Thus, the importance of introducing at the end of this book some perspective on what we may perceive as a watershed moment, a tipping point, and an existential threat to America as we know it.

This brings us to the most important question raised by this book: Should you still delude yourself into the belief that Pinocchio-Trump is the Messiah who will save you from Armageddon of your world? Or, more explicitly, from a new world order led by children blood-sucking pedophile Democrats, from the "*Big Replacement*" of the white race, from socialism, communism, and from that Antichrist Joe Biden?

Answering the question is not a futile exercise in assessing your psychological ability to discern reality from what you want to believe as true, but the realization of who you truly are when faced with only yourself as a minuscule player in the developing story of the human race. **Indeed, you alone is insignificant, but millions like you are strong enough to create a resonance frequency wave that could alter one way or another matter and reality of the visible world**. All past civilizations understood the causality between intent and manifestation in one's reality. In other words, be careful of what you wish for because you do not know its unintended consequences. *"We are not makers of history. We are made by history."* Martin Luther King, Jr.

AFTERMATH

TO THE FALL OF THE AMERICAN EMPIRE

America is so far down the rabbit hole that maybe God will say, "This time, I am giving up. America does not deserve to be saved. I will just let the Devil and the golden statue[88] worshipers do their work."

---

[88] In reference to Trump Golden statue at CPAC

What goes up must come down, so the saying goes, and so do empires.

Rome was not built in one day, but its fall still took about 500 years, which in comparison seems puny to the more than 1,500 years for the Byzantine and Assyrian empires. The Persian Empire was the last one that stood the test of time, 869 years. But when it comes to the longevity of modern empires, they don't even compare.

The French and British empires lasted between 450 and 500 years, depending on when they started and ended. But their fall came quickly: 8 years for France and 17 years for Great Britain. The fall of the Soviet Union, which many thought to be eternal, came crashing down in only two years. **American hegemony that constituted the hay days of American imperialism started at the end of WWI until the end of the Vietnam War in 1975, a puny 30 years**. Of course, many may dispute what history is teaching us, but the fact that the United States remains to this day the first economic and military power in the world does not constitute an empire.

The fall of American democracy can be seen as the harbinger of the rapid decline of the West. **Without the leadership of America as a superpower, the model of Western liberal democracies is in peril of a slow and inevitable demise**.

Today, our republic is on its way to becoming a full-fledged banana republic. Not because we have problems unlike any other nation, but because, as described earlier, our issues are multiple and systemic, and **we do not have the will to solve them**.

We do not want to admit it, but even though we can hide the sun with one finger, that does not deny its existence. The same goes for our vision of ourselves and our denial that:

- Our model of democracy is in shambles because our house is divided.
- In all our attempts at nation-building, we have only managed to export our corruption and moral decay.
- We have been incapable of governing ourselves and addressing the numerous systemic problems that plague our society.
- We are the only democratic country that has more guns than inhabitants. That explains why, at 73% of homicides, we have the highest gun-related killing in the world.
- Despite our zillion-dollar military might, we have stumbled from one military debacle to the next and have not won a single war since WWII. Asymmetric wars don't care about how many aircraft carriers, stealth bombers, or even how many nuclear tactical warheads we can muster. The next warfare will be psychological, hybrid, and ideological, including the larger cyber-warfare threats.
- Our goals and ambitions are short term, the time of a presidential term, while centralized autocratic countries like China take the long view of their goals.
- Our political system is based on a zero-sum game, with only two parties where there can only be winners or losers, with no room for cooperation or compromises.
- We are the only country in the world with right-wing armed militias with rights entrenched in the Constitution.

- More than any other country, our lack of self-education has made us more susceptible to conspiracy theories, fake news, and opportunistic political lies.
- Because we are persuaded that socialism is a communist ideology, we do not believe in redistributing the nation's wealth to its citizens.
- Our sense of community, shared beliefs, respect, empathy, and core values are down the toilet.
- By any other democratic country standard, our voting system is arcane and undemocratic.
- We are in denial of fundamental life extinction threats and still believe that our planet has unlimited resources for us to spoil.

But the main two reasons that foretell our doom are

1. that half of America does not share the same planet and reality, and.
2. that a morally corrupt charismatic individual and his henchmen are determined not to fail a second time to hijack our democracy.

Finally, it is more than appropriate to conclude the somber perspective that our republic is going down the toilet by quoting in full a dire warning that is fully relevant as the next U.S. presidential election draws closer. If God is customarily referred to as such in the context of religion, it also applies to his substitutes in the case of the new sect we call Trumpism.

"Truly, whoever can make you believe absurdities can make you commit atrocities. If the God-given understanding of your mind does not resist a demand to believe what is impossible, then you will not resist a demand to do wrong to that God-given sense of

justice in your heart. As soon as one faculty of your soul has been dominated, other faculties will follow as well. And from this derives all those crimes of religion which have overrun the world."

François-Marie Arouet, known by his pen name as Voltaire

IN LIVING MEMORY

Like *"E pur si muove!"* (And yet it moves) attributed to Galileo Galilei when forced to recant his claim that the earth revolves around the sun, it did not matter whether you believed it or not. Still, it is an irrefutable fact, just like America's grand experiment with democracy was doomed to fail. But that, we already knew since John Adams, one of our founding fathers, warned us:

"Remember, democracy never lasts long. It soon wastes, exhausts, and murders itself. There never was a democracy yet that did not commit suicide."

Those prophetic words were a warning that we did not heed or believe, but here we are. Two hundred and forty-eight years later, this is exactly what we did: we committed collective political suicide and murdered our democracy ourselves.

In a divorce, when two parties can no longer live together, we call it *"irreconcilable differences."* The great irony of our nation is that the difference that divided us was the same: failure on both sides to face reality.

One side of America believed in things of which there was no proof. We call that faith, and it was the reason why religion was invented.

The other side refused to believe that we would deliberately forfeit the dearly paid[89] capability from God: the ability to think and tell good from evil.

It had been a long time coming, but if one single man had been able to accelerate our downfall, our commitment to truth and democracy could not have been very strong to begin with.

Our nation, which was born out of two Capital Sins, genocide and slavery, has never been able to get rid of that pervasive violence that defines us as people. We are a violent society, and as such, we are accustomed to killing things. Other than people, we killed our willingness to live together, hope, empathy, and truth. Truth is now dead; social media have accelerated its demise and, with it, our grand experiment in liberty and exchange of ideas: democracy.

So, if America was a person, what epitaph should be written on its tombstone in memory of a great moment deserving to be remembered?

---

[89] By being casted from Paradise

What should remain in our memory is a moment when America truly shined.

*Not in 1776 for the signing
of our Declaration of Independence*

*Not in 1945 when the Marines
raised Old Glory at Iwo Jima*

Not in 1964, when the Civil Rights Act was instated

Not in 1969 when we landed on the moon

*But in 1985, when forty-five of our most talented
music artists sang*

"WE ARE THE WORLD,"

This is the America we should remember.

PROUD, GENEROUS, TALENTED, UNITED, AND FREE

GOODBYE, AMERICA, WE HAD A GOOD RUN.

OUR SELFISHNESS AND LACK OF FAITH IN OURSELVES

FINALLY, DID US IN.

WE WERE NOT THAT EXCEPTIONAL AFTER ALL

POSTFACE

At first glance, one might wonder what weird notions like Oneness, doomsday, and philosophical questions like what is time, intelligence, or reality have to do with a book dealing essentially with politics and the future of Americans as people, especially since nobody can bring a definite answer to any of them?

But bringing up those topics at the close of an exposé on an existential threat like the future of our country is neither out of topic nor trivial since it may bring the reader to contemplate his personal responsibility in the great alignment of planets that regulate the fate of humankind.

ON ONENESS

"We experience ourselves, our thoughts and feelings as something separate from the rest. A kind of optical delusion of consciousness." Albert Einstein.

Throughout the course of human history, the only constant of civilization has been *"us against them."* From tribes to cities, nations, and empires, humanity has not ceased to fight, kill, and divide itself into characteristics that differentiate people as opposed to what unites them. Since ancient times, territories, language, beliefs, skin color, and religion have all been pretexts for annihilating the other. For a time, it was hoped that civilization would evolve thanks, among other things, to writing and printing and that the widespread diffusion of free information would push people to learn more about each other's differences and commonalities. After all, wasn't it the original goal and purpose of the internet and social media? Instead, now we can only ascertain that the contrary has happened, as we are today more divided than ever before. But why?

Throughout the world, many cultures, religions, philosophical and spiritual traditions share the same belief that everything in the universe is part of the same fundamental whole that unifies every living and unanimated thing. Now, even quantum physics appears to support the notion that, indeed, there is a fundamental oneness that connects everything that exists in the universe. So why are we in the West so slow to even contemplate what has been for centuries an evidence in the East?

Is it because our Judeo-Christian civilization, from which we source our morals, values, and logical thinking, is the source of our egocentrism? In the West, our belly-centric obsession with ourselves has rationalized and legitimized our dominance over any other living things, including other human beings. Christianity, may God forgive its sins, bears a considerable responsibility for the egocentric way we see ourselves. By placing man above all God's creatures, the Roman Catholic Church has effectively cut him off from the rest of all living things. That is the primary reason why today we consider the "*environment*" to be something to exploit without limits, since we reject any connection between nature and us humans. Let's just hope that before it is too late, we will realize that we need the Earth, but that the Earth does not need us.

In the rest of the world, many cultures have entirely different views of the world, reality, and our connection to all living things. For them, we are all connected and interdependent on each other. They all believe in a concept utterly foreign to Western thinking: "*Oneness,*" or the spiritual concept that we are all connected as part of some fundamental entity. Sure, at the molecular level, science has now put in evidence that all matter in the known universe has a common origin, stardust, created after red giant stars exploded eons ago on distant galaxies. But that scientific fact was already intuitively known by ancient people before modern science confirmed it. Indeed, ancient people, Native Americans, and everybody in the East believe that a "*spirit*" or a form of energy resides in all living and inanimate matter. We now know that everything vibrates, even rocks. On that belief, modern sciences have confirmed that everything in existence has a common origin and that even quantum physics is compatible with the notion that there is indeed a fundamental oneness of the universe of which we are all part. But part of what?

We now know that all matter, including ourselves, is made of atoms, even though nobody, in fact, knows exactly what an atom is. Atoms, protons, neutrons, electrons, quarks, gluons, etc., we know what they do. They have a charge, are in perpetual motion, and circle each other that is it. In other words, we know what they do, but do not know what they are. In other words, we know what matter *does* but not what it is. It is like saying that you know John because he is a doctor, and you know what doctors do. In short, we know diddly-squat about what we are, in fact, made of. So why not contemplate the notion that we are all ONE, whatever that means? That sure would change our optic on the world, who we are, and our connection to others.

"In our quest for happiness and the avoidance of suffering, we are all fundamentally the same and therefore equal. Despite the characteristics that differentiate us - race, language, religion, gender, wealth, and many others - we are all equal in terms of our basic humanity." — Dalai Lama

At this time, when America is more fractured and divided than ever, perhaps you should start wondering why you think your ideology is the best one and anybody who does not share your worldviews and beliefs deserves to die. This might have been a very Christian thing to do in the past, but today, just consider that if you and everybody else on this planet are one, the other is also you, and you are, in effect, killing yourself.

Besides, before trying to determine who or what we are, perhaps we should question our understanding of reality and time.

ON REALITY

"Reality is merely an illusion, albeit a very persistent one." Albert Einstein.

According to quantum physics, the evidence is in: everything is just energy. The scientific proof that everything is energy and that what we call reality isn't real validates the previous point that posits that all matter is just energy that vibrates to a specific wavelength. Perhaps we all live in a gigantic video game where nobody decides anything. After all, isn't it what we mean when we rationalize the bad things that happened to us by saying, *"It's God's will"*? So, are we the puppets, and God, the master puppeteer, pulling the strings?

Leaving aside the scientific, philosophical, or psychological aspects of this illusion, reality deserves a further investigation to understand on what basis people interpret reality for one important reason:

It will be on the interpretation of their reality that every American will vote in the next presidential election.

So, on what basis do people interpret reality?

From a clinical point of view, people who make it their business to answer such a question will, with confidence, advance the following reasons:

☐ **Beliefs and Values**: Individuals often interpret reality based on their existing beliefs and values. These can be shaped by religion, philosophy, or personal convictions.

☐ **Experiences**: Past experiences play a significant role in shaping how individuals perceive reality. Positive or negative experiences can influence their interpretations of similar situations in the future.

☐ **Cultural Background**: Cultural norms, traditions, and practices greatly impact how individuals perceive and interpret reality. What is considered acceptable or taboo varies across cultures and can influence perspectives.

☐ **Education and Knowledge**: Formal education and knowledge acquired through learning influence how individuals interpret reality. Education provides frameworks for understanding complex issues and can shape critical thinking skills.

☐ **Emotions and Psychological Factors**: Emotions can color perceptions of reality. For example, fear can distort perceptions of safety, while love can influence perceptions of others positively.

☐ **Biases and Prejudices**: Cognitive biases and prejudices can distort interpretations of reality. These biases stem from ingrained stereotypes, assumptions, or judgments about certain groups or situations.

With all those well-established reasons, new ones have now been added to an already varied list of triggers that determine someone's worldviews, social values, and reality. Such as:

☐ **Media and Information Sources**: The media and information sources individuals are exposed to can shape their interpretations of reality. Different media outlets may present information with varying perspectives, leading to diverse interpretations.

☐ **Social Influences**: Peer groups, social circles, and societal norms can influence how individuals interpret reality. Conformity to group beliefs or societal expectations may affect individual perspectives.

☐ **AI**, **fake news, conspiracy theories, lies, and demagogue politicians**. The reason why all those last reasons are bundled together is that they are all interconnected to achieve the same goal.

☐ Finally, because it is the most recent one and appears to be most prevalent in America: **feelings**.

Whatever the reality is, it seems that many Americans have surrendered any sense of reality to the way they feel. This emotional trigger is based on four things:

- Wishful thinking.
- False memories.
- Amnesia.
- Alternate reality.

Wishful thinking: This is the trigger mostly used by politicians promising anybody who has a reason to be dissatisfied that they are the solution to all their problems. This trigger is especially successful when used by demagogues and politicians surfing on the populist wave to reach their autocratic agenda. Wishful thinking distorts the decision-making of voters who prioritize their desires over a rational assessment of reality.

False memories: False memories are triggers that mostly affect conservatives in their conviction that everything was so much better before and that, consequently, nothing should change. The power of false memories is based on the fact that people tend to forget the bad times and only remember the way they wish they were.

Amnesia: Closely related to short-term memory, this trigger explains why voters keep re-electing bad people who are the heirs of leaders who either ran their country into the ground, murdered countless of their people, plundered the resources of the country as their personal property, and repress any form of liberty with violence. This has been the case in many countries that experience a bout with democracy to revert with nostalgia to the good old days when everything was decided for them, and they were dreaming of liberty.

Alternate reality: Of all the triggers that affect rational decision-making, alternate reality and alternate truth are the most powerful ways to manipulate people into thinking your way. It takes a very charismatic leader with a messianic message to achieve this miracle.

It is now a scientific fact: Quantum teleportation exists on Earth. Most political observers now accept the proof that Donald Trump acts as a Stargate Portal to a parallel universe where his supporters can have access to an alternate reality. The only remaining question is when they go there, will they ever come back?

ON TIME

What is time? For us Americans, the answer is obvious: time is money.

For most people, time is perceived in the way it flows. Time goes fast or slow, but always in one direction, from the past to the present and towards the future. When time goes fast, we say it flies, and we don't know where it went, as if time in reality goes somewhere. When time goes slow, we say that we are killing time, which is strange, considering that it is time that is killing us. But what about the present? Eastern tradition teaches us that we should live in the moment. Why? Did they already know what science has just discovered?

"People like us who believe in physics know that the distinction between past, present, and future is only a stubbornly persistent illusion." Albert Einstein.

In other words, time is just like reality, an illusion because the past, present, and future happen simultaneously. There is only one moment in time: the present.

It is a brief moment in time, but it is our time.

To paraphrase Stephen Hawking, the events that we are living in now are only important to us because they affect us directly today. This is not history for something that happened in the past nor a projection of something that might happen in the future. It is important to us because it is today that we are alive, responsible for our actions, creating a future for our children, and writing history. **In the grand scheme of things, whether America remains the democratic beacon to the world or becomes a banana republic is a non-event.** On the cosmic scale of the Universe, our 6,000 years of recorded history or the

60,000 years of non-recorded history counts for naught. Even the six million years it took our ancestors to evolve into the human race we recognize today barely register as a blimp and a ripple in the ocean of time.

This is why, regardless of how special we think we are or how unprecedented we believe our time is, it is hardly unique. Many empires have risen and fallen before, and the American empire or its hegemony on the world and perceived superiority is no exception.

Even if time is an illusion, this is the way we perceive it, and as such, it is your reality. Therefore, whether you participate in the fall of your country as a democracy or not, your actions today will be written in the history books, impact your present, and decide the future of your descendants.

Remember, your past, present, and future are all happening right at this moment. What are you going to do about it?

ON BELIEFS

Why do we believe what we believe?

This is a great question with multiple answers since the reason for our beliefs determines our mindset, our view of the world, what we consider as true, and ultimately, our reality.

There is nothing more personal than belief since it is altogether determined by a combination of cultural and societal Influences, personal values and ethics, personal experiences, family and upbringing, peer influence, religion and spirituality, psychological factors, education and learning, critical thinking and rationality, emotional needs, psychological factors, and of course, the big one: media and information sources. All those factors explain why the reasons for beliefs are complex, deeply rooted, and difficult to change once acquired.

Of course, in a perfect world, anybody should be able to believe whatever they want as long as they do not try to force their own beliefs on others. So, who cares if someone believes that the Earth is flat or that fairies are real as long as they don't blow up something to prove their point? However, in the real world, things are very different, and beliefs, especially when forced on others, could have dramatic consequences for the people subjected to them. In that department, religion has done more than its share of molding societies into beliefs geared at preserving privileges, impeding knowledge, controlling the mind, and enshrining the patriarchal dominance of men over women.

If today, more than 2.5 billion women and girls across 155 countries still face discriminating laws based on religious beliefs, mostly in Muslim countries, it is easy to forget that for millennia, Christianity had done just the same. Is it because the Church never got over the claim that Mary Magdalene was the first person to whom Jesus appeared after his Resurrection, as well as being the one Jesus loved the most over the Apostles, that they had to brand her a prostitute? Let us also not forget the Original Sin, for which women are still paying the price. But thank God if today in America, where women have far more equal rights than in most countries, we still can make jokes saying that:

If the Israelites had given more liberties to their women to speak, they would have asked someone for directions instead of wandering in the desert for forty years.

But let's not be complacent. Religious beliefs in the U.S. are on a warpath to revert hard-won civil rights for women. No doubt that the newly enacted anti-abortion laws in many States will have a significant impact on the voting preferences of many women.

Beliefs are also well at work in America, where there is not a single school board under siege from vocal parents who even use death threats to voice their opposition to the teaching of certain parts of our history, critical race theory, transgender issues, The Theory of Evolution, etc. And as always, politics are also starting to enter the fray, turning local school boards into ground zero of political discourse.

Beliefs have not only been a big impediment to the spreading of knowledge and progress, but have also been an active contributor to the eradication of ancient knowledge and know-how accumulated over centuries of human evolution. Indeed, if we were hard-pressed to choose among the many examples of ancient knowledge destroyed by the belief of intellectual and cultural superiority, there is at least one that still affects us today: the knowledge of medicinal plants. If beliefs of intellectual superiority had not eradicated thousands of years of practical knowledge, Big Pharma would not desperately be on the lookout for the next cure among plants, which would make them billions at little cost. How many thousands of women with knowledge of plants were burned at the stake as witches because they could cure better than traditional medicine could kill? The Americas had extensive knowledge of medicinal plants until the Spaniards made a bonfire of Aztec and Mayan Codices containing centuries of information about their history, science, and beliefs. If we are rediscovering the power of plants today, it is mainly because the Far East has been able to perverse traditional medical knowledge out of the reach of Christian missionaries.

But again, why talk about beliefs in a book that deals with the fall of America? The reason is in the close proximity of belief with faith. What they both have in common is that neither one requires any proof to be believed, which, when used in politics, has the power to move mountains or bring down the most powerful country on Earth.

Like two failed impeachments, the January 6th, 2021, Committee Report on the Capitol insurrection and four indictments for attempting to overturn voting results precisely demonstrate that nothing will convince Trump's supporters that he did anything wrong. That is what he keeps telling them, and this is what they believe. In all cases, there is no absence of proof that makes up their beliefs; it is just irrational blind faith in their leader, no matter what. In some respect, this is similar to cult members who, as a proof of faith in their leader, commit collective suicide on the promise of meeting Jesus or being picked up by a UFO before Armageddon. After all, this kind of faith is well documented, especially after WWII, when thousands of ordinary German citizens committed suicide rather than live in a world without their Fuhrer. For the others, it took seeing their cities reduced to rumbles, atrocities committed in deportation camps, and less than human soldiers (Russians) take their capital to start doubting that they may not be the master race after all. His is the same kind of blind faith that leads a terrorist to blow himself up to kill unbelievers with the promise to be met in Paradise by 72 virgins.

It remains to be seen if Trump's unconditional supporters will commit collective suicide if their Messiah ends up the rest of his life in the slammer.

When your tribe's beliefs are under attack, even if you do not share them, unless you are a strong-willed individual, it will be hard not to defend them.

ON INTELLIGENCE AND STUPIDITY

We should find a way to harness stupidity to produce clean energy. It is cheap, renewable, and plentiful.

Here is a not-so-stupid question:

Can you be intelligent and stupid at the same time?

Although there is no consensus on what intelligence admittedly is, it is generally accepted that it entails the cognitive ability to think, reason, understand, plan, create, be self-aware, learn, do critical thinking and problem-solving, among many other things. We believe we are at the top of all the animal kingdoms because, in our Judeo-Christian civilization, God gave us dominion over all living things to use as we wish.

Stupidity, however, is not so easy to define. To simplify things, we could just say that stupidity is the absence of intelligence. Fortunately, we do not require all the cognitive abilities identified above to be recognized as intelligent; otherwise, most people would be classified as functionally stupid. A more scientific definition would be an incapacity to connect the dots, process the information, and draw the right conclusion. In this case, we must differentiate between a stupid person as a personality trait and a stupid act that unfortunately affects us all. Finally, there is the theory of stupidity, which, like the Big Bang or the Evolution theory, relies on a series of hypothetical laws to prove their validity. Among the most important:

- Stupidity is universal and uniformly distributed. It means that, like male/female, the distribution is equally distributed, regardless of social, gender, race, or political color. This may explain why, when people vote, they are almost equally split between those who want to be free and those who wish to remain slaves.
- A stupid person is one who harms others and also himself while incurring no gain for himself.
- Ignorance or overconfidence pushes people to do stupid things by taking risks of any kind, although they lack the skills or knowledge necessary to face them.
- People, the ones who know little but profess to know a lot, can be said to be truly stupid. In this department, we all know at least one.
- Most commonly, out of laziness, wishful thinking, short-term interests, or adverse to change for ideological

reasons, stupid people tend to do nothing to prevent a situation from going from bad to worst.

One thing scientists have not yet determined is whether stupidity is genetically predetermined or if education can root out stupidity not merely by teaching facts but by teaching people how to attain facts and how to discern a good source of information from a bad one. Given the importance of social media in how we consume information, we are far from winning.

But why talk about intelligence and stupidity in a book about the fall of America and its ineluctable crash against the wall of stupidity? It is because the cause of this predictable event is not solely due to the degradation of our society as Americans, but more generally as the shortcoming of the human race's cognitive abilities. In short, we can almost excuse ourselves by saying that we were wired that way and that acting stupidly is not our fault. Now, instead of blaming the Devil, we can excuse ourselves by saying, "*My genes made me do it; stupidity is in my DNA.*"

Man is said to be God's greatest achievement. The reality is that if man were a product, it would have been recalled a long time ago for manufacturing defects. It is true that, indeed, God himself realized his mistake and tried to destroy his creation by sending a universal deluge to eradicate all humans. Unfortunately, God being God, he could not help himself to give humanity a second chance by allowing Noah and his family to escape the apocalypse. Since then, God has probably realized that man was perfectly capable of annihilating himself from the surface of the earth, so he figured, why bother?

In our examples of human intelligence superiority over the rest of the animal kingdom, we routinely malign birds as the epitome of lack of intelligence and stupidity. Being qualified to have a "*Bird brain*" is not a compliment. But we should take it as one. First of all, birds are the last descendants of dinosaurs that were wiped out of the earth's surface some 65 million years ago. We should all wish to be like birds. Of course, we could argue that all the physical and cognitive feasts performed by birds are wired and the results of millions of years of evolution. Unfortunately, as far as the human race is concerned, despite its increase in size, no significant brain changes have taken place since Homo sapiens started to walk upright on their two legs, and waiting for Darwin's natural selection to take its course until we become less stupid is a losing proposition. To this day, since Cain and Abel, and despite the veneer of civilization, humans have never ceased to look for a better and more efficient way to kill each other.

If humans were not stupid, they would not sleepwalk through predictable outcomes that menace their very existence. Yes, we know how to connect the dots and predict future outcomes. This is where intelligent people would act to prevent the prediction from becoming a reality. But what do we do? We collectively sweep the problems under the rug and don't think about them because, of course, if you do not think about them, they do not exist.

Let's take climate change as an example. Of course, between the melting of the ice caps and all the glaciers throughout the world, the burning of California, global rising temperatures, and droughts, climate change deniers are on their last leg. But what are we doing about it? Governments throughout the planet are slapping themselves on the back, congratulating each other for committing to a carbon-neutral economy by the year 2050. Seriously? This is exactly what stupid people would do.

In the meantime, industries, transport, and intensive agriculture are spewing poison into the atmosphere as if there is no tomorrow, which is about to become true.

It would be incorrect to say that we do nothing except for the fact that when we decide to do something, we tackle the problem with more stupid solutions. For air pollution, for instance, we usually point to cars as the source of most of our respiratory problems for spewing nanoparticles of metal that clog our lungs and arteries. However, another form of transportation has flown unnoticed under the radar, and it has more dangerous consequences: sea freight fuel used by freight container cargo ships. Each one of those ships produces between 3,000 to 3,500 ppm (part per million) of sulfur dioxide. For comparison purposes, cars in the European Union are limited to 15 ppm of nanoparticles. Studies have now revealed that a single of those ships produces the equivalent of 50,000,000 cars, so just 20 of those ships produce more nanoparticle pollution than all the cars in the world. Considering that more than 60,000 cargo containers plight the ocean, addressing the car problem is obviously not the solution. In the meantime, the European Union will ban all fossil-fuelled cars by the year 2035 to be replaced with electric cars. Of course, nobody has been asking where all the electricity needed to power all those cars will come from. Perhaps from the coal-power plants that Germany has been forced to re-open after foolishly ditching their nuclear power plants? Could Europeans be so stupid?

Soon, overfishing will result in the fact that by the year 2050, there will be more plastic than fish in the world's oceans.

- Ten million tons of plastic are dumped in our oceans annually.
- Less than 10% of all plastic is recycled.
- Annually, approximately 500 billion plastic bags are used worldwide. More than one million bags are used every minute.
- On average, it takes between 200 years and forever for plastic to degrade.
- Without exception, all marine life has been contaminated by plastic pollution, and by way of consequences, us.

And what are we doing about it?

It has been estimated that China has at least twenty-seven hundred distant-water fishing ships. Those are ships that stay at sea for months, depleting the oceans 24/7 from all living creatures on a scale not seen since an asteroid killed off 80 percent of all life on planet Earth 65 million years ago.

Large bottom trawler boats continue to drag the ocean floor and destroy all marine life while at the same time discarding and rejecting close to 56% of their catch. Of course, restricting areas where fishing is allowed would go a long way toward making commercial fishing sustainable, but this is what intelligent people would do. With only 7 percent of the world's oceans protected, we have a long way to go.

With nearly 8 billion people on the planet to feed, we should seriously start thinking about how we produce our food. It is a fact that most of the corn and cereal produced in the world are not grown to feed people, but cattle. Regarding meat, in terms of efficiency, we are using 25 calories to produce one calorie of beef. The ratio for pork is 15 to 1 and 1 to 9 for chicken. Any way you slice it, it is like spending $25 to make one dollar, a rather stupid proposition. But that is what we have been doing forever, and if the meat industry has anything to say about it, things will not change anytime soon. In addition, it has been estimated that most of what we produce is thrown away. Of course, plant-based protein would be a solution, but until the three main criteria that firstly concern consumers, price, taste, and convenience are addressed, nothing will happen anytime soon.

On this planet, water is the source of life and energy. On average, we are composed of between 50 to 65 % of water. So, it is easy to say that water is essential to our survival. If it is a fact that 75% of the earth is covered with water, **only about less than 1 percent of all water is fresh and available for human consumption**, which should make it a rare element that we should protect and cherish as if our life depended on it. Almost all the freshwater (excluding glaciers) available is groundwater, which provides approximately 40% of drinking water. Groundwater or aquifers are regularly recharged by atmospheric water in the form of rain or snow, which until now have served us well. But that was the past since we discovered that because of *"forever chemicals,"* even rainwater is now unfit for human consumption. This discovery means there is no longer a place on Earth where rainwater is safe to drink, with life-and-death consequences for millions of people who rely on rainwater as their unique source of survival. The chemicals of concern are perfluoroalkyl and poly-fluoroalkyl substances. They are highly resistant to degradation and can persist in the environment or human body for years and sometimes infinitely. As a palliative, we are now forced to drill deeply into the earth for aquifers containing fossil water formed some 40,000 years ago[90]. This is what stupid people would do: kicking the can down the road instead of implementing conservation policies to conserve a unique resource that is only partially renewable.

The latest COVID-19 epidemic has alerted us, humans, to how susceptible and exposed we are to the tiniest of deadliest of all organisms: viruses. If this time, science has, like the U.S. cavalry who comes just in time to rescue us from an epidemic potentially more severe than **the 1918 Spanish Flu that killed more than 500 million people worldwide**, an underrated, equally deadlier pathogen is menacing humanity: bacteria.

Even though bacteria are, in general, less deadly than viruses, the leading cause for alarm is that the world only has less than a handful of antibiotics left to combat them, especially due to the emergence of "*superbugs*" such as MRSA and *C. difficile*[91] that have become resistant to any antibiotic left on the planet. What this also means is that soon, there won't be any cure for potentially deadly infections such as Anthrax, Tetanus, Leptospirosis, Tuberculosis, Pneumonia, MRSA infections, E. Coli, Meningitis, Botulism, Cholera, Gonorrhea, Syphilis, and the Bubonic Plague.

The first question we should ask is why antibiotics are no longer effective. For this, there are two answers:

1. Thanks to doctors, Big Pharma's drug pushers, who have overprescribed the use of antibiotics, bacteria have acquired a quasi-immunity to most generic antibiotics.

---

[90] In the United States, the Ogallala or High Plains Aquifer sits under 450,000 km^2 of 8 states and is one of the largest freshwater deposits in the world.
[91] According to the CDC, at least 2.8 million people become infected with pathogens that are resistant to antibiotics and at least 35,000 people die as a direct result of these infections each year in the U.S.

The CDC has estimated that approximately 50% of outpatient antibiotic prescriptions are unnecessary.

2. Antibiotic use in animal feeds and farming is widespread in the U.S. It is used by the majority of chicken, pork, and beef producers not to prevent diseases, but to promote animal growth. Estimates on antibiotics given to livestock range from 17.8 million to 24.6 million pounds, compared with around 3 million pounds used by humans in medicine. So here you have it: profits come before human health.

Why should we worry? Because the World Health Organization predicts that worldwide death rates from drug-resistant infections will rise from 700,000 per year to 10 million by 2050, making them the leading cause of death in humans, and because little research is done to find new antibiotics.

In the U.S., any research in this field has been impeded by the numerous regulatory hurdles and roadblocks imposed by the Food and Drug Administration as well as the low return on investment by Big Pharma companies for a drug typically prescribed for just a few days as opposed to drugs used to treat lifelong or chronic disease. For those two main reasons, the U.S. has lost virtually all of its industrial base to make generic antibiotics and generic drugs such as penicillin, which are now made in China. If, for whatever reason, the U.S. enters into conflict with China, the latter may, in retaliation, cut off supplies altogether. We then will not be able to provide chemotherapy for cancer treatment or treatments for Alzheimer's, HIV/AIDS, diabetes, Parkinson's, and epilepsy, nor provide anti-depressants and birth control pills to Americans. The consequence of our stupidity is that medicines can now be used as a strategic and tactical weapon against the United States.

It is now time to explain what all the examples of stupid human responses to major global challenges have to do with the fall of

American democracy. What global warming, the pollution of plastic in our oceans, the rarity of drinkable water, antibiotic-resistant bugs, and the fall of American democracy have in common is that in all cases, we know the facts and have used our intelligence to predict the probable outcome. What would make a difference is how we will respond to the most existential challenges our country has ever faced: the upcoming 2024 presidential election.

We know the undisputable facts:
- The Republican Party has a long tradition of fascism and is about to fulfill its long-time aspiration.
- The Trump Party has become a sect.
- Trump has never been coy about his authoritarian tendencies and has proved it many times through his actions and his open love for dictators.
- The Trump Party has put in place state legislation and the legislators who will decide the validity of the votes and who wins the election.
- The next time that Trump asks to find him votes, the answer will be, "*Yes sir, how many do you need.*"
- If replacing valid ballots with fake votes did not work the last time for Trump, the next time will be different.
- Should any election challenges reach the Supreme Court, the Trump Party may be assured that the Court will rule in his favor.
- Should legal challenges to voting results don't go the way they should, an army of "*patriots*" is willing, able, and ready for an armed insurrection.
- America is not leading the anti-democratic movement led by populist political parties. Still, it is following the trend led by countries like Brazil, Hungary, Poland, India, Turkey, and Indonesia, which had a Constitution modeled on ours or one of their former colonial powers.

For all of the above facts, the die is almost cast on the final outcome that would see the end of the American democracy as we dreamed it. Of course, the intelligent thing to do would be to bridge our differences and try to work together towards common aspirations, moral values, and reality. But we also know what stupid people would do, and judging from the global challenges earlier described, the proposition that they would act differently is merely wishful thinking.

90 SECONDS TO MIDNIGHT

"Mankind is not likely to salvage civilization unless he can evolve a system of good and evil which is independent of heaven and hell." George Orwell

90 seconds to midnight is the time left on the Doomsday Clock[92] before humanity blows itself up into oblivion. When the clock

---

[92] https://thebulletin.org/doomsday-clock/

reaches midnight, it is game over for all of us and most living things on our only home, planet Earth.

Since 1947, at the onset of the first atomic bomb, atomic scientists across the world have kept checks on humanity's potential to annihilate itself.

To come up with this clock, anything from nuclear threats to bioterrorism, artificial intelligence, genetic engineering, cyber-attacks, climate change, weapon development, unchecked scientific and technical advances, the militarization of space, energy, diplomacy, politics, etc. In short, anything that could take us back to before the Stone Age is taken into consideration.

As a sidebar piece of information, recent studies have estimated that within the next 50 years, whether by intent, accident, or malice, humanity will drive itself to oblivion.

In the meantime, welcome to the SIXTH mass extinction.

- Nearly half of the 177 mammal species surveyed lost more than 80% of their distribution between 1900 and 2015.
- Of 3000 species, 50% of individual animals have been lost since 1970.
- Current rates of extinction are between 1000-10,000 times higher than previous extinction rates.
- The current rate of vertebrate genus extinction exceeds that of the last million years by 35 times.
- 48% of species have declining populations, and just 3% have rising populations.
- Up to 1 million species are threatened with extinction, and some could be lost within decades.

But why worry about that? How is humanity going to feed itself if birds, insects, and bees are gone to pollinate plants?

The last mass extinction occurred after an asteroid struck the Earth roughly 66 million years ago. Still, as humans, we are perfectly capable of doing the same thing in less than half a century, or even sooner, if we create our own apocalypse.

But what if there is evidence that a nuclear apocalypse has already happened before? Could we learn from history not to repeat it?

Very ancient Hindu texts written in Sanskrit relate with great detail to a mythological war in the sky that led to an Armageddon of their world.

"I am Death, the destroyer of worlds," [93] Bhagavad Gita.

"A single projectile charged with all the power in the Universe...An incandescent column of smoke and flame as bright as 10,000 suns, rose in all its splendor...it was an unknown weapon, an iron thunderbolt, a gigantic messenger of death which reduced to ashes an entire race," The Mahabharata, 6500 BCE.

In this epic poem, flying sky chariots and terrifying weapons brighter than the sun were used to obliterate entire cities with all their inhabitants. Western scholars routinely dismissed such stories as fabulations of ancient people with an unbridled imagination until recent discoveries wiped the smirk off their faces.

Archeologists have recently unearthed in Rajasthan, India, an ancient city where evidence shows that an atomic blast dating back **8,000 to 12,000 years** destroyed most buildings and probably a half million people. Researchers estimate that the

---

[93] Also quoted by **Dr. J. Robert Oppenheimer C**hief scientist of the Manhattan Project that led to the first atomic bomb.

nuclear bomb used was about the size of the ones dropped on Japan in 1945. Just like the Mahabharata[94] distinctly describes it, a catastrophic blast that we can now identify as a nuclear blast. The radiation is still so intense that the Indian government has cordoned off the entire region.

However, India is not the only country where evidence of nuclear obliteration took place. As related by many ancient cultures throughout the world, a great war between the gods took place in the sky, taking humanity back to the Stone Age. Ancient cities that have literally been vitrified can be found not only in India but also in Ireland, Scotland, France, Turkey, and other places. If there could be an interpretation for the vitrification of forts, there is no logical explanation for the vitrification of entire cities except for an atomic blast.

So, we were not the first ones to discover nuclear technology. Why do I care?

Of course, in our unfettered belief that our modern society is the apex of human civilization, it is understandable that we don't give such considerations a second thought. Still, we should, and this is why:

For starters, we should pause at the evidence that humans are stupid enough to annihilate and drive themselves back to the Stone Age. So, should we stop worrying about what will happen to our children and grandchildren if we are all doomed? Unless if, and that is a big "IF," we stop deluding ourselves that our

---

[94] The *Mahābhārata* is the longest epic poem ever written. With 1.8 million words, it is roughly ten times the length of the Iliad and the Odyssey combined.

beliefs are the only possible truth or reality and start learning from the past.

"Everyone who wants to know what will happen ought to examine what has happened: everything in this world in any epoch has its replicas in antiquity."
Niccolò Machiavelli.

Learning from the past? For starter, which past?

In contradiction to some people who, contrary to evidence, still insist that history started 6,000 years ago, **modern archeology has carbon-dated artifacts and civilizations that go past before the last earth's glaciation, the big meltdown, and the universal flood**. Along with this standard chronology, all past civilizations attest that they owe their knowledge to the "*gods*" who came from the stars. Of course, such claims are easy to dismiss until you enter into the details of such "*myths.*"

One such myth was told by the Dogon, a tribe of about 300,000 people in Mali, West Africa, when they were studied in 1930 by Marcel Griaule, a French anthropologist who studied ancient myths.

According to the Dogon, they are custodians of a very ancient tradition that they were visited by people from the stars around 3,200 B.C.. Their claim is not any different from many native people around the globe, with one exception: their knowledge of astronomy, of the Orion Belt Constellation and the Sirius Star System, cannot be comprehended since it pre-dates modern technology by thousands of years and far exceeds the capabilities of the Dogon Tribes.

The Dogons gave him specific information on where the race of people who came to visit them ions ago came from. They call them "*Nommos*," and according to the Dogon, the Nommos lived on a planet that orbits other stars of the Sirius system, that they are ugly amphibious beings resembling mermaids, a description that matches many other ancient cultures such as the Sumerians, the Egyptians, and some Native American tribes.

They also revealed that Sirius A, which was only discovered in 1862 and is the brightest star in our night sky, has a far dimer companion star, making it a binary system.

Sirius's companion star is invisible to the naked eye, and we did not know that it even existed until the late 1920s. The companion star that scientists now call "*Sirius B*" was only discovered and photographed by a large telescope in 1970. The Dogon also explained that Sirius A orbits the companion star on a 50-year elliptical orbit, that Sirius B is extremely heavy, and that it also rotates on its axis. All that information turned out to be accurate. It was confirmed as recently as 2005 by the Hubble space telescope, which also confirmed that Sirius B is a white dwarf with a density of approximately one metric ton for one tablespoon (2204 lb) of material. Put another way, a 150-pound person would weigh 50 million pounds on its surface. The Dogon also refers to a third star in the system that has not been discovered yet.

The Nommos also gave the Dogon some interesting information about our own solar system: Jupiter has four major moons, Saturn has rings, and the planets orbit the sun. These are facts that were only discovered thousands of years after Galileo invented the telescope. It should also be noted that the same interest in Sirius appears in Babylonian, Accadian, Sumerian, and Egyptian myths. Of course, we can all act like the mainstream scientists who conveniently dismiss and ignore anything that does not fit the official consensus because if you don't talk about it, it just does not exist. But some other facts are just as hard to ignore.

More recent studies into Dogon's mythology have revealed more unsettling evidence about their knowledge of the cosmos and astrophysics.

Their understanding of how matter is formed, including chaos theory, wave and vibration, and the existence of sub-atomic particles, is compatible with our current scientific knowledge. Moreover, they believe that matter has three levels of reality and that our world is not one of them and is an illusion (also posited by Einstein).

They also believe in a cosmology close to our multi-universes and String theories that we are still trying to make sense of. But that is not all.

All ancient civilizations, from China, India, Sumer in Mesopotamia, Egypt, and Mesoamerica, have what we call Long-Count calendars[95]. Contrary to our modern calendars, Long-Count calendars are cyclical and span hundreds or thousands of years.[96] This implies that past civilizations had a precise understanding of the Precession of the Equinoxes[97] created by the gradual shift in the orientation of the earth's axis of rotation in a cycle that moves backward through all the twelve

---

[95] Ancient Hindu calendars even have a cycle that span 306,720,000 years

[97] In the West discovery of the precession of the equinoxes is attributed to the 2nd-century-BC Greek astronomer Hipparchus.

signs of the Zodiac in precisely 25,772 years. That knowledge presupposes that the ancients knew:

- that the earth is not a perfect sphere but an oblate geoid flattened at the poles and swollen at the equator because of centrifugal forces. This knowledge is important because, without it, the earth would not tilt on its axis like a gyroscope.
- that at some point in time, the travels of the Earth in our galaxy will come back exactly to the same place it started in the sky.
- that the ecliptic of the earth was divided into twelve equal zodiacal arcs of 30° each[98].
- that the point vernal of the equinoxes, the time of year the Sun is in a given constellation, moves backward in the Zodiac and arrives a fraction of a second early every year, the reason why it is called "*precession.*"
- that they had computed the mean diameter of the earth, which was very close to the actual 12,742 km.
- the ancients had very precise instruments to measure the planetary precession shift, which amounts to a rotation of the ecliptic plane of 0.47 seconds of arc per year or at a rate equal to 1 degree every 72 years.
- that you had to have experienced a complete cycle of the Zodiac of 25,772 years before knowing that the earth's axis would point back where it started to the exact same stars in the sky.

---

[98] The origin of the Zodiac is attributed to Babylonians because they refer to it in their writings even though we know that the. Babylonian techniques of observational measurements were in a rudimentary stage of evolution. So obviously, they did not invent it.

All that knowledge ions before 1633 when the Inquisition of the Roman Catholic Church was still forcing Galileo Galilei to recant his theory that the Earth moves around the Sun and at a time when it was universally accepted that the Earth was flat.

When you consider that during a single lifetime, a person went from horse and buggy to landing on the moon and AI, think where humanity would be today without the more than 1400 years of religious obscurantism, intolerance, and mind control. After all, it took the Catholic Church 16 centuries before allowing you to read the Bible in English without being burned at the stake. And it did not do it voluntarily but was forced to by the publication of the King James Bible in 1611.

The takeaway

You must be wondering yourself: great, good to know, but what does all that have anything to do with me?

Nothing if you consider the preceding as a lot of bunk and that QAnon's claims are more believable than ancient myths.

Everything, if you entertain the possibility that time is cyclical and that history that we usually ignore is bound to repeat itself. It should also make you aware that,

1. America is not exceptional,
2. In the great book of history, the fall of American democracy is rather inconsequential,
3. It is up to us to decide if our actions, or lack of them, will precipitate the next apocalypse.

America's foes are numerous and determined. Some have biological and nuclear capabilities, with rogue leaders who would not think twice before pushing the nuclear button if faced with an existential threat. Because of China's determination to bring back Taiwan under communist rule, an armed conflict between the U.S. and China is not only possible, it is inevitable. When this happens, who do you want to be in control of America's nuclear button? There was a reason why U.S. General Mark Milley, chairman of the Joint Chiefs of Staff in the Trump Administration, called China's counterparts, promising to warn them first if he were ordered to attack. Apparently, the Chinese feared that Trump might attack Beijing in his final months in office.

But even if a near-future military confrontation with China does not materialize, there are plenty of reasons to dread the future. The U.S. is spending 100 billion to build a new weapon of mass destruction in the form of a nuclear missile 20 times more powerful than the atomic bomb dropped on Hiroshima. Do we veritably need the capability to blow up the planet 100 times over instead of 10? Apparently, yes, if we want to catch up with China and Russia, who have already built hypersonic missiles capable of reaching close to ten times the speed of sound, or 7672 mph, that can change course in flight, and which are virtually impossible to detect and intercept before they reach their targets. Those new developments alone will surely advance the Doomsday Clock by a few seconds.

Of course, if Dear Leader Trump makes his second Coming, that surely would please Evangelical Christians who would be ecstatic at the thought of advancing the date of Armageddon and the Rapture, that End of Time belief in which believers would rise *"in the clouds, to meet the Lord in the air."*

This is all fine and dandy if you are a believer, but is it fair to the billions of other people who believe in a different God?

Viewed from that angle, America's democracy apocalypse seems consequential, at least for us. Because If America's democracy falls, economic and geopolitical consequences will be as unpredictable as unfathomable.

So, what can you do about it? Just consider that you might have a role to play in this doomsday scenario.

As a citizen of the world's first economic and military power, your responsibility is that American politics does not move the minute hand of the Doomsday Clock closer to a zombie Apocalypse.

Here is an anti-B.S. that works all the time. On a clear summer night, just contemplating the open sky that displays our Milky Way Galaxy will make you realize how petty, small, and insignificant the ramblings of a sad clown like Donald Trump truly are.

POST SCRIPTUM

"The longer I live, the more convinced am I that this planet is used by other planets as a lunatic asylum."
George Bernard Shaw.

One indication that our generation might be living extraordinary times is that finally, after more than 75 years of denials and cover-ups, the U.S. government, along with others across the planet, is coming clean in acknowledging the possibility that we might not be alone in the Universe after all. That is exactly what the ancients have always affirmed. That people from the stars came and went, promising to return[99]. Maybe they have never left, and it is only now that our technology is sufficiently advanced for not to interpret what we saw as "*gods*" descending from heaven but as the evidence of more advanced beings riding on a technology that we could not comprehend.

Maybe the "*aliens*" are just watching us from afar in what could be for them, nothing more than a big experiment or simple curiosity. After all, we are doing the same thing when watching a colony of termites. We may find their social organization interesting, but what need would we have to interfere in whatever they do?

Finally, interestingly enough, one of the most controversial books of the Ancient Testament that did not make the cut into the new one was the Book of Enoch. The early Christian censors banned it as *Apocrypha* (the hidden knowledge)

---

[99] That is exactly what the Mayans believed when they saw the first Spanish Conquistadors landing on their shores. Unfortunately, instead of knowledge and civilization, the Spaniards were real humans that could bring them only one thing: Apocalypse.

explicitly because it refers to the "*watchers*" and to Enoch as being taken in space above the Earth.

In the Book of Enoch, the Watchers are angels dispatched to Earth to watch over the humans.

Until an alien spacecraft lands in front of the White House with the message "Take me to your leader," humanity will continue to fuck up and perpetuate the great cycle of time that always goes back to where it started. Alternatively, the Alien might just say the equivalent of "Beam me up, Scotty, there is no obvious sign of intelligence on this planet" and take off.

QUOTES

From the Author

"We should find a way to harness stupidity to produce clean energy. It is cheap, renewable, and plentiful."

"The ultimate moron is someone who is proud of something for which he does not deserve any credit, like his gender, his place of birth, or the color of his skin."

"Shit never happens at random. It is just a failure of the imagination to forecast the future and accept the possibility that the worst may happen."

"It is now a scientific fact: Quantum teleportation exists on Earth. Most political observers now accept the proof that Donald Trump acts as a Stargate Portal to a parallel universe where his supporters can have access to an alternate reality. The only remaining question is whether they go there. Will they ever come back?"

"Without knowledge of geography and historical facts, you are not entitled to have an opinion to judge people's behavior without understanding the context and the circumstances. So until you go and educate yourself, shut the fuck up!"

"Even if time is an illusion, this is the way we perceive it, and as such, it is your reality. Therefore, whether you

participate in the fall of your country as a democracy or not, your actions today will be written in the history books, impact your present, and decide the future of your descendants."

"Dispensing insults is the hallmark of people with low intelligence who need to lower others in order to raise themselves above the dirt level where they belong."

"To say that half of Trump's supporters are complete idiots would not be politically correct, so let me rephrase my statement: half of Trump's supporters are not complete idiots."

"The mother of all ironies is that for centuries Christians have vilified, despised, hated and murdered Jews indiscriminately while at the same time adoring Jesus as their God, a Jew."

"Hey, America, if you don't want to be compared to a banana republic, stop acting like one."

"Stop asking God what to do; that is why he gave you free will."

"When you do the sum of all fears, only three pose an existential threat to America. AI, Donald Trump, and stupid people. And if we do not eliminate two of them, the third one will eliminate us."

"It is a paradox that never in the history of the world has so much information been made available to so many ignorant people without any positive results."

"In America, we believe in three things: God, money, and bullshit, and not necessarily in that order."

"Happiness is not knowing what you don't know."

"If you are an Evangelical Christian and believe in the power of prayers, stop praising the Lord for sending you Donald Trump as the antichrist who will bring you Armageddon and the Rapture, where you will meet Jesus in the sky. Instead, stop being selfish and pray for America instead. It needs everybody, even you."

"To those who still believe that God created man in his image and are denying the theory of evolution, please explain why God had a tail and why humans lost it?"

"We Republicans don't care about democracy or the sharing of governance. Our only mission until we achieve complete power has three goals: obstruct, obstruct, and obstruct."

"In America, truth has been replaced by feelings; no evidence is necessary. So, if I feel that you are a complete idiot, that must be true."

"It would be unfair to label all Trump's supporters as morons and complete idiots. After all, we do not judge

the people that a hypnotist makes flap their arms thinking there are chickens."

"It is an error to compare Trump to Hitler. Yes, they both share many similarities and sized power by being democratically elected. But at least Hitler was articulate."

"America is unique indeed. It is the only country in the world where the more a politician is a sleazebag, the more he is popular."

"The simplest way to compare France and America is that the French believe that they live in Hell while living in Paradise. For Americans, it is the other way around. Never mind that they are both wrong since Hell and Paradise are subjective and may not exist outside of being a figure of speech."

"In the final analysis, what if the fall of America was simply just due to an increasing shortage of good men? Men who do not confuse their wishes for reality, men who do not equate compassion with a lack of virility, and men capable of admitting when they are wrong. In short, men that women would like to see as the father of their children as a model of the moral values you expect from a human being."

"The modern definition of a banana republic applies to a country incapable of governing itself. On that

criterion alone, America has already become a de facto banana republic."

"*Contrary to what pundits are saying, our republic is not on the verge of becoming a banana republic; we are already there.*"

"*Those who still believe that America will never become a banana republic are like the Jews after the fall of the Weimar Republic, deluding themselves. It will happen, and sooner than you think. Those who had the foresight to face reality got out in time, for the others…..*"

"*Anyone who wants to know what will happen in the future only has to look in the rear-view mirror.*"

"*You know that the internet has turned the world on its head when a robot asks you to prove that you are not a robot.*"

"*You should always pay attention to what narcissists and psychopath leaders say because, contrary to most politicians, they usually do what they say.*"

"*An election says more about the people who do the voting than the people they elect.*"

"*Collective amnesia is the only rational explanation for voters who keep re-electing politicians and leaders who only care about themselves.*"

"Democracy is not unlike life insurance that you buy and forget about until your beneficiaries realize that it is no longer there. You need to keep paying the premiums, or it will lapse."

"When you let yourself be robbed of your rights, your moral compass, and your democracy by electing corrupt, liars and self-centered politicians, you are not a victim; you are complicit."

"It has been advanced that American voters are not so stupid to re-elect a demagogue. You wish.

"Grandpa, where were you during the war? Daddy, for whom did you vote before the fall of America?"

"It is a mistake to think that the Trump Party goes off the rails pretending that the January 6, 2021 *Capitol insurrection was an FBI plot and that Joe Biden is the biggest threat to American democracy. On the contrary, their rhetoric keeps them well on track to achieving their long-time aspiration: authoritarian rule.".*

"The biggest shortcoming of the Democratic Party was their naivety in believing that the Republicans would impeach Trump. Doing so would have been like the Nazi Party putting Hitler on trial for burning the Reichstag."

*"If there is one single thing that all Americans should learn from their history, it is that fascism has been a long-term goal of the Republican Party. Now that the Second Coming of their Messiah is about to fulfill the **rapture** of our democracy, they are all in ecstasy in hypothetical Heaven."*

Rapture: from Middle French "*Rapture,*" means "*taking away, rape and kidnapping.*"

"Truth is the last thing voters want to hear because it is not a feel-good feeling. They would rather listen to fairy tales from snake oil peddlers telling them that they are their only hope to bring closer the light at the end of the tunnel of their shitty life. But hope is like the horizon; it recedes as you advance, and that is even more depressing."

"The only reason why America has now been officially designated a "Flawed democracy" [100] is that until now, nobody had dared to say it explicitly, but "flawed" it was from the start."

"What do religious faith and conspiracy theories have in common? They are both based on the belief of unproven allegations. No wonder fundamentalist Christians, QAnon, and Trump believers in B.S. are often the same people."

---

[100] Global democracy Index

"These days, a patriot is someone bent on destroying the very institution he is pretending to defend."

"The big scam of democracy is to make people believe that because they elect the puppets, they control the puppeteers."

"If you are advocating the burning or banning of books with passages that offend your moral susceptibility, you should start with the one that condoned genocide, rape, slavery, human sacrifice, misogyny, incest, cannibalism, murder, and dismemberment: The Bible."

"In America, you still have the right to disagree, but only in your head. Don't tell anyone because it could be hazardous to your health."

"Of course, you can find a politician that is not morally bankrupt. After all, it is not impossible to find a four-leaf clover."

"When millions of Americans have elected and are on their way to re-elect a pathological liar, a cheat, and a narcissist psychopath with the moral values of a slug to represent them, this is a clear sign of the moral decay of our society."

"According to Republicans, the word socialism, after Democrat, is the dirtiest word in the American vocabulary. So you can imagine what social democracy means to them."

"There are only three things important in a democracy. Who votes?
Who counts the votes?
And who decides who wins?
Everything else is just farting in the wind."

"For the Republicans, Donald J. Trump represents the Party's messianic hope to fulfill its long-awaited agenda to establish a fascist form of government in America. For this fulfillment to be realized, the messiah must first disappear to give the faithful time to prepare for his Second Coming, where he will re-appear in all his glory."

"If you want a country where trying to topple democracy is a patriot act while revealing all the lies and bad deeds committed by your government will put you in the slammer for life. Welcome to America."

"If you have received any financial support from the government, directly or indirectly, this is socialism. So, have you returned your COVID check yet?"

"I hate to bring it to you, but free speech is dead; social media killed it. Where is freedom of expression when everybody is entitled, holier-than-thou, a critic, a judge, and an executioner?"

"When ignorance is bliss and stupidity divine, we call it freedom of expression."

"Liberty is like free speech; we like it for ourselves, not so much for others."

"Liberty is a free electron and, like space-time, is all relative."

"The problem with intelligence data gathering, algorithms, and artificial intelligence is the lack of human intelligence to analyze the data."

"In any event, liberty may end up being just a state of mind, a sort of illusion that we strive to achieve but never reach. For that reason, we should never take it for granted because it is when it is gone that we know we were free."

"A country where people cannot talk freely with one another, cannot govern itself and work together towards the common good. In America, we used to call it a banana republic."

"Justice is the opposite of a fishing net; it only catches small fry fish."

"America prides itself on being a country of law, but it is not. It is a country of lawyers."

"If God knew in advance all the atrocities that were going to be committed in his name, is he a sadist or just not as omnipotent as we think he is? In that case, does he deserve to be a God?"

"From the day Christianity ceased to be persecuted, it started persecuting others. That is when Christianity became a religion."

"America has a new religion, and Trump is his prophet. Donald Akbar!"

"The Devil invented God to see what we would do with it. He has not been disappointed. That is how he gets his best recruits for Hell."

"America is exceptional from any other country. That is why we do not have to abide by international laws. This is exactly what America First means."

"America has not won a single war since the end of WWII, and even our role in ultimately defeating the Axis was not as crucial as portrayed in our history books."

"Next to a planned financial crisis, war is the best way to make money. This is why the Industrial-military complex will never forbid politicians ever to start a war."

"A real friend tells you what you need to hear, not what you want to hear."

"I had a dream," said Martin Luther King. Our certitudes, attitudes, and ineptitudes killed it."

"Whether we admit it or not, we are an imperialistic power. That is not a strength, but a weakness."

"When will the U.S. ever learn that nation-building has to come from the people and that shoveling it down their throat and throwing money at it is not the solution, but the problem?"

"Don't draw a line in the sand if you do not intend to carry it through."

"The clear and present danger is not that the barbarians are at the gate. They are domestic and already in."

"It would be nice to think that we have learned anything from a myriad of military debacles in foreign lands, but this will never happen. Because the big U.S. industrial-military complex that owns the politicians will ensure that the latter will never prevent them from inventing perpetual wars for their profits."

"Thank you, Jesus, for allowing America to go back on the merry-go-round of its addiction: perpetual war."

"No more foreign military adventurism. Today, the enemy is within. America is at war with itself."

"Is a patriot someone who loves his country without question or someone who still loves his country after getting the answers he does not like?"

"Sometimes, in order to predict the future, one only has to look in the rear-view mirror."

"Donald Trump talks like a fascist, thinks like a fascist, and acts like a fascist. Therefore, according to Republican's logic, he is not a fascist."

"One proof of the decadence of America today is that too many political decisions are made based on people's feelings. Striving to prevent people from feeling bad is like preventing them from making mistakes. The only thing they will learn from it is that everything is beautiful and that the world owes them. This is hardly an attitude to build resilience and face the vicissitudes of life."

"America's foreign policy: bomb, invade, fuckup, retreat, repeat."

"It is a fact that bare some exceptions; people have a history of voting against their own interests."

"At this time, when America is more fractured and divided than ever before, perhaps you should start wondering why you think that your ideology is the best one and anybody who does not share your worldviews and beliefs deserves to die. This might have been a very Christian thing to do in the past, but today, just consider that if you and everybody else on this planet are one, the other is also you, and you are, in effect, killing yourself."

"Fear the printed words, for when burned, like the phoenix, they have a habit of resurrecting from their ashes with a vengeance."

"When someone tells you what reality is, that everything else is a lie, and you accept it, he has become your God. Your thoughts are no longer yours, and you are just an avatar being manipulated, just like in a video game."

"In the same way that streams go to rivers and rivers to the ocean, some events are ineluctable. The history of this country has already been written; it is a done deal. America will become a de facto banana republic. The only thing in doubt is the timing of the tipping point."

"WE ARE Q-less AND PROUD OF IT!"

"If Christians are blaming the Jews for Jesus's death, they should, at least, be consistent and thank them instead. Because if Jesus had died in any other way, like falling off a ladder, of pneumonia, or drowning while trying to walk on water, for example, there would not have been a claim for a resurrection, and with no resurrection, no Christianity. So, thanks to the Jews."

"There is no point in identifying for you how many horrible character traits describe Donald Trump. But if you do not recognize that he does not possess any, it

could mean that your identification with Donald Trump is the reason for your affinity with him and your inability to acknowledge that he is a reflection of you."

"People who laud Teflon-Trump capability should know that Teflon eventually wears off and that it becomes toxic when heated, just like Trump."

"Is Donald Trump faking to be stupid, or is he too stupid for faking it? Donald Trump is neither smart nor stupid. He simply gave the impression of being stupid because whatever comes out of his mouth is not filtered by his brain."

"Regardless of his presidential rating, Donald J. Trump, as a person, deserves to enter the history books as the greatest illusionist, con man, and escape artist of all time."

"It would be incorrect to attribute Trump's success to any particular of his character traits. His success resides in the failure of our imagination to accept the possibility that there is anyone who can lie and cons as shamelessly and effectively as he does."

"The Republican Party has no morals, no integrity, no honesty, no balls, no shame, and is proud of it. That is why it has now become the Trump Party as a true reflection of Trump's personality."

"Whatever you think of the TADPOLE-GOP, you have to give them credit; they have a gift: they can look you

straight in the eyes and scream rape while squeezing your balls."

"How not to admire Pinocchio-Trump's capability to use his growing nose to evolve from a puppet to a puppet master?"

"The problem with a cold war with China is that contrary to our short attention span, they are playing the long game and can afford to keep it warm on the back burner for a long time."

"It is perplexing to comprehend why a Christian would see Trump as the new Messiah considering that he acts more like the Anti-Christ, meaning the opposite of what Jesus teaches."

"We are obsessed with social media, and as a result, we are today dumber than our parents, and our children will be even dumber than we are."

"Because whatever comes out of Trump's mouth is not filtered by his brains, the fastest way to get his thoughts out is to talk out of his ass as verbal diarrhea."

"When you go to an echo chamber to hear voices validating your way of thinking, don't call it critical thinking."

"Birds aren't real, but dummies are. They all flock and quack in unison as a show to display the deepness of their stupidity."

"Civility? Isn't that a word for sissies or something French? If someone takes my parking space, I will express my civility with my gun hanging at the back of my truck. This is the American way."

"In the old days, we used to lock up insane people. Today, we double and triple down on insanity to see if it is contagious, and it is."

"Normally, people who have lived under an authoritarian regime fight for a more democratic one. America is the only country in the world where people fight to overthrow their democracy to live under an autocratic ruler."

"If you are gullible enough to think that the Big Lie is about democracy, think again. It is about the only things that drive American politics: money and power."

"Do you want to hear a good joke? What used to be called a Retweet when retweeting a lie on Twitter is now called a Re-Truth on Truth Social. No joke!"

"If you are going to lie, make it big. The bigger the lie, the more believable it becomes."

"America is so far down the rabbit hole that maybe God will say "This time, I am giving up. America does not deserve to be saved; I will just let the Devil and the golden statue worshipers do their work."

do his work."

"The attack of the Capitol was our own Reichstag Fire planned as a setting stage to use emergency powers to seize control of the election, just like Hitler did."

"Perhaps it would be a good thing if Trump becomes president again because we have not reached rock bottom yet. It will only be after America experiences the fascist government of Trump that America will be ready, like the phoenix, to be reborn from its ashes."

"Our democracy is going down the toilet, and Donald Trump is the one flushing it. The tragedy is that in doing so, nearly half of America is cheering him on while draping themselves in the patriot flag of the Star-Spangled Banner."

"When you yell "fire" in an echo chamber, do you expect the echo to return "water"?'

"Here is an anti-B.S. that works all the time. On a clear summer night, just contemplating the open sky that displays our Milky Way Galaxy will make you realize how petty, small, and insignificant the ramblings of a sad clown like Donald Trump truly are."

"It is when the sad ramblings of a demagogue become the hymns of the faithful and the Parrots' choir starts singing the caws of the crow that you know that the

TADPOLE-GOP is so far down the rabbit hole that it has become a Golden Mole."

"Historians, like scientists, have a big problem admitting evidence contradicting their hypothesis. That is contrary to the scientific approach that consists of having an open mind, investigating, following the evidence wherever it leads them, and drawing a reasonable conclusion as close to the facts as possible."

"When you want to believe in something that is impossible to conceive, trying to represent it diminishes the way we think about it. This is the reason why Jews, Muslims, and early Christians forbade the representation of God. Conversely, the word can wire the brain where it triggers emotions that implant our beliefs. Here lays the power of the demagogue."

"In a democracy, it appears that people want the right to say whatever they want to be coupled with a strong leader who tells them what to do so they do not have to think. Of course, those two things are mutually exclusive, and until we find a way to reconcile the two, democracy is doomed to fail."

"In the same way, you cannot say that you are anti-plague or anti-cholera; being anti-Trump is meaningless: Trump just is."

"Until an alien spacecraft lands in front of the White House with the message "take me to your leader," humanity will continue to fuck up and perpetuate the great cycle of time that always goes back where it started. Alternatively, the Alien might just say the equivalent of "beam me up Scotty, there is no obvious sign of intelligence on this planet" and takeoff."

"Voters are not rational but emotional. Find the chord that makes them vibrate, and you can play them like a violin."

"The problem with demagogues is that once they have tasted one drop of power, they get drunk and addicted to it and will never give it up."

"If octopuses had a god, it would have eight arms, nine brains, and a beak, so it does make sense that we think that God created us in his image, although I don't see what use God would make of two legs, two arms, two ears, a nose, and a mouth."

"All mini-Trump of the world, unite. A New World order is coming!."

"That Trump's own Department of Homeland Security declared the 2020 election "the most secure in history." That it was also the fairest and the most thoroughly scrutinized election in U.S. recent history that found Zero, zilch, nada, rien, walou, nichts, niente, nashi, widespread voting fraud, means absolutely nothing to

those who are still sleepwalking through reality. They are waiting for their revenge when they will wake up in 2024 for Donald Trump's Second Coming."

"*People get the character they inherit and the government they merit.***"**

"The gulf that separates Republicans and Democrats is greater than the Gulf of Aqaba separating the Sinai from the Arabian Peninsula in the Red Sea. "Even Moses would find it daunting to try to find a path bridging the two sides of their political divide."

"Donald Trump is a RINO (Republican In Name Only). If he does not get the Republican nomination, he will run under a new Party, his."

In a democracy, whoever you elect to represent you is, at the subconscious level, a reflection of who you truly are. Your character, your moral values, and your worldviews.

"The best way to lose a war with good soldiers is to lead them with incompetent leaders, including political ones. The opposite corollary is also true."

"When you consider that during a single lifetime, a person went from horse and buggy to landing on the moon and AI, think where mankind would be today without the more than 1400 years of religious obscurantism, intolerance, and mind control? After all, it took the Catholic Church 16 centuries before

allowing you to read the Bible in English without being burned at the stake. And it did not do it voluntarily but was forced to by the publication of the King James Bible in 1611."

"Who in his right mind would have thought that politics would be the main reason for the fall of our democracy? But who in his right mind did not think it would not?"

"American voters should understand one thing: they do not elect presidents; the Electoral College does, and even Trump understands that. That is why he orchestrated a fake elector's fraud to overturn the election."

"It is not fair to Russians to compare Trump's with Putin's supporters. In America, they have access to free information and the truth. It is their choice if they prefer to label it as lies. In Russia, they don't have the choice. Speaking the truth will lend them in a re-education gulag."

"It is quite natural to hate everything you are not. Like liars if you seek the truth, and the truth if you are a liar."

"You cannot blame Trump for using every trick in the con book he wrote himself."

"The problem with sleepwalking Trumpsters is that they take their dreams for reality and will never wake up."

"If Trump is not a genius, he is a genie. He can make all your wishes become a reality in exchange for your ability to think for yourself."

"America has a new religion, and Trump is his prophet. Glory to the Commander of the faithful. Donald Akbar!"

"Isn't it ironic that the term "Banana Republic" coined by us to describe a country incapable of governing itself has come full circle to bite us in the butt?"

"It is great that your snowplow or lawnmower parents took care of you by sparing your feelings from the vicissitudes of reality. But what are you going to do when reality takes care of you?"

*"The love phrase **"**I love you more than yesterday, but less than tomorrow" is a perfect analogy to global warming since every year is warmer than the one before while being the coolest than it will ever be in the future. We can deny reality, but reality does not care because one day, nobody will be left to deny its existence."*

"Truth is the last thing voters want to hear because it is not a feel-good feeling. They would rather listen to fairy tales from snake oil peddlers telling them that they are their only hope to bring closer the light at the end of the tunnel of their shitty life. But hope is like the horizon; it recedes as you advance, and that is even more depressing."

"We Americans don't give a F%$# about how the world sees us. What counts is how we see ourselves. That is your problem said the mirror, I am just reflecting what you are, not what you see."

"Sometime in the near future, history books will summarize the ascent and fall of America in two words that start the same way: **LI**BERTY and **LI**ES."

"Somebody should remind Christians who have massacred Jews for centuries that their God Yahweh is a very ancient God from Akkadian and Mesopotamian myths, recycled by the Hebrews some thirty centuries ago, and that Jesus was a Jew."

"Here is an easy question: When Trump is talking about loser, bird brain, dumb, and crooked. Who do you have in mind?"

"If you are advocating the burning or banning of books with passages that offend your moral susceptibility, you should start with the one that condoned genocide, rape, slavery, human sacrifice, misogyny, incest, cannibalism, murder, and dismemberment: The Bible."

"Grandpa, where were you during the war? Daddy, for whom did you vote before the fall of America?"

"It is a mistake to think that the Trump Party goes off the rails pretending that the January 6, 2021 Capitol insurrection was an FBI plot and that Joe Biden is the biggest threat to American democracy. On the contrary, their rhetoric keeps them well on track to achieving their long-time aspiration: authoritarian rule."

"Instead of poking fun at those who believe that they will one day disappear from the surface of the Earth without anybody noticing to meet Jesus up in the sky, you should instead pray for those who believe in Trump's fairy tales. What! You say that they are the same people. What are the odds?"

"It is a statistical fact that in any given population, about one-third are complete idiots. Since only two-thirds of the same population bothers to vote that explains why a minority of dummies governs most countries, and nothing gets done."

"If someone's nose is in cow dung, how do you convince that person of the contrary if he continues to insist that it is chocolate pudding? Because if there is anything more futile than trying to convince an imbecile, it is trying to convince a person of bad faith. You will always lose, for he has more experience defending something with no arguments than you do."

"When you do the sum of all fears, only three pose an existential threat to America. Donald Trump, stupid people, and AI. And if we do not eliminate the first two, the third one will eliminate us."

Quotes from Donald Trump's little voice in his head

"*Dear Leader of the New America, I like that!*"

"*Mirror, mirror on the wall, who is the most intelligent of all? You are, oh great one.!*".

"*I can't believe that those suckers are actually gobbling up all the bullshit I feed them.*"

"*Critical thinking? I am the best critical thinker in the world. I criticize everything.*"

"*The truth is whatever serves me best, and whatever I say it is. It is flexible and can change overnight.*".

"*The next election will be the most corrupt election in U.S. history; I will make sure of that, believe you me!.*"

"*I have demonstrated that I can do whatever I want. The next time, no more Mister Nice Guy.*" (After getting scot-free from two impeachments)

"*Fraud, fraud, fraud, I have to stop repeating it before people start realizing I am a fraud.*"

"*I heard that some people consider me as the Second Coming of Christ. That is false. I have already created my own religion.*"

"*Memo to myself: Make a list of who I am going to insult today.*"

"Memo to myself: Practice mugshot. Look mean. I bet I can make money out of it."

"Of course, I know I lost the election. I am not stupid. But I have to keep repeating it because if I admit it now, I would just prove my indictment charges, and that would be stupid. Besides, that is what my fan base expects me to do."

"Be nice to Putin. Remember who holds the pee-pee tapes."

"Who said I am a racist? I love niggers, alligator baits, Beaners, Brownies, Ching Chongs, Mexican hombres, Dinks and Pocahontas. I am the least racist person that God ever created."

"Calling me a liar, a cheat, and a con man does not insult me. I don't believe in truth."

"Maybe I should shoot someone in the middle of Times Square and get indicted for murder. Think how much money I could raise to fight such a politically motivated charge."

"I orchestrated an insurrection to overthrow democracy, so what? It is not illegal to contest voting results. I have done nothing wrong, I have done nothing wrong, I have done nothing wrong."

"Oh Putin and Xi Jinping, how I envy you! But when I come back, me too will make my opponents disappear."

"Damn you, lawyers and tax accountants! Sure, I am a fraud expert, but do I have to do everything myself not to get caught? "

"Memo to myself: I got to get re-elected president, God damn it! It is the only way to stay out of jail."

"What shining object can I throw to the media today to stay on top of the news cycle?"

"I did not do anything wrong; I just told others to break the law. They are the ones who should go to jail."

"People are funny: The more I insult them, the more they kiss my ring."

"91 felony charges? Bring them on. The more I get, the more popular I become."

"I am not a whiny little bitch, and there is nothing little about me."

Annotated quotes from Donald Trump

There is nothing more revealing about a person's view of the world, character, and what he truly believes than unscripted answers to impromptu questions or tweeted at 3 a.m. to get something off your chest. Here are some insights into the inner character of the man we choose to represent us once and prepare to re-elect again.

Wise, funny, outrageous, silly, stupid, take your pick.

"I have the absolute right to PARDON myself." **Imagine that! However, that would be redundant, since others are pardoning you for whatever you do. So, go ahead and shoot someone in the middle of Times Square!**

"You see the mob takes the Fifth. If you're innocent, why are you taking the Fifth Amendment?" **So said the man who pleaded the Fifth more than 450 times in a four-hour deposition into his business practices.**

"Part of being a winner is knowing when enough is enough. Sometimes you have to give up the fight and walk away and move on to something that's more productive." **So, why don't you follow your own advice instead of running again?**

"Anyone who thinks my story is anywhere near over is sadly mistaken." **This could have been Hitler's last words in his bunker in 1945.**

"People love me. And you know what? I have been very successful. Everybody loves me." **Everybody likes**

to hit their head against the wall because it feels so good when you stop.

"When you open your heart to patriotism, there is no room for prejudice. The Bible tells us, 'How good and pleasant it is when God's people live together in unity." **That is rich coming from someone who relishes chaos.**

" I am the most honest human being, perhaps, that God ever created," **So said the man who, according to the beans counters, made at least 30,573 lies during his presidency, and we are still counting.**

"I am the Most Innocent Man in the History of Our Country." ***Oh, Jesus, this man has suffered enough; please prepare for him his well-deserved place in Paradise.***

"I've always won, and I'm going to continue to win. And that's the way it is." **That is what your father told you, but he was also a psychopath.**

"What do you have to lose? It's going to be tremendous. We're going to have jobs, we're going to bring back the wealth, we're going to take care of our military, we're going to take care of our vets. We're going to start winning again.". **When you say "*winning again*," does that mean that you acknowledge that you lost before?**

"I will be the greatest jobs president that God ever created." **As if God gives a hoot about what you are doing.**

"I think Viagra is wonderful if you need it, if you have medical issues, if you've had surgery. I've just never

needed it. Frankly, I wouldn't mind if there were an anti-Viagra, something with the opposite effect. I'm not bragging. I'm just lucky. I don't need it." **Melania did not say. But Stormy Daniels did not think it was worth the money she received.**

"All of the women on The Apprentice flirted with me – consciously or unconsciously. That's to be expected." **You forgot all the women on Miss USA Pageant.**

"She does have a very nice figure… If [Ivanka] weren't my daughter, perhaps I'd be dating her." **Jared Kushner must not be too happy about that!**

"You know I'm automatically attracted to beautiful -- I just start kissing them. It's like a magnet. Just kiss. I don't even wait," "And when you're a star, they let you do it… You can do anything." …"Whatever you want,….."Grab them by the pussy". "You can do anything." **Once a pig, always a pig! So proud he was our president.**

"I have tremendous respect for women." **Now, that is rich!**

"One of the key problems today is that politics is such a disgrace. Good people don't go into government." **Did you just acknowledge that you are not a good person?**

"I was a great student. I was good at everything." **That is not what your professors said. Unless being the *"Dumbest G-damned student I've ever seen,"* is a compliment.**

"If you're the President of the United States, you can declassify just by saying: 'It's declassified.' Even by thinking about it. Now we get it. You thought that you had won the 2020 election and that just thinking about it would make it so.

"Sorry, losers and haters, but my I.Q. is one of the highest – and you all know it! Please don't feel so stupid or insecure, it's not your fault.". **That is not what many of your Cabinet members who worked closely with you say. Unless idiot and moron are compliments.**

"I'm intelligent. Some people would say I'm very, very, very intelligent.". **Of course, if it comes from someone who is mentally retarded, anybody else is a genius.**

"I'm like a smart person. I don't have to be told the same thing in the same words every single day for the next eight years.". **A "*dope*," and "*An idiot with the intelligence of a kindergartener*," from former National Security Advisor HR McMaster.**

"Nobody has better respect for intelligence than Donald Trump." **So you have learned a new word. Do you even know the meaning of the word "Respect"?**

"I know more about ISIS than the generals do. Believe me." **Are you talking about Isis, the goddess of ancient Egypt?**

"Nobody knew health care could be so complicated." **Duh!**

"I could stand in the middle of 5th Avenue and shoot somebody, and I wouldn't lose voters.". **Yes, sadly, that is true.**

"You know, it really doesn't matter what the media write as long as you've got a young and beautiful piece of ass." **Are you talking about those Russian prostitutes? You know, the ones Putin has with you on the pee tapes?**

"The beauty of me is that I'm very rich." **Not as rich as you are pretending to be.**

"My fingers are long and beautiful, as, it has been well documented, as various other parts of my body." **What other parts of your body? If you are talking about your dick, that is not what pornographic star Stormy Daniels said. In fact, she was very diminutive about it.**

"I'm the most successful person ever to run for the presidency, by far. Nobody's ever been more successful than me. I'm the most successful person ever to run. Ross Perot isn't successful like me. Romney – I have a Gucci store that's worth more than Romney." **And still, you lost to "*sleepy Joe.*"**

"I would bet if you took a poll in the FBI, I would win that poll by more than anybody's won a poll.". **Sure, if the question was, "Who was the stupidest president ever?"**

About naming a special prosecutor to investigate his opponents if reelected.

"That means that if I win and somebody wants to run against me, I call my attorney general, and I say, 'Listen, indict him!' " .....*"[If the attorney general says], 'Well, he hasn't done anything wrong,' [I'll say], 'I don't know, indict him on income-tax evasion. You'll figure it out.'* **"Tax-evasion? That is rich. Shouldn't the prosecutor start by investigating you?**

"[John McCain is]... not a war hero. He's a war hero – he's a war hero cause he was captured. I Like people that weren't captured, OK, I hate to tell you." **So said the guy who used all the tricks in the book to dodge being drafted for Vietnam.**

"To be blunt, people would vote for me. They just would. Why? Maybe because I'm so good-looking.". **Please shoot me! Have you seen your face in a mirror recently?**

"If Hillary Clinton can't satisfy her husband, what makes her think she can satisfy America?". **That was funny!**

"You could see there was blood coming out of her eyes. Blood coming out of her wherever.". **Were you referring to her menstruation? Classy!**

"Border Wall: "I will build a great, great wall on our southern border, and I will have Mexico pay for that wall. Mark my words.". **We did mark your words and are still waiting for Mexico to pay for it.**

"The concept of global warming was created by and for the Chinese in order to make U.S. manufacturing non-competitive.". **The Chinese must have had a good laugh about that, along with anybody who lives in California.**

"The line of 'Make America great again,' the phrase, that was mine, I came up with it about a year ago, and I kept using it, and everybody's using it, they are all loving it. I don't know, I guess I should copyright it, maybe I have copyrighted it." **You wish. Jimmy Carter and Ronald Regan had used the same slogan before you.**

"I love the poorly educated." **Sure, they are most susceptible to believe in bullshit.**

"Kim Jong-Un] speaks, and his people sit up at attention. I want my people to do the same." **At last, a candid acknowledgment of why he loves dictators**.

"It's freezing and snowing in New York – we need global warming!" **Aren't you confusing weather forecasting with global warming? Even a goose knows the difference.**

"It's really cold outside, they are calling it a major freeze, weeks ahead of normal. Man, we could use a big fat dose of global warming!" **Like in California?**

"I watched Hillary Clinton tonight. … And she lied again like she's been lying for the last 15 years. She's a liar." **It is the one who says it who is** (French saying).

"Barack Obama is the founder of ISIS. He is the founder of ISIS, OK? He's the founder. He founded ISIS. And I would say the co-founder would be crooked Hillary Clinton." **It's not because you repeated it four times that makes it true. Besides, ISIS sprang from al Qaeda in Iraq and was founded by Jordanian Islamist Abu Musab al-Zarqawi. It gained its popularity as the main insurgency against the U.S.-led forces that toppled Saddam Hussein in 2003. So, the co-founder of ISIS is George W. Bush.**

"The only card she has is the woman's card. She's got nothing else to offer, and frankly, if Hillary Clinton were a man, I don't think she'd get 5 percent of the vote. The only thing she's got going is the woman's card, and the beautiful thing is, women don't like her." **That is not totally wrong. There is no better bitch towards a woman than another woman.**

"I think the only difference between me and the other candidates is that I'm more honest, and my women are more beautiful." **You are not wrong about the woman, but more honest? That was a joke, right?**

"I have evidence that Barack Obama was born in Kenya. I have a birth certificate." **We are still waiting to see it. By the way, Bill Maher also has a certificate that your mother F%@&ed an orangutan.**

Commentary

In 2013, on his program "Real Time with Bill Maher," Maher made the following joke:

"Look, I'm not saying your mother was repeatedly ****ing an orangutan back in the 1940s. I don't know if that's true. I hope it's not true. But given your face, your physique and your intelligence level, and of course, your hair, the American people deserve some real proof that your mother did not spend most nights in 1945 covering her body in banana oil sneaking into the monkey cage, and compulsively humping an orange orangutan."

When Trump filed a suit against comedian Bill Maher, the latter than appeared on NBC's "The Tonight Show," proclaiming that he would give $5 million to charity if Trump could prove that he is not the son of an orangutan.

"An 'extremely credible source' has called my office and told me that Barack Obama's birth certificate is a fraud." **We also hear that an 'extremely credible source,' called your office and told you that you were a fraud, not the election. What do you have to say about that?**

"Thanks – many are saying I'm the best 140-character writer in the world. It's easy when it's fun." **It sure helps when you have a limited vocabulary and small fingers.**

"Well. I do think there's blame, yes I think there is blame on both sides, I think there is blame on both sides". **See, I told you that his vocabulary was limited. I told you that his vocabulary was limited. I told you that his vocabulary was limited. I told you.......**

"Sure, he is a tyrant and a low-life human being, but he likes me, so I love him." D. Trump referring to Kim Jong Un, the North Korean. How can you be more narcissistic than that?"

"Why is Obama playing basketball today? That is why our country is in trouble!". **We could say, "Why is Donald Trump playing golf today? That is why our country is in trouble."**

"Our country is in serious trouble. We don't have victories anymore. We used to have victories, but [now] we don't have them. When was the last time anybody saw us beating, let's say, China in a trade deal? They kill us. I beat China all the time. All the time.". **You cannot have it both ways. Either China is still beating us, or you are beating China.**

"My favorite part [of Pulp Fiction] is when Sam has his gun out in the diner, and he tells the guy to tell his girlfriend to shut up. 'Tell that bitch to be cool. Say: Bitch be cool.' I love those lines.". **Why some women are still supporting him is a total mystery.**

"While @BetteMidler is an extremely unattractive woman, I refuse to say that because I always insist on being politically correct." **Somewhere else, you said, "*I do not have time to be politically correct.*" So which one is it?**

"*I will prevent WWIII very easily, very easily….and you can have WWIII by the way.*" Please stop the world; I want to get off.

"I'm the least racist person you have ever interviewed." **So why do white supremacists think of you as their leader?**

"So they're investigating something that never happened." **That is rich coming from someone still**

investigating something that never happened, like a rigged election.

"I look very much forward to showing my financials because they are huge." **Yes, you fought for six years in court to not have to release your financial and tax records like it is customary for all presidents.**

"I loved my previous life. I had so many things going. This is more work than in my previous life. I thought it would be easier." **So why are you trying so hard to get elected again?**

"You know, I go to Washington, and I see all these politicians, and I see the swamp. And it's not a good place. In fact, today I said we ought to change it from the word swamp to the word cesspool or, perhaps, to the word sewer." **And you did just that, restocking the swamp with your own bottom-crawling, spineless slugs.**

Miscellaneous quotes

"Remember, democracy never lasts long. It soon wastes, exhausts, and murders itself. There never was a democracy, yet that did not commit suicide," John Adams.

"In our age, there is no such thing as 'keeping out of politics.' All issues are political issues, and politics itself is a mass of lies, evasions, folly, hatred, and schizophrenia." George Orwell.

"Kill one man, and you are a murderer. Kill millions of men, and you are a conqueror. Kill them all, and you are a god," Jean Rostand.

"In politics, stupidity is not a handicap." Napoleon Bonaparte.

"We know that no one ever seizes power with the intention of relinquishing it." – George Orwell, *1984*.

"Half the U.S. population owns barely 2 percent of its wealth, putting the United States near Rwanda and Uganda and below such nations as pre-Arab Spring Tunisia and Egypt when measured by degrees of income inequality." Eric Alterman.

"Inequality provokes a generalized anger that finds targets where it can. Immigrants, foreign countries, American elites, government in all forms, and it

rewards demagogues while discrediting reformers." George Packer.

"I disapprove of what you say, but I will defend to the death your right to say it," Attributed to Voltaire.

"What is freedom of expression? Without the freedom to offend, it ceases to exist." Salman Rushdie.

"Arguing that you don't care about the right to privacy because you have nothing to hide is no different than saying you don't care about free speech because you have nothing to say," Edward Snowden.

"Religion is the opium of the people," Karl Marx.

"Those who believe religion and politics aren't connected don't understand either." Mahatma Gandhi

"The truth will set you free, but first it will piss you off!" Gloria Steinem

"My country, right or wrong." Attributed to Stephan Decatur.

"In war truth is the first casualty," Aeschylus, 550 B.C."

"A terrorist is someone who has a bomb but doesn't have an air force," William Blum.

"It is always more difficult to fight against faith than against knowledge." Adolf Hitler.

"I don't know it for a fact....I just know it's true." Real Time with Bill Maher.

"The real danger is not inaction. The real danger is when politicians and CEOs are making it look like action is happening when, in fact, nothing is being done." Greta Thunburg.

"I love the smell of napalm in the morning." From Apocalypse Now.

"We'll be remembered more for what we destroy than what we create." Chuck Palahniuk.

"Kill them all, God will recognize his own." Arnauld Amalric, Papa; Legate.

"They plunder, they slaughter, and they steal, these things they misname empire, and where they make a wasteland, they call it peace."[101] Tacitus.

"Insanity is doing the same thing over and over and expecting different results." Albert Einstein.

"To be a good patriot, you must become the enemy of mankind." Voltaire.

"The longer I live, the more convinced am I that this planet is used by other planets as a lunatic asylum." George Bernard Shaw.

---

[101] In reference to the Roman Empire.

"Someone said that patriotism is the last refuge of cowards; those without moral principles usually wrap a flag around themselves, and those bastards always talk about the purity of race." Umberto Eco.

"If you don't know history, then you don't know anything. You are a leaf that doesn't know it is part of a tree." Michael Crichton.

"The object of life is not to be on the side of the majority but to escape finding oneself in the ranks of the insane." Niccolò Machiavelli.

"*The worst thing a son of a bitch can do is to turn you into a son of a bitch,***"** Frank Oppenheimer.

"You're such a big BABY. So cry me a river, build yourself a bridge, and GET OVER IT." Rachel Renée Russell.

"It is when you see a mosquito landing on your testicles that you realize that all problems cannot be solved by violence." Chinese proverb.

"*Either you deal with what reality is, or you can be sure that reality is going to deal with you.***"** Alex Haley, author of Roots.

"A fanatical neo-fascist political cult in the TADPOLE-GOP, driven by a strange mixture of corrosive hatred and sickening fear, who are recklessly determined to

either control our party or destroy it." Republican Senator Thomas Kuchel

"*Patriotism is, fundamentally, a conviction that a particular country is the best in the world because you were born in it,*" George Bernard Shaw

"*There's none as blind as those who will not see,*" Proverb

"*Americans like to talk about (or be told about) Democracy but, when put to the test, usually find it to be an 'inconvenience.' We have opted instead for an authoritarian system disguised as a democracy. We pay through the nose for an enormous joke of a government, let it push us around, and then wonder how all those assholes got in there.*" Frank Zappa

"*Men are so simple of mind, and so much dominated by their immediate needs, that a deceitful man will always find plenty who are ready to be deceived,*" Niccolò Machiavelli.

"*We learn from history that we do not learn from history.*" Georg Wilhelm Friedrich Hegel

"*We are not makers of history. We are made by history.*" Martin Luther King, Jr.

"*Truly, whoever can make you believe absurdities can make you commit atrocities.*" Voltaire.

"If people cannot write well, they cannot think well, and if they cannot think well, others will do their thinking for them." George Orwell.

"A politic and diapers must be changed regularly, and for the same reasons." George Bernard Shaw.

"We experience ourselves, our thoughts and feelings as something separate from the rest. A kind of optical delusion of consciousness." Albert Einstein.

"In our quest for happiness and the avoidance of suffering, we are all fundamentally the same and therefore equal. Despite the characteristics that differentiate us - race, language, religion, gender, wealth, and many others - we are all equal in terms of our basic humanity." Dalai Lama.

"What good fortune for those in power that people who do not think," Adolf Hitler

"Mankind is not likely to salvage civilization unless he can evolve a system of good and evil which is independent of heaven and hell." George Orwell

"Reality is merely an illusion, albeit a very persistent one." Albert Einstein.

"People like us who believe in physics know that the distinction between past, present, and future is only a stubbornly persistent illusion." Albert Einstein.

"It is the one who says it who is," French proverb.

"Everyone who wants to know what will happen ought to examine what has happened: everything in this world in any epoch has its replicas in antiquity." Niccolò Machiavelli.

"Man's principal trait is a readiness to believe anything. Otherwise, how could the Church have survived for almost two thousand years in the absence of universal gullibility?" Umberto Eco.

"Liberty means responsibility. That is why most men dread it." George Bernard Shaw

"Let me speak plainly: The United States of America is and must remain a nation of openness to people of all beliefs. Our very unity has been strengthened by this pluralism. That's how we began; this is how we must always be. The ideals of our country leave no room whatsoever for intolerance, anti-Semitism, or bigotry of any kind— none.." – Ronald Reagan.

"The best argument against democracy is a five-minute conversation with the average voter." Winston Churchill.

"The most effective way to destroy people is to deny and obliterate their own understanding of their history." George Orwell

"In the United States, the majority undertakes to supply a multitude of ready-made opinions for the use of individuals, who are thus relieved from the necessity of forming opinions of their own." Alexis de Tocqueville

"There is hardly a political question in the United States which does not sooner or later turn into a judicial one. There are two things that a democratic people will always find very difficult - to begin a war and to end it." Alexis de Tocqueville.

"As one digs deeper into the national character of the Americans, one sees that they have sought the value of everything in this world only in answer to this single question: how much money will it bring in.? Alexis de Tocqueville

GLOSSARY

BASKET OF MORALLY BANKRUPT DEPLORABLE

If you have found yourself dazed, speechless, and out of words to describe Trump's supporters' outrageous behavior and claims, you may be excused. Think what you want of Hillary Clinton, but at least her vocabulary is a notch higher than Trump's 4th-grader level. Despite the hacks she got from her self-flagellating Democrat colleagues, we should thank her for finding an apt word that encapsulates the meaning of **disgraceful, shameful, dishonorable, submissive, despicable, lamentable, pathetic, contemptible, base, sordid, revolting, obsequious, and loathsome** into one single word: DEPLORABLE.

BASKET OF MORALLY BANKRUPT DEPLORABLE is, _therefore,_ the updated version of "**_Basket of deplorables_**" attributed to Hillary Clinton, describing half of Trump's supporters as racist, sexist, homophobic, xenophobic, and Islamaphobic. The new version reflects the TADPOLE-GOP evolution, based on their words, actions, and sickening obsequious servility to Donald Trump that led to their moral bankruptcy.

DEAR LEADER

Now that the Republican Party is dead and has morphed into a sect/cult, giving it a new name is entirely appropriate. We still should call it a party because running a country as a sect does not seem serious and does not invite respect. However, until Donald Trump insists on being called by a new name like "Your Excellency, Great One, Boss or Majesty," this book will simply refer to him as "_Dear Leader_" in reference to Kim Jong-un of

North Korea, whom Donald Trump particularly admires and even love.

TADPOLE.

A new name for the GOP should reflect its past and present. Given the GOP's anti-democratic history, it sounds perfectly appropriate to give the "*Great Old Party*" a brand new name:

TADPOLE: **T**rump **A**nti-**D**emocratic **P**arty **O**f **L**ies & **E**ntitlement

Tadpole: A tadpole is the larval stage in the life cycle of an amphibian that lives, along with other spineless and bottom-feeder creatures, in the pond after Donald Trump drained it of its former creatures.

Question without an answer

Was the GOP already morally bankrupt, or was it contaminated by Donald Trump, who corrupts everything he touches?

Today, the primary role of the TADPOLE's elected politician is to support everything the "*Dear Leader*" says or does out of fear of the electoral base, who may not elect or re-elect them in office.

The secondary role of a TADPOLE politician is to obstruct any laws and regulations proposed by the Democrat Party. His primary role is getting re-elected to secure a political career and the perks it entails.

What motivates a TADPOLE Congressman/woman or Senate member? Fear, self-preservation, and money. Not necessarily in that order.

What makes the TADPOLE Party look strong?

They all sing from the same partition written by "*Dear Leader.*" They never, never apologize for anything. Instead, they double or triple down on their screw-ups and lies.

In the old days, we used to lock up insane people. Today, we double and triple down on insanity to see if it is contagious, and it is.

If silence is consent, we can assume that, with a few exceptions, the vast majority of the TADPOLE gives tacit approval of the most outlandish claims. However,

Whatever you think of the TADPOLE, you have to give them credit: they have a gift: they can look you straight in the eyes and scream rape while squeezing your balls.

This talent for telling something that is so blatantly untrue can only be performed by a few other people. Aside from the TADPOLE, only one type of person can make you flap your arms and jump like a bird while making buck-buck sounds: a hypnotist who makes you think you are a chicken.

The need for a new word to describe the TADPOLE "*signature move.*"

TRUMPILATE

There is not a strong enough word in the English language to describe something that neither the telling nor the receiving party knows to be true.

A new word must, therefore, be invented to truly convey the meaning of such action.

To *TRUMPILATE;* verb, like to Trump-Pilate somebody.

From the word "*Trump*" is derived from the word "*trumpery,*" meaning falsehood, nonsense, rubbish, trash, and the word "*Pilate,*" like Pontius Pilate.

Pontius Pilate, the Roman Prefect of Judea until 36 A.D., who tried Jesus, did not believe the accusations thrown at him by his accusers. He even clashed with the Jewish population and at first dismissed the case. But he finally acted as if the allegations were true and washed his hands of Jesus' crucifixion sentence.

To "*Trumpilate*" somebody is, therefore, to tell something nobody believes to be true, but the person saying it acts as if it is. Example:

Recent attempts in red states to enact voter-suppression legislation to prevent eligible voters from exercising their right to vote have been portrayed by the TADPOLE as necessary laws to protect democracy. An explanation that neither the Democrats nor the Republicans truly believe in, since they both know the genuine attempts of such legislation.

Such a "*Trumpilate*" explanation would be like proposing a law to kill all elephants to eradicate poaching and the illegal ivory trade and actually going ahead with it.

On that topic, a counter-law proposition would be to replace photo safaris with "*poacher safaris,*" where people would be allowed to hunt and kill poachers for a fee. This proposition would undoubtedly be very lucrative and popular, especially in the United States, where people like Trump's two sons would pay good money for the privilege. However, mounting a poacher's head as a trophy would be forbidden; that would be too cheesy.

Obviously, this latter example is only given to illustrate the absurdity of the rhetoric and dangerous mindset in which the Trump Party has fully engaged and adopted.

One last Trumpilate example to show that the action is not essentially limited to politics. Vladimir Putin signed a law to force French Champagne to be labeled "*sparkling wine*" in Russia. Real Champagne is a complicated manufacturing process that is only made in the Champagne region of France. It is a protected label that is recognized in 120 countries across the world[102]. What makes this move a "*Trumpilate*" action is that now only Russian-made sparkling wine can be called "*Champagne*." while real Champagne must be called "*sparkling wine*." Obviously, nobody is fooled by the new appellation, and even if you are not a connoisseur, the price alone, which is ten times more expensive, will dispel any doubt in determining which one is the real Champagne. This example is even more interesting because no official reason was given in this case. However, in TADPOLE style, Putin could have said that the move was made to protect the production of Russian vodka.

TRUMPGASSING

In English, we have a word for a person who does good deeds, is virtuous, puts the welfare of others before his own, and goes above and beyond what is generally expected from normal good behavior. We call it a saint. For the layperson, being a saint does not mean being beatified by the Church and performing miracles. But what is the opposite of a saint? A person who does ill as a second nature and corrupts everything he touches. Words like sinner, evildoer, malefactor, or villain don't seem to

---

[102] The United States is one of the last countries in the world to not reserve the Champagne name exclusively for wines from Champagne.

fit the bill to describe a person like Donald Trump. Using the word "*Trump*" as an antonym to "Saint" would be too easy. Of course, we could use it in a context like "*Trump made me do it*" instead of "*the Devil made me do it,*" a legal defense already used by some of Trump's enablers who faced criminal charges.

One particularity of a saint is to lead by example and inspire people to follow his words and actions to surpass themselves to improve their lives and those of others.

In a way, this is precisely the role that Donald Trump is playing, except that following his examples inspires people to strive in chaos and toxic behaviors. Since no word already exists in the English language to describe such behavior, a new one must be invented.

TRUMPGASSING is a new word that describes the effect of gaslighting people for the purpose of manipulating them into questioning their own reality, perception, or moral values. It is like passing toxic gas, either by words or actions, to intoxicate others to do bad things and incite them to do the opposite of that of a saint.

GASTRUMPING

Gastrumping is a special form of gaslighting, which means accusing others of things you do yourself or are about to do. A typical example of someone who routinely used gaslighting is Vladimir Putin, who made it his hallmark. The problem with gaslighting is if you abuse it, your accusations will end up being ignored and even act as a signal that it is exactly what you intend to do.

If Gaslighting "*Is a form of psychological manipulation in which the abuser attempts to sow self-doubt and confusion in their victim's mind. Typically, gaslighters are seeking to gain power and control over the other person by distorting reality and forcing them to question their own judgment and intuition."* [103]Gastrumping goes one step further.

---

[103] Newport Institute

ANNEX

The "*How to subvert democracy for "A Dear Leader" Wannabe*" elaborated for this book is reprinted here **without the commentaries** to let the reader assess for himself whether or not Donald Trump has so far checked all the boxes of the "*How to subvert democracy for "A Dear Leader" Wannabe*" playbook. This assessment will reveal the chances that Donald Trump will "*steal*" the 2024 presidential election, as he has accused his political opponents of stealing the previous one.

How to score.

At the end of each rule, the reader is asked to assess how Donald Trump is performing in implementing each step of the playbook by giving a note represented by a checked mark as follows:

- Trump has not implemented that step: TWO POINTS ☐
- Trump has partially implemented that step: 1 POINT ☐
- Trump has implemented most of that step: 0 POINT ☐

When completed, simply add all the points to determine how Donald Trump is fairing in implementing all the steps to win the next presidential election and become an autocratic ruler.

How to subvert Democracy self-test

In twelve easy steps

Subverting a democracy by democratic means is relatively easy. Countless charismatic politicians, military men, or your average Joe Blow have surfed on the nationalist wave of their country to do just that. It is, therefore, a well-defined and time-tested playbook that Donald Trump, who has never been coy about his admiration for dictators, is following to the letter.

- **Rule number one**: **Assess your potential.**

For aspiring dictators, the first thing to consider is your personality traits. You must be a psychopath or, at the very minimum, a narcissist, and preferably both. You must be able to lie easily, think that you have a Messianic mission, and have a complete lack of empathy. Those basic character traits are essential for any chance of success.

Does Donald Trump have the character traits required to become an autocratic ruler?

- Trump does not have any of those character traits: 2 Pts. ☐

- Donald Trump has some of those traits: ONE POINT ☐

- Donald Trump has most of those traits: ZERO POINT ☐

- Rule number two: **Become a Messiah of some cause.**

You must be imbued with a messianic mission that makes you special or even unique. You alone have the ability to save the people from a looming catastrophe or the reality of their social condition. Better still, find a cause that would appeal to everybody's desire to protect, especially women. Anything with the words "save the children" is a guaranteed winner.

Has Donald Trump managed to portray himself as the only person who can solve all our problems?

- No, Donald Trump has not: TWO POINTS. ☐

- Yes, Donald Trump has indicated that: ONE POINT ☐

- Yes, Donald Trump can solve everything: ZERO POINT ☐

- Rule number three: **thrive on chaos.**

Chaos is your friend. Your goal is to make people angry and frustrated about something. Try to make them economically insecure and anxious. Provoke their anger, incite civil disobedience, protests, riots, and even armed conflicts. You must act like a firefighter pouring gasoline on a fire while pretending to be the only one who can extinguish it.

Has Donald Trump succeeded in creating political or social chaos?

- No, Donald Trump has not: TWO POINTS ☐

- Yes, sometimes: ONE POINT ☐

- Yes, most of the time: ZERO POINT ☐

- **Rule number four**: **Invoke internal and external enemies.**

You must portray yourself as the only strong man who can protect the country and fix anything. If you can't rely on the traditional scapegoats, the Jews, fall back to alternative choices, like the blacks, the yellows, the browns, in short, anybody who does not look like you. Capitalize on people's fear of differences, social or religious. Your goal is to sow divisions, discord, and distrust of the other who does not belong to your tribe.

Has Donald Trump met this requirement?

- Trump has never invoked external enemies: 2 pts . ☐

- Yes, sometimes: ONE POINT ☐

- Yes, all the time: ZERO POINT ☐

- **Rule number five**: **Undermine the institutions.**

If you want to control any facet of government, you must first dismantle all existing institutions controlled by the State.

How has Donald Trump performed on this task while in Office?

- Trump has never undermined our institutions:2 Pts ☐

- Yes, sometimes: ONE POINT ☐

- Yes. All the time: ZERO POINT ☐

- **Rule number six: secure the allegiance of an army of thugs.**

From the smallest to the biggest countries, any well-respected dictator ought to be able to count on his personal Praetorian Guards who only swear allegiance to him.

Can Donald Trump rely on an army of thugs to do his bidding?

- Yes, he can: TWO POINTS ☐
- Not sure :   :   ONE POINT   ☐
- Definitely: ZERO POINT ☐

- **Rule number seven:** (This is a great one) **Pack the Courts with like-minded Judges.**

Military coups could be hazardous and not guaranteed to succeed (for example, in Turkey). Packing the Courts is less obvious, bloodless, perfectly democratic, and so much more efficient. Today, as the number of autocratic countries worldwide outnumbers the democratic ones, we should be more than alarmed that many of them were fully democratic countries. We should indeed be wary that a good number of countries run by de facto dictators had a Constitution mirroring the United States. Many of those who were too complacent in believing that such a thing could happen to them are either in prison, dead, or in a clandestine opposition.

How well has Donald Trump managed to pack the Courts in his favor?

- No, Donald Trump has not: TWO POINTS   ☐
- Not sure: :   ONE POINT   ☐
- Definitely: ZERO POINT   ☐

- **Rule number eight: Make people cynical of democracy.**

Subverting democracy is relatively easy. Much easier, in fact, than in an established dictatorship or when only one party rules, where it is difficult to identify friends from foes and where the slightest miscalculation can send you directly to the firing squad. In a democracy, however, the parties to beat are clearly identified and are no threat to your health.

Democracy's weak point: the voters

To achieve your goal, your first order of business is to make people cynical about democracy. In a democratic country, military coups would be too obvious and counterproductive. Therefore, the best approach would be to use democracy against itself and use democratic elections to achieve your goal. If this had been the royal road to many dictators, starting with Hitler, it is not as straightforward as a military coup and requires patience, preparation, and commitment, especially if you are not certain of winning.

Of course, that strategy does not preclude you from cheating yourself, but this old tried-and-true strategy does not guarantee you a victory like the new one.

How successful has Donald Trump managed to disparage democracy?

- Trump has never disparaged democracy: TWO Pts. ☐

- Trump has sometimes disparaged democracy:1 Pt ☐

- Very successful   ZERO POINT ☐

- **Rule number nine: Set up your own propaganda apparatus** dedicated to disseminating your vision to the broadest audience possible.

You must also have noticed that things with a word in their name to describe them are often the contrary to what they purport to be. For example, "Democratic Republic of something," like "*The Democratic People's Republic of Korea*" (North Korea), "*The Democratic Republic of Congo,*" or "of Afghanistan" are either a dictator or a failed state. The same goes for "*Institutes*" or "R*esearch Centers*" for lobby companies or "*Planned Parenthood Centers*" masquerading as abortion clinics.

Enters "*Truth,*" Trump's new social media platform.

How efficient has Donald Trump been in using the media to his advantage?

- Trump does not use media to his advantage:2 Pts ☐

- Trump uses media to his advantage: ONE POINT ☐

-

- Trump always uses media to his advantage: 0 Pt ☐

- **Rule number ten: Make lying and deceit the principal means to achieve your goals.**

"If you tell a lie big enough and keep repeating it, people will eventually come to believe it.[104]. Remember, people are so easily manipulated that the challenge to make them believe anything is almost boring. But it is a must.

All great dictators are master manipulators of the truth. It does not matter if the lie is benign or enormous. In fact, the more preposterous, the better because the more people question and repeat it, the more plausible it becomes.

How proficient has Donald Trump been at manipulating the truth?

- Donald Trump never lies: TWO POINTS ☐
- Donald Trump sometimes lies: ONE POINT ☐
- Donald Trump lies most of the time: ZERO POINT ☐

- **Rule number eleven: Use the Justice system as your personal "*special op*"** striking force to go after whoever opposes you.

If your autocratic rule has not yet reached full maturity to the point where you can arbitrarily arrest, torture, make disappear, or execute by firing squad people you don't like, you can always fall back onto your "independent" justice system.

---

[104] Attributed to Joseph Goebbels , Hitler's Propaganda Reich Minister

The beauty of this approach is that you do not even have to control the entire justice system. All you need is to have the person in charge of it in your pocket. In addition, as a bonus, it gives the whole process the veneer of legitimacy and deniability in case something goes wrong.

If you cannot openly take out your critics (political opponents, journalists, minorities, religious leaders, etc.), at least ensure they cannot muster an opposition that could challenge your power. Use your "independent" justice system to vigorously investigate your political opponents on trumped-up charges if necessary. You do not even have to go through the trouble of setting up kangaroo courts to prove anything. In the mind of most people, the simple fact of investigating someone is sufficient to ruin a person's reputation and create enough doubts about his lack of guilt.

Short of a military coup, controlling the justice system is the modus operandi of choice to subvert democracy.

Has Donald Trump fulfilled this requirement?

- Trump has not implemented that step: 2 POINTS ☐

- Trump has partially implemented that step:ONE Pt ☐

- Donald Trump has implemented that step: ZERO Pt ☐

- **Rule number twelve**: **BE RUTHLESS.**

    Ban empathy and the rule of law from your vocabulary. You are strong, and you have a mission: power. Be prepared to do anything necessary to achieve your goal. You are, above all, a winner.

Has Donald Trump demonstrated that he can be ruthless?

- No, Trump is gentle and cares about people: 2 Pts ☐

- Yes, Donald Trump could be ruthless:　1 POINT ☐

- Donald Trump only cares about himself:　0 POINT ☐

SCORING

What is your assessment?

✓ Between 13 and 26 points: your view is that Donald Trump has not been trying to subvert democracy: **you are a MAGA supporter.**

✓ Between 13 and 19 points: your view is that Donald Trump has implemented most of the steps necessary to subvert democracy, but there is only a 50/50 chance that he will be using them to win the next presidential election: **you are an independent or have not made up your mind yet.**

✓ Less than 13 points: Donald Trump has implemented most of the steps to subvert democracy, and there is a 99.99 % chance that he will use them to win the next presidential election or will not accept the voting results: **you better start packing your belongings and move to Canada.**

Interpreting the score.

It might surprise you that the score you gave to the implementation of the "*How to subvert democracy for "A Dear Leader" Wannabes*" guide by Donald Trump was less an assessment of his readiness to subvert democracy than a reflection of you, your own cognitive ability to think, reason, and do all the critical thinking required to vote intelligently in a democratic election.

Winston Churchill said it best:

"The best argument against democracy is a five-minute conversation with the average voter."

INDEX

Oppenheimer: 64, 335, 389, 417
Orbán Viktor: 227, 417
Orwell George: 81, 224, 333, 386, 391, 392, 417

P
Palestine: 62, 347, 417
Paramilitary: 125, 222, 418
Pathological liar: 34, 115, 354, 418
Pathological lying: 10, 30
Patriot Act: 73, 225, 355, 418
Patriotic: 70, 91, 268, 418
Patriotism: 74, 153, 376, 389, 390, 418
Pearl Harbor: 41, 67, 73, 141, 142, 146–49, 156, 159, 225, 418
Pence Mike: 16, 68, 140, 141, 179, 186, 267, 418
Pennsylvania: 107, 108, 118, 138, 166, 418
Pentagon: 52, 149, 172, 174, 194, 418
Plato: 128, 418
Poland: 86, 331, 418
Political divide: 246, 263, 280, 367, 418
Political party: 4, 79, 151, 225, 246–48, 252, 254, 256, 257, 260, 263, 418
Politician: 21, 23, 55, 156, 167, 266, 350, 354, 395, 418
Politicians: 13, 16, 24, 33, 54, 81, 87, 114, 115, 120, 153, 165, 189, 218, 285, 313, 351, 352, 357, 358, 385, 388, 402, 418
Populism: 44, 19, 73, 216, 313, 331, 418
Presidential
       Presidential campaign: 38, 199, 202, 204, 208, 220, 418
       Presidential character: 156, 157, 163, 418
       Presidential characteristics: 157, 165, 418
       Presidential election: 222, 274, 275, 291
       Presidential eligibility: 183, 184, 418

T

Other publications by Axel de Landalay

PAPERBACK

The Second Coming of Trump The First – Part I

The Second Coming of Trump The First – Part I

Pictures & Quotes from *The Second Coming of Trump The First*

EBOOK

How to subvert a democracy for *"Dear Leader"* wannabes

The Second Coming of Trump The First – Part I

The Second Coming of Trump The First – Part II

How to subvert a democracy for *"Dear Leader"* wannabes

AUTHOR'S WEBSITE
https://www.trumpthe1st.com/

www.ingramcontent.com/pod-product-compliance
Lightning Source LLC
Chambersburg PA
CBHW050449270326
41927CB00009B/1664